Educational Provision for our Youngest Children: European Perspectives

Edited by Tricia David

P·C·P
Paul Chapman
Publishing Ltd

Copyright selection and editorial material © Tricia David
1993. All other material copyright © Paul Chapman
Publishing 1993.

Paul Chapman Publishing Ltd
144 Liverpool Road
London
N1 1LA

British Library Cataloguing in Publication Data

David, Tricia
    Educational Provision for Our Youngest
    Children
    I. Title
    372.21
ISBN 1 85396 204 X

Typeset by Inforum, Rowlands Castle, Hants

A B C D E F G H   9 8 7 6 5 4 3

Dedicated to our youngest children, and all those who act as their advocates throughout the world

Contents

Biographical details of contributors   ix
Preface and acknowledgements   xii

1   Young Europeans   1
    Tricia David
2   Nursery education in Belgium   7
    Jacqueline Andries and Tricia David
3   Provision for preschool children in Denmark   18
    Karin Vilien
4   Preschool education in France   35
    Madeleine Goutard
5   Early childhood education and care in Germany   56
    Hedi Colberg-Schrader and Pamela Oberhuemer
6   Preprimary education in Italy   78
    Lucio Pusci
7   Provision for preschool children in Spain   93
    Teresa Aguado Odina
8   Early childhood care and education in Sweden   112
    Monica Bergman
9   Educating children under 5 in the UK   133
    Tricia David
10   Overview: issues and implications   155
    Tricia David

Bibliography   171
Appendix: useful information   184
Index   187

Biographical Details of Contributors

Teresa Aguado Odina holds a doctorate in Sciences of Education, and a licenciate in Educational Psychology. She is a teaching assistant in the Department of Research Methods in Education at the Universidad Nacional de Educacion a Distancia (UNED), in Spain. Her current work involves collaboration with Spain's Ministry of Education, in the in-service education and training of preschool teachers.

Jacqueline Andries is the current President of the Belgian National Committee of OMEP (l'Organisation Mondiale pour l'Education Prescolaire). She was the principal of a primary/nursery school (2½–10 years) before her retirement. As well as her teaching qualification, she is the holder of a diploma in Special Education.

Monica Bergman holds a degree in Art History supplemented with Sociology. Since 1980 she has been a lecturer in Social Sciences at the University College of Falun Borlange, in Sweden, where she is mainly involved in in-service and supplementary courses for preschool and primary teachers. For the last seven years she has been a member of the National Board of the Swedish Association of University Teachers (SULF), where she brings to bear her interest in the interconnections between higher education and employment for women, and the education and care of young children.

Hedi Colberg-Schrader is head of the section Children and Childcare at the German Youth Institute in Munich, a non-university sociological research institute. Her work is focused on applied research on the living conditions of children, and on innovatory projects concerned with kindergartens and childcare services. She was involved in the last

Government-commissioned report on children and youth which was published in 1990. Hedi lectures and holds in-service seminars for kindergarten teachers and advisers in Western and Eastern Germany, and she is a member of the federal committee concerned with early childhood care and education. She has published widely and is a member of the editorial board of Welt des Kindes.

Tricia David is a lecturer in Education at the University of Warwick. Her earlier career has included teaching at almost every level of the education system from age 3 to 83; headship in nursery and primary schools; and membership of one of the 1970s early years research teams, led by the late Dr Corinne Hutt. Having two daughters who are now the age she was when they were born, she has grown more and more frustrated and passionate about the need for proper policies and action in ensuring high quality edu-care in the UK – equality of opportunity for young children and their mothers. Her previous publications include *Under Five – Under-educated?* and *Child Protection and Early Years Teachers: Coping with Child Abuse.*

Madeleine Goutard is known worldwide for her work with OMEP, as she has been a member of the World Executive for many years. She has also been OMEP World President and the representative to UNESCO in Paris. She has published widely. Her works include *Preschool Education in the European Community* (OECD 1980) and *Mathematiques sur mesure* (Hachette 1970).

Pamela Oberhuemer is a research worker at the State Institute of Early Childhood Education and Family Research (IFP) in Munich. Areas of focus include: child development, education and care; educators and professional development; intercultural education; children's literature and childlore; children's social concepts. Previous experience includes working in an infant school (London) and a school-kindergarten (Munich). Alongside her work in research and innovatory projects, Pamela Oberhuemer lectures and holds in-service seminars for kindergarten educators and advisers in Western and Eastern Germany. She currently chairs two working parties on the development of in-service training and advisory services in Bavaria; and she is Vice-chair of the Pestalozzi-Froebel Association, and a member of a federal committee concerned with issues of early childhood education and care (AGJ – also the OMEP German National Committee). Pamela is an editorial board member of the journal *Kinderzeit – Socialpadagogische Blatter (Paderborn)* and *The International Journal of Early Years Education.* Publications include books for educators and students on children's play, organizing learning in the kindergarten, and numerous journal articles. She has also co-edited a series of anthologies, audio-cassettes and video-cassettes for inter-cultural work in kindergartens and primary schools.

Lucio Pusci is a researcher at the Centro Europeo dell'Educatione in Frascati, Rome, where he is national co-ordinator of the IEA Preprimary Project. He is an experienced teacher, and holds a doctorate from the University of Rome. His publications include an edited comparative text evaluating new curricula in the primary education systems of ten European countries, and *Ricerca e politica educativa in prospettiva europa*, published by Armando in Rome.

Karin Vilien BA, MA has been Director of the Department for Early Childhood Studies at the Royal School of Educational Studies, Copenhagen since 1984, working in the field of continuing education for pedagogues. Her earlier experience includes teaching and directing in daycare institutions, involvement in the development of 'co-ordinated school start', and methods teaching in a college for preschool teachers.

Preface and Acknowledgements

As editor, my first debt of gratitude must be to the colleagues who have contributed their work to this volume, for their interest and enthusiasm, their tolerance of my inadequacies and, at times, my demands. Further thanks are due to Donna Jay, Mary Graham, and Sandra Dowse, who patiently wordprocessed various parts of the manuscript; to Professor Bridie Raban, catalyst and mentor; to colleagues Audrey Curtis and Ann Lewis, who have given time to read and comment on the manuscript; and to staff at PCP whose support I have valued. I am also grateful to the Nuffield Foundation, whose research award allowed me the opportunity to undertake work abroad, so enlarging my own horizons and sensitivity to the inter-relationships between various aspects of life in different countries, with different geographies, histories, and so on, resulting in different attitudes towards childhood and family life.

This book would not have been possible without the opportunities offered by OMEP, the World Organization for Early Childhood Education, to find friends and collaborators from other countries, to explore our roots and our inheritance, in work with and for young children and their families. All royalties from sales are being kindly donated to OMEP by the contributors.

Acknowledgements for permission to reproduce extracts from publications:

Tables 1 and 2 are reproduced by permission of Professor D. Sommer. Tables 3 and 4 are reproduced by permission of Stig Lund of BUPL, Denmark. Table 8 is reproduced by permission of the National Children's Bureau, from Pugh (ed) (1992) *Contemporary Issues in the Early Years*, Paul Chapman. Table 9 is reproduced by permission of the European Commission, from *Childcare in the European Communities 1985–1990*, EC, (1990).

1

Young Europeans

Tricia David

On a recent visit to another European country, where primary school admission age is currently 7 and where daycare provision is far more abundant than that in the UK, I was struck by the apparent lack of evidence for early, or emergent, literacy engagement in the daycare centres I visited. The colleague who was conducting our tour explained that such activities would only be available for children if they themselves asked for the necessary materials, and that it was highly unlikely they would do this, there being so many other exciting aspects to learning at this stage. 'But what happens when you walk down a street with a four-year-old, don't they ask about signs in shops, print on labels, and so on?' I asked. 'No, I have never had a four-year-old ask me those kinds of questions,' came the reply. The surprise must have shown in my face, for she continued, 'It's your society. You put a lot of pressure on your children to start reading early, so they learn early to ask those kinds of questions, that it's expected of them.'

Statements such as this, taken together with research evidence that in the country concerned 'reading failure' at 11 years and above is far lower than in the UK cause one to pause for some considerable time for reflection. Learning about the way of life, education, societal organization, and so on, in another country is not only informative in the obvious sense, as straightforward, new knowledge, it is also a way of providing oneself with a kind of mirror, but a mirror similar to those in a funfair, where an image comes back to meet the eye, but some features are larger than one thought, others smaller, emphases have been altered and provide a special focus on something one had earlier considered taken for granted, or insignificant. Further, it is important to probe the ways in which similarities and differences which are not apparent until comparative information is available highlight the ways in which governments and their supporters respond to particular pressures. For example, Moon (1990) discusses the fact that reforms in France, the Netherlands and the UK have been undertaken, with increasing intervention by central governments, on the pretext of raising standards. He argues that in spite of differing structures and histories, these education systems have been 'worked similarly, where orchestrated reform is vigorously pursued' (p. 127). Moon also debates the revolution in communications, the currency of ideas such as 'resource targeting' in response to financial constraints, and the internationalization of issues.

In this book leading early childhood specialists discuss provision outside the home for the youngest children in their own countries, exploring in particular the ways in which their society delineates forms of that provision as educational, aimed at ensuring high quality learning experiences for the children, rather than from a starting point of care, so that mothers (for it usually is mothers, not fathers, who stay at home to look after small children in countries where provision is scant) may go out to work.

That is not to say that the contributors are not interested in equal opportunities for women, far from it, but they recognize that the two sets of rights and opportunities must go hand in hand, and that parents will not be fulfilled in their work if they feel their children are paying a price for their own adult right, or need, to work outside the home. Elly Singer (1992), well known for her work in Holland, takes to task the psychologists who have given the impression that they are solely interested in children's development and learning, without recognizing the ways in which the contexts in which those children live (i.e. perhaps with a mother who wants or needs to work or study but whose opportunities are not being provided equally to those of men, and whose talent is going untapped). It is this type of ecological perspective which forms the underlying theoretical basis of the contributors to this text.

In each of the chapters the authors, from Belgium, Denmark, France, Germany, Italy, Spain, Sweden and the UK, consider the ways in which provision has evolved; political and economic factors which have influenced that development; philosophical underpinnings and the effects of research; the extent to which provision is expected to be deemed 'educational' and the form taken by curricula; and the links between home and provision, and between this phase and the primary school sector. Chapters concerning the other EC countries – Greece, Portugal, Luxembourg, the Netherlands and Ireland – would indeed have strengthened (but considerably enlarged) this book. Sadly, space and time have resulted in their being left until a possible future volume, as have the Eastern European, and some of the EFTA countries.

Readers need to be aware that terminology is sometimes tricky, and that although a word may be used in the English translation of a particular chapter, it may not have exactly the same connotation in the country concerned that it does in England itself. One such example is 'infant education', which in the UK means education for children aged 5–7, but as the translation from Spain's new system of 'educacion infantil' means education for children aged 0–6 years.

Another, but different, kind of example of issues arising because of working in English, is the use of the word 'teacher'. While at present UK nursery teachers are educated and trained to the same level of graduate status as teachers for other sectors, but as early childhood specialists, teachers in some of the other countries share neither this level of education, nor the equivalent status, pay and conditions of teachers in the primary and secondary sectors. However, issues such as training and status, among others, are debated in the final chapter, the overview, which attempts to challenge the reader to consider the prospects for early childhood education in the free market of post-1992 Europe, a Europe in which there is currently considerable cause for concern, with the problems of recession, unemployment, increasing racial harassment, disagreement about the status of non-EC nationals and the definition of a refugee, yet a Europe which is avowedly on the side of children's rights, as enshrined in the 1989 UN Convention, and on the side of a highly educated populace, fit for life and work in an advanced democratic society.

Other interesting discrepancies arise in connection with the way 'early childhood' is defined, particularly in relation to provision outside the home. In some countries the younger children, those aged under 2 or 3 are seen as the responsibility of health or social services departments, rather than education – does this mean that in the countries involved children under this age are seen as ineducable, that learning begins at the age designated by the first rung of a school career? In particular, the chapters discuss the early childhood curriculum, if this has in fact been delineated in any way, in each of the countries concerned; who has produced the definition adopted, and on what basis? For example, is it the result of traditional beliefs and pragmatism, or informed by research, and if so, what kind of research? For some early childhood specialists the idea of a compulsory preschool curriculum is anathema, partly because they insist on the importance of harnessing the young child's spontaneity, over-planning suggesting formal, inappropriate tasks. Others see such a requirement as potential interference in family affairs – the parents being the primary educators, especially at this crucial early stage. However, if high quality, educational early childhood services are provided for only some children in a community, and if they raise the levels of children's achievement, both in the present and in the future, should not all the children in that society be entitled to such services? Rigorous research into the interconnections between the type of provision experienced by children *and* ecological factors influencing their families, and the resultant effects on academic achievement, remains to be carried out (Hennessy and Melhuish 1991), but the authors included in this book explore the evidence they already have concerning early childhood education in their countries.

One aspect of work with the young which early childhood educationists are beginning to tackle is that of metacognition – awareness of one's own learning processes and achievements. For example, Ingrid Pramling in Sweden, and Mirjana Pesic in ex-Yugoslavia, have both carried out research in this field. My own fieldwork in the UK and Belgium, through a Nuffield Grant, enabled me to spend time with children asking why they thought they attended nursery schools – not one child talked to me of learning. There is no reason why we cannot ensure that children know of the skills and concepts they have developed, even though we adhere wholeheartedly to the idea that learning should be enjoyable, and that our curriculum in the early years be based on child-directed play.

In her chapter on Sweden, Monica Bergman draws attention to the lack of academic credibility in early childhood studies. She points to the fact that there are few university Chairs in Early Childhood Studies, or Education, in Sweden, and this could also be said of any of the other countries. She asks whether it is significant in this regard that the majority of those who work, research, lecture and study in this field are women.

Discrepancies in the ages of admission to primary schools are a further example of the historical differences between the countries in Europe. The UK, with a statutory age of admission set at 5 years old, is the only one of the countries represented here with such an early entry to the primary sector. Furthermore children are in reality entering school before they attain this age, and in most areas of the country four-year-olds are being admitted to school with the blessing of the majority of their parents, on the assumption that the sooner they begin academic work the more successful they will be later. Similar arguments to those now raging in Scandinavia, focused on a primary school admission age reduced from 7 to 6, have been aired in relation to these UK four-year-olds. This raises a further question regarding 'Europeanization' – will a European age of admission ultimately evolve, with children entering primary school at 6?

What most of those in the field of early childhood education, Europe-wide, are concerned about is the appropriateness of the teaching and learning methods for children in this first, important, phase in life. New research (for example that carried out at Edinburgh University by Professor Colwyn Trevarthen on brain development) is reiterating the crucial nature of what happens during the early years, despite some intervening years of rejection of the Jesuits' credo 'Give me a child until he is seven, and I will give you the man'. Young children, as active learners, need opportunities to observe, explore, experiment, represent, and transform materials and their environment, and there is anxiety that large classes and the more formal world of primary schools will not allow for these needs. Forms of provision in which there is adequate resourcing, in terms of appropriate levels of equipment, space, and adults, for such learning opportunities are costly, and even those governments in countries where there has, hitherto, been generous resourcing, are looking for ways of cutting back (e.g. Norway and Sweden). What we must ask, then, is – should high quality/high cost early childhood education and care be seen as an investment in the future, rather than as an expensive drain on current economic resources?

In the final chapter, the overview, we will explore what evidence the accounts presented here offer to support the claim that children are important, so important that funding for high quality provision is a priority in the countries to which they belong. On the other hand, is there evidence of systems where early childhood care and education are the victims of ideological myopia – storing up trouble for the future, because young children have not been accorded the respect as people at a particular, but 'perfect in its own right', stage in development they deserve? This neglect may have been made manifest through a deliberate, or unintentional, under-development of provision, or the tailoring of provision to the future needs of society at the expense of individuals, so provision becomes very much 'preschool', a preparation for life in formal schooling. Yet it must be acknowledged that children who are in a sense prepared for the next stage, and are ready to meet it with joy and enthusiasm, already possessing some of the skills and learning strategies they will need, are more likely to succeed and therefore to have their self-esteem, their feelings of autonomy, competence and mastery, bolstered, than those who enter the primary system lost for words, unable to make sense of events, and regarded as deficient in some way. Readers might like to consider whether it appears that each society expects its youngest children to be prepared for and adapted to the primary school, or the primary school for the children.

Researchers in the Scandinavian countries have been exploring the ways in which different societies define childhood for their young (e.g. Dahlberg 1991), overlaying physiological constraints with their own concepts, or models, of how children 'should be' at certain stages in their lives. Where children are left to 'be children' the model is defined as 'child as being'; where their lives are mapped out for them, the model is 'child as project'. Both types of model could leave children at a loss – the child as being is potentially ill-prepared for the expectations of school and society; the child as project lives under tremendous pressure to achieve. By examining the systems and expectations of each of the countries discussed in this text, readers may begin to consider what different European societies consider to be an appropriate concept of childhood.

The role of parents is also discussed for, as Joyce Watt (1990) comments, early childhood education is complex because 'it is firmly rooted in the families and communities of which it is a part . . . at its best, it recognizes that adults and children have reciprocal effects on each other's learning . . . making provision for the needs of adults is an important element in meeting the educational needs of children' (Watt 1990, p. 3).

Family policy in the different countries depends on ideological factors – how much, or how little, a government considers it appropriate for a state to 'help with', or 'interfere in', family life. Again, this may become clear to readers as they compare country with country. However, 1994 will be the International Year of the Family, and a European conference is being organized by the Confederation of Family Organizations in Europe (COFACE) at which it is intended family policies will be examined (Cohen 1993). The first-ever Council of Europe Recommendation on Childcare Policy was published in March 1992 and it requires member states to inform the European Commission of action taken on its four areas of concern, within the three years following its adoption. The areas of concern are as follows: services for children; parental leave; changes in the environment, structure and organization of parental employment in response to children's needs; and the promotion of sharing responsibilities for children between women and men. Action is expected of not only governments, but also on the part of trade unions and employers. Let us hope the Recommendation will create a climate in which high quality services in which education is embedded will flourish.

What is exciting about a comparative collection such as the papers presented here is that it provides an opportunity to examine the situation in seven EC member countries, plus one EFTA country (European Free Trade Area) – Sweden, which is due to enter the EC in a couple of years' time – and reflect on our collective and individual commitment to young children, families and communities, and their educational development. The status and role of early childhood professionals as advocates of children's rights are currently important topics of debate in many of the countries included in this book. Looking beyond national boundaries is a vital ingredient in early years teacher education.

2

Nursery Education in Belgium

Jacqueline Andries and Tricia David

During the last twenty years important legislation has influenced the ways in which the education system in Belgium is 'delivered'. The original structure of the Belgian State had remained largely unchanged since its creation in 1830. The central principle underpinning this structure was the unity of the State, through legislation and government covering the whole country, despite the fact that the country was split linguistically and culturally. Following legislation in 1970, 1971 and 1980, power became divided between central government and other, regional, local and provincial authorities, according to the cultural communities served.

The (around 10 million) inhabitants of Belgium fall into three main linguistic and cultural groups – one French-speaking, one Flemish-speaking, and a smaller German-speaking community. The region around Brussels itself is 'bi-communautaire' (French and Flemish). Approximately ten per cent of the population come from ethnic and linguistic minorities.

In 1988–89, there were 155,589 children attending *écoles maternelles* in the French and German communities combined, and 213,735 attending Flemish nurseries (Eurydice 1991). Since 1 January 1989 the linguistically determined community authorities took over responsibility for the administration of education. The Belgian constitution states that there must be freedom of education, and that laws are in place to deal with any infringements or hindrances to that freedom (Article 17). The organizing power relating to education has been devolved to various official and private bodies, and the latter are dominated by the Catholic group, which is in fact a political party in Belgium.

Primary education is compulsory between the ages of 6 and 12. From the age of 2½, children in Belgium may attend nursery schools and classes, which are clearly deemed educational, and recent estimates suggest that currently over 95 per cent of children in the appropriate age range (2.5 to 6 years) do so. Before this, there is some 'care' provision, but surveys indicate that the levels are inadequate (Humblet 1992).

The école maternelle/kleuterschool *in Belgium*

Nursery education in Belgium began at the end of the last century. While there may be confusion in some countries concerning the aim of early childhood provision and accusations of 'child-parking' so that mothers may go out to work, Belgium has always held a clear line, signalled by the fact that the overarching administrative body is the Ministry of Education, not Health or Social Services.

The historical roots of early childhood services in Belgium go back to the early part of the nineteenth century. In 1826, an English woman, Caroline Colson, founded the first *salle d'asile*, the precursor of day nurseries, in Brussels. During the ensuing years, the work of Froebel became more widely known, and in 1830 the State declared an interest in provision for very young children. The first *jardin d'enfants* was opened in Brussels in 1857, and in 1879 a law was issued requiring local authorities (communes) to annex group childminding facilities to existing primary schools.

Although little action followed the institution of a course of training lasting one month, leading to a diploma, for those working in the care facilities, a Circular was issued to this effect in 1880. Froebelian methods continued to exert an influence and to become widely accepted in local communes, and with the foundation of the first *école normale* (training college) in 1910 at Mons, the stage was set for the diploma to become obligatory in 1919. In 1921 four new colleges were opened, at Bruges, Brussels, Laeken and Liege, and a course of two years' duration was initiated. By 1926 the required qualification had been extended to one demanding three years of training, and by 1927 the theoretical underpinning of the course had shifted, and the ideas of Maria Montessori gained precedence (Delvaux-Furnière and Malisoux-Gillet 1985).

A further important influence on teaching approaches in Belgian nurseries was the work of Ovide Decroly, a doctor whose original interest lay in the needs of children with disabilities. Decroly believed that the nursery curriculum should be a 'programme for a school of life' (Peers 1942). He wrote about first-hand experience; learning through the senses; taking account of the interests of the child; the importance of encouraging children to observe and to explain their thoughts. Further, he was an advocate of the judicious employment of spontaneity.

Anne-Marie Delvaux-Furnière and Marie-Jose Malisoux-Gillet (1985) and the team of nursery teachers with whom they conducted an action research programme and evaluation of provision, concluded that since the early part of the twentieth century the following tendencies had existed in Belgian nursery education:

- children's development and learning are not the result of an accumulation of facts and knowledge, but a slow construction which the children themselves craft;
- children should not be left to their own devices all the time, supposedly to learn spontaneously. Intervention is vital, especially for those who are disadvantaged.

Contemporary inspectors of nursery schools claim that teachers of such young children do not espouse dogma, or limit themselves to one particular theory (Le Soir, 1992). They suggest that, while theoretical links and reflective practice are essential, early years teachers in Belgium are open to change, are aware of the changing needs of children and their families, and are more concerned with *education*, i.e. the child's learning, than with 'teaching'. They identify the need for teachers to find the key to arousing each child's individual achievement and learning, and that this should be undertaken in partnership with the family.

Perhaps one of the most important points to be made concerning nursery education in Belgium at the present time, especially when comparing systems, is the fact that nurseries are part of the way of life in Belgium, they are seen as part of the education system, the first step in each child's educational career.

Attitudes towards provision

Belgium has for some time taken the issue of parental involvement very seriously, and this has included parental participation in classroom activities (Macbeth 1984). Perhaps because the school is seen very much as part of the community, parents, when questioned about any improvements they could suggest in order to make their child's nursery come closer to their 'ideal', had few changes they could put forward (David 1992). One frequent point, however, was that the nursery classes are too large, teacher : pupil ratios too high. (These ratios vary according to the administrative body overseeing the school. In State nurseries the ratio is officially 1 : 20, but in some other establishments the figure is far higher.) Staff too endorsed this point, and in 1992 teachers across the system held one-day strikes for a number of reasons, including class sizes in the early years. In a sense the size of classes reflects the demand for provision.

Management and funding

Parents are not required to pay a fee for nursery education, but they will normally be asked to contribute to the costs of out-of-hours care, any food supplied, or trips in which children participate.

Out-of-hours care

Many schools now offer a care facility early in the morning and after the school day, some being open from 7 in the morning until 6 in the evening. The school day itself is usually from 8.30 a.m. until 3.30 p.m. A scheme run by the Ministry of Labour for the Flemish community is currently providing training for women who are long-term unemployed, training them to lead out-of-hours care groups. Short courses provide participants with some knowledge of child development and behaviour, play activity ideas, and liaison with parents. Although the courses are well-thought-out and structured, the scheme itself is creating some anxieties among those in the field, for a number of reasons. Firstly, qualified, unemployed nursery nurses are not being considered for either the posts or the training, since the central thrust is to engage women who might otherwise have no training or expertise; the women are low paid (little over their normal rate of unemployment benefit); work with children could be perceived as being devalued, especially if that work involves play provision; the opportunities in after-school play centres could deter any development of child-directed learning in schools, because school could begin to be perceived as the place where 'serious, teacher-directed and controlled learning' takes place.

The curriculum

The overall aims of nursery education in Belgium are said to be:

- a global education, embracing all aspects of the child's personality, and providing for cognitive, aesthetic, moral, and physical development, among others;
- the education of the emotions through the provision of a secure environment, with attention to the prevention of events likely to cause socio-emotional problems for the child;
- the encouragement of communication skills, divergent thought, logic, and self-expression, through opportunities to work in carefully managed groups;
- continuity of experience at points of transition;
- to help children become autonomous, responsible, and co-operative;

- to foster respect for individual needs and to individualize learning;
- to reduce school failure.

Curriculum documents stress the importance of classroom organization, the use of space, appropriate resourcing and use of materials, encouraging a widening of the 'team' coming into contact with the children, collaboration with parents and the need to ensure their understanding of learning methods, relevance to real life and the broadening of children's 'world' (Delvaux-Furnière and Malisoux-Gillet 1985; Ministere de l'ERF 1985).

Teachers are exhorted to guard against formal preparation for the primary school, to see their role as one of being child-centred, of providing an education which is neither rigid nor cloistered, but is practical and based on activity. The curriculum document issued by the Ministry of Education, Research and Training (ERF) in 1985, divides the content of the curriculum according to activities, which equate to a curriculum based on areas of experience. These areas are: mathematics; language; plastic/artistic activities; music; physical/movement; and science. Within each of these areas, the document demonstrates how the other areas cut across, so that, for example, in the section on *activités d'art plastique* there is some introductory discussion concerning creativity, the management of space and materials, adult roles and intervention, followed by some examples from practice in which the links with other areas of experience are clear, e.g. using vegetable dyes (links with science), construction and exploration of three-dimensional shapes (links with mathematics). Within the section headed *activités psychomotrices*, scientific and mathematical connections are again highlighted in examples such as 'looking at oneself in a mirror, making faces . . . filling and pouring water containers' (Ministère de l'ERF 1985, p. 26). Links with language components include 'playing with puppets' – from the physical development point of view, good for hand–eye co-ordination, muscular development and control, etc., as well as being an activity which promotes language development.

The document stresses the need for assessment and evaluation, stating that children will be aware of their own successes and achievements, and that each child should feel valued and stimulated in order to progress. Evaluation of each teacher's own performance, of the ways in which children's needs are provided for, is also stressed, and that this is an integral part of their work in education, something teachers carry out constantly in their roles as educators, greater effectiveness deriving from this aspect of the work being undertaken consciously.

The school day

The daily routine naturally depends on the needs of the individuals comprising the group, and in particular, on the age group in question. The activities for the youngest children, who are usually placed in smaller groups, with nursery nurses rather than teachers, take account of their need for movement; encourage play in pairs; provide for progression in physical development; help children begin to look after their own toilet and washing, eating habits, naps (all the youngest children usually sleep after lunch), etc.; broaden experience with objects, animals, events. At times they will come together to sing, to listen to a story, to celebrate someone's birthday.

The eldest children, who will soon move on to the primary school, will have a PE session, discuss the day's project, share ideas, then move on to particular activities, individually, or in pairs or a small group. Before playtime, the whole group may come together to sing or recite rhymes. After playtime, children may be grouped for particular tasks (Figure 1 shows how these can be arranged, depending on the organization of the staff team, extra/specialist staff for subjects such as PE, etc.) and in the afternoon they join 'workshops' in which they make things, paint, etc., or play in the different class areas provided, such as the grocer's shop, hairdresser's, kitchen, dressing-up clothes, book corner, toy car track, dolls' house, puzzles, construction equipment, and so on. Most classes are organized in same-age groups, but in some cases, by choice or because the school is in a small rural area, classes are vertically grouped, and some headteachers initiate a flexible staffing structure, such as that illustrated in Figure 1.

Links with other facilities

The use of the term *accueil* (welcome) underlines the importance paid to the positive nature of nursery school attendance and admission. Home–school links are valued, and when children begin attendance at 2½ years old, attempts are made to ensure more favourable adult : child ratios, so this 'welcome' can be a warm extension of family care.

On 6 May 1981 a Commission (called, in the Francophone region, the Commission de Renovation de l'Enseignement Fondamental (CREF)) was set up to review and make recommendations concerning basic education. Nursery education was naturally seen as a part of this and, in particular, the links between nursery and the first years of the primary school became a focus of attention. One aim of the Commission was to ensure *continuity and coherence* at this interface.

Figure 1 A week in a Belgian nursery school

	Monday	Tuesday	Wednesday	Thursday	Friday
8.45–9.15	WELCOME	Books, writing materials, games, play etc.			
9.15–9.45	REGROUP on the carpet		Calendar, surprise, day's plans, project discussion etc.		
9.45–10.25	Activities – eldest group have PE; younger children choice of activity		Workshops (rotate groups)	Activities – eldest group have PE; younger children choice of activity	
11.00–11.45	Cognitive activities			Cognitive activities	
	Younger children – sensory activities, emergent literacy and mathematics, etc.				
1.30–3.00	Craft/ creative workshops techniques	Craft/ creative workshops (rotate groups)		Craft/ creative workshops (rotate groups)	Free play
3.30–3.55	Dancing, singing, poems, directed games etc.			Dancing, singing, poems, directed games etc.	

(Adapted and translated from Delvaux-Furnière and Malisoux-Gillet, 1985.) p 25

Certain targets for reflection were advocated, as follows: that between 1983 and 1984 there was to be discussion focusing on pedagogy in the nursery; the five- to eight-year-old phase; equality of opportunity; obligatory entry to the system at 5; initial and in-service training of teachers; provision for pupils with special educational needs; innovation in teaching methods; the schooling of children of migrant workers.

During the following year (1984–85) there were to be additional foci: home–school relations; physical education and fitness/sport provision; setting down of basic competencies; teachers were to have the right to certain days when they could speak out and make their opinions heard, and access to documentation and information through the establishment of centres.

Although, as stated earlier, previously unemployed women have been targeted for training to provide out-of-hours care facilities, either in school (if there is appropriate and available space), in their own homes, or in local halls, some out-of-hours facilities are run by schools, staffed by nursery nurses whom the children already know. This system then provides a good link with the rest of the day, and also precludes the need for different people to pass on messages, for example, if a child has been ill, had an accident, etc., and the reverse is also true – that parents do not feel their children are moving from one place, or carer, to another, with subsequent demands on them to liaise. On the other hand, the 'down side' of this practice is that if the nursery nurses employed by the school during the school day are being asked to extend their hours of work, the relatively low rates of pay such personnel traditionally receive in any country may mean they are being exploited, working extra hours for a small remuneration, in conditions which may not always be sufficiently adapted for the task.

Children with special educational needs

The first special schools in Belgium were founded in 1897 in Brussels and Antwerp. These had had several antecedents, for example, the Royal Institute in Liege, founded in 1819 for those with hearing and speech impairment, and certain religious groups had set up charitable institutions for the blind during the 1830s. The influence of Dr Ovide Decroly was in evidence in the developments around the turn of the century. Between 1901 and 1915 Decroly founded a number of homes for those with different types of special needs, ranging from mental handicaps to socio-emotional disturbances. Later, special centres were instituted for those suffering from tuberculosis and other diseases affecting the respiratory tract, and for other debilitating conditions, such as diabetes and haemophilia.

Between 1958 and 1970 a Bill was presented to parliament each year relating to special education, and this was finally adopted. This law applied to anyone between 3 and 21 years of age with a disability. It set out their right to be educated, to take a place in society, to be enabled to take part in the workforce.

The decision to provide special education is taken jointly by a multi-professional, medical-psychological-social team together with the parents. There are special schools, provided by the State, the provincial and communal (local) governments, or privately. The State finances all these schools.

This means that children with severe learning difficulties may be placed in a special school after the age of 3.

Children from ethnic and linguistic minorities

Around a tenth of the population of Belgium comes from a non-indigenous background. Many of the children from linguistic and cultural minorities were born in Belgium, and there is an awareness of their rights (Decat, Sant'Angelo and Louveaux 1989), and of their linguistic and learning needs (Delvaux-Furnière and Malisoux-Gillet 1985). Home language is seen as the essential learning medium for a young child, the first language through which to encourage cognitive development and to help children make sense of their world. As the inspector for nursery education in Namur stated (quoted in Delvaux-Furnière and Malisoux-Gillet 1985) 'we can enrich our education provision through our involvement with young children and families from minority groups; we must beware of the ease with which children can be classified as difficult, simply because these children are posed enormous challenges, which stick simply because they have brown skins' (p. 12).

The aim must be to engage with parents, to develop multicultural perspectives, so that children recognize the ways in which their own cultural background is valued, and for the teacher (who is perhaps the 'odd one out' linguistically) to find ways of communicating with children who are very capable of interacting in their own language.

Staff qualifications, education and training

In 1957 the education and training of nursery teachers was extended a further year to make this a four-year course, and the courses were aligned with those for primary phase teachers. During the 1970s this alignment was further strengthened, and the national government instituted a demand for two years of coursework to focus on the humanities, giving a common basis to nursery and primary teaching qualifications. In 1984 the Diploma in Nursery School Teaching was reduced to a three-year course, with a minimum entry requirement of the certificate of higher secondary education, and a minimum age of 18. Students who do not fulfil the certificate (entry) requirement may be offered the opportunity to gain access to the diploma by sitting special entrance examinations.

The diploma provides a specialized qualification to work with children aged 2½ to 6 years old, but despite the fact that training is equivalent to graduate level, salaries are lower than those of other teachers.

Monitoring and inspection

Since 1972 there have been specialist teams of inspectors who have encouraged teachers and nursery nurses to make great strides in developing provision. Their work has been much in evidence during the reviews between 1983 and 1985, and they have both an inspectorial as well as an advisory and in-service training responsibility.

Parental partnership, community involvement

Information is provided for parents, who may choose the school their children will attend. In one area outside Brussels, the local paper occasionally contains a special section to help parents in this choice. Information about the schools in the area is published alongside one another, so that parents may compare not only the school size, organization of classes etc., but also the curriculum, including additional activities – for example, for nursery children swimming may be an extra option not available in all the schools listed.

Research and development

Since 1975, the universities and field researchers have been engaged in work exploring pedagogy. More and more frequently this has entailed a research partnership with staff in schools.

Examples of the type of work carried out in the field, or in conjunction with practitioners include a University of Liege/Van Leer Foundation project concerned with the education of ethnic minority children from a Turkish community. This is an action research project aimed at developing the curriculum and parental involvement in children's education.

Another example is the project involving one representative from the psychology departments of the three Flemish Universities at Ghent, Louvain and Brussels. The steering committee of the project includes members of the Catholic daycare centres, members of the neutral daycare centres, members of the Federation of Family Daycare schemes, and the staff of a new training centre set up with the project's funds. The project team not only provides training, it also develops materials which can be used, for example, by Flemish childminders. (This pack is based on the British 'Childminding pack, materials for learning and discussion' developed by the Community Education Development Centre in Coventry, and the National Childminders' Association).

A third example is the workshop on equal opportunities set up by the Centre for Research and Sociopedagogical Innovation, at the University of Mons-Hainaut in 1991. This work was particularly concerned with gender effects in nursery and primary schools, and it was intended to set in train a review of practices in the schools, by bringing research evidence to the attention of those in the field.

As a result of the similarity of the two systems and, in part, the use of French, Belgian and French nursery education are each able to benefit from research carried out in the other country. An example of this is the circulation of a research paper from France (Jarousse, Mingat and Richard 1991), indicating that children who begin nursery at 2 years of age, not 3 as is often the case, make long-term gains in their later academic achievement which surpass those of their counterparts who do not start until 3, 4, or 5.

Conclusion

Belgian nursery education is seen as a basic entitlement for all our children. While it is expected to provide a foundation for primary school it is not expected to 'prepare' children by putting them through formal drills and lessons, but by offering meaningful, often individualized, activities.

Scheuer (quoted in Delvaux-Furnière and Malisoux-Gillet 1985) stated: 'what is the role of the school? Is it to select children according to their socio-economic background, or instil in some a sense of failure? Or is it to foster the growth and flowering of all our children, especially those who are most disadvantaged?'

3

Provision for Preschool Children in Denmark

Karin Vilien

In Denmark there is a long tradition of close co-operation between the government and the public and private sectors to provide good quality daycare based on developmentally appropriate programmes for children below school age. Much work has been done in order to form a long-term policy for all aspects of early childhood education in families, daycare centres and in the society as a whole.

Most young children in Denmark live in urban surroundings and in families where both parents are working. The typical child has few sib-lings; 25 per cent of families have one child, 44 per cent have two chil-dren and only 17 per cent of families have three or more children (Langsted and Sommer 1988).

The majority of children in Denmark need a place in a daycare centre. This fact is a major change which has developed in Danish society during the last twenty years. It is in fact a very dramatic change which has had a great influence on children's everyday life. It has influenced the educa-tional pattern of the family and is also having a major impact on parents' and teachers' understandings of their own task.

Danish society has not yet comprehended the fact that daycare is a necessity in a modern community, both for the children's education, and so that parents may be employed. Thus society is failing to meet the needs of both children and their parents.

Daycare for all, or at least most, children is such a heavy demand on the public purse that politicians would be well-advised to take a greater interest in the quality and structure of early childhood services. So far, however, politicians in Denmark have been mainly concerned with the finances. The quality of daycare has been of minor importance in legislation.

Apart from the demand on economic resources, the most significant single factor relating to daycare is that it involves almost all children in the age group 0–7, and attending daycare has become an integral part of modern childhood in Denmark. In fact what is needed is a change in attitudes in society, in order that preschool matters are attended to in the same serious way as those pertaining to primary education.

There are two issues which indicate that society in Denmark still does not deal with preschool matters as phenomena closely connected to life in a modern society.

Firstly, neither central government nor the local authorities set out any demands concerning the curriculum in the daycare centres. What children actually experience is left as the responsibility of the teachers, in close co-operation with the parents, whereas this is not the case for primary education.

The other issue is that society, and especially politicians, believed that the falling birth rate would result in a decreasing demand for daycare provision (the birth rate has fallen from approximately 80,000 in 1974 to 60,000 in 1986. It has remained steady at around 60,000 every year since). However, contrary to expectations, there is a demand for places which continues to rise every year. The BUPL (the Danish National Union of Preschool Teachers), whose officers examine daycare waiting lists throughout the country on an annual basis, has ascertained a shortage of at least 30,000 daycare places (Lund 1992).

This growing demand has several causes. First, there is a powerful economic cause, because the average family cannot maintain an acceptable standard of living on one average income, thus there has to be one-and-a-half or two incomes coming into the home. Another important factor is that younger women are personally strongly motivated towards being employed outside the home. Seventy-five per cent of young mothers have undertaken courses in further and higher education (Christoffersen 1987a), and they wish to use their qualifications and expertise.

These two motivating factors (economic and personal) are apparently the most frequently cited reasons why the demand for daycare places has not decreased with the falling birth rate, but instead rises each year. With so many parents working and almost all children spending the major part of their day in daycare centres, residential areas are somewhat deserted during working hours. As a result, parents and children who stay at home feel isolated, and this creates another reason for yet more parents to want daycare provision for their children, in spite of the fact that they could look after their children at home. In other words, early childhood care and education services are not sought solely because of parents' work.

During the last twenty years, interest has focused on children's living conditions. In 1976, the government established the Child Welfare

Commission, which in 1981 formulated long-term goals for a policy on the child. These were:

- to respect the child as an individual in the family and in society;
- to give the child a central position in the life of grown-ups;
- to promote – in a wider sense – the physical conditions in which children grow up;
- to promote equal opportunities, in the conditions of life of children, both in a material and in a cultural sense.

The Minister of Education has appointed a number of committees to deal with problems related to primary school admission age, following the submission of proposals and recommendations to the Minister of Education in 1984, by members of an earlier committee.

In addition, in 1986 the Minister of Social Affairs appointed a committee to explore and report on young children's daily life. The committee examined matters concerning health conditions and, in particular, cooperation between parents and institutions.

In 1987 the government appointed a permanent committee of civil servants from thirteen ministries, delegating to members responsibility for following all matters relating to the conditions affecting children's lives.

All these initiatives concerning children's everyday lives have involved the identification of problems, and solutions have been offered in the form of advice, and/or by the presentation of facts which could be taken into consideration when relevant legislation was being formulated.

Public debate has been very active and engaged, and parents' organizations, the Danish National Union of Preschool Teachers, researchers and other interested individuals have participated in these discussions, all in order to give children a higher priority. Unfortunately the result so far has been a lot of concern and good wishes, rather than tangible results.

Parental working patterns

The number of mothers of very young children in the labour force in Denmark has changed over the last twenty years. In 1974 approximately 50 per cent of mothers stayed at home with young children, whereas today only 10 per cent of mothers with young children are either housewives or in full-time education (i.e. they are not included in the employment statistics). Very few families with small children, except for one-parent families, have less than two incomes (Christoffersen 1987a).

Naturally, parental employment patterns have an essential influence on the everyday life of the child and the life of the family. It is now well-documented that in Denmark, mothers with young children rarely stay

Table 1   Working hours for mothers and fathers with children 0–6 years

Hours per week	Mothers	Fathers
0–35 hours	50%	4%
More than 35 hours	50%	96%

(*Source:* Langsted and Sommer 1988 p. 23)

home after the baby is born, they go back to work immediately after maternity leave. This pattern has developed over the last twenty years, and the pattern is the same in both cities and rural areas (Langsted and Sommer 1988).

In Table 1 we can see not only the high levels of employment of both mothers and fathers of young children, but also the extent of the working day outside the home, resulting in many hours' attendance at daycare centres for children.

Concomitantly, children today spend fewer hours in the family than ever before. It means that adults other than the parents have a great influence on the upbringing and education of the child and this is one of the major changes in the life of our young children within the last twenty years.

Maternity leave

Mothers' right to maternity leave was extended from only six weeks to six months in 1984. However, this is not six months' fully salaried leave, but a combination, with some weeks on full pay, some at a reduced rate.

When the law on maternity leave was implemented in 1984, fathers were also granted the right to take parental leave. Before the birth, mothers have the right to four weeks' leave, and they are entitled to a further fourteen weeks after the birth. The ten weeks following this period may be taken as parental leave by either the mother or the father, and additionally fathers are also entitled to a further two weeks' leave as a separate right, and these two weeks are often taken as soon as the mother and the child come home from the maternity ward (Langsted and Sommer 1988).

The right to leave is independent of economic and benefit factors/allowances. Benefits, as compensation for loss of earnings during parental leave, will vary from one person to another and a number of families are granted insufficient benefits, especially in the case of some fathers. In fact, very few fathers (around only 3 per cent) take more than the basic two weeks' paternity leave, whereas about 49 per cent take advantage of that two-week entitlement (Carlsen 1990).

Because it is very difficult to get a place for a baby either in day nurseries or in approved family daycare, many mothers have to stay home longer than the six months allowed. This situation creates not only economic difficulties for families, but it also causes psychological problems, with unrest in the family and stress in the developing relationship between mother and child. Where a family has the problem of not knowing when and where their child will be offered a place in daycare, and the mother is uncertain when she will be able to return to her job, thus running the risk of getting fired, this is a far from beneficial start for everyone involved. Very little or, in fact, no research has been conducted to find out what kind of influence the uncertainty and unrest in the family has on the relationship between the mother and her baby.

Over the last few years, there has been some debate concerning the role of the mother, should she stay at home and be the central person in the care of the family or should she keep her job and have the double role of being a mother and a working housewife? This discussion has been both ideological and political and has involved views on equal opportunities for women, as well as ideas of a 'new' order, where the women should again stay home and care for the family.

The interesting point here is: how has this discussion influenced the young mothers' wish to continue their employment, and what effects have there been on the length of their own working hours and those of fathers? (Langsted and Sommer 1988).

Research (see Table 2) clearly indicates that young mothers want to keep their jobs. Nevertheless about half of them want to work shorter hours, and half of them also think that their partners' working day is too long (the fathers were not questioned). The statement that the young mothers want to work is so clear and strong that it is vital it be taken seriously. What Table 2 also tells us is that there is a considerable gap between the mothers' ideal wishes and real life, where 50 per cent work more than 35 hours a day, and this figure is increasing.

Table 2 Young mothers' desire for short working hours for themselves and for the fathers

Answer	Mother	Father
Right number of hours	46%	43%
No, prefer shorter hours	50%	56%
No, prefer longer hours	3%	1%
No, would like to give up work	2%	0%
Total	101%	100%

(*Source:* Langsted and Sommer 1988)

An integrated part of a child's life

In a modern society the demand for daycare is not simply a matter of the family wanting a place where they can 'park' a child while they are working, but the assurance of high quality provision both for children between 3–6 years, and for those who are babies, infants and toddlers.

In Denmark most families want places for their children from approximately nine months of age. The majority want public care, which means a day nursery or approved family daycare.

Having somewhere to send your child while you are working is far from the only reason why parents want a place for their child in a daycare centre. The point of view that childcare is only a women's rights issue, relating to equal opportunities and employment, is an overly narrow angle on the value of daycare. The debate which is currently going on all over Europe, about whether daycare is only 'care' or whether a daycare centre also has an obligation to provide 'education' is also one with which we are concerned in Denmark.

Mothers were asked how they preferred the family to be organized in order to meet the needs of a family with small children. The survey demonstrated a dramatic change in expressed wishes between respondents questioned in 1970 and those in 1985. In 1985, 86 per cent of the mothers questioned wanted their children in half-day daycare, 3 per cent wanted full-time daycare and only 11 per cent wanted their children to stay at home (Christoffersen 1987a). In 1970 each of these figures was considerably less, since 68 per cent wanted their children to go to half-day provision, 1 per cent wanted full-time daycare and 31 per cent wanted the children to stay at home. This significant change in mothers' attitudes towards daycare has to do partly with economic factors, and partly with personal motivation. But it must be added that it is also the understanding that children living in small families with few or no siblings need the experience derived from attending daycare. The benefits in terms of socialization and education are considered essential for their development. Daycare provision with a developmentally appropriate curriculum is considered just as important for a child in a modern society as primary education is for older children.

The large-scale research project about modern childhood in Scandinavia deals with the term 'double socialization'. The group carrying out the research suggest that double socialization indicates that the child's life condition takes place in two different contexts, home and daycare, at the same time and at a very early stage in life. They add that there are likely to be developmental consequences of growing up in these two different contexts, and that it is not enough to simply merge the two, because their nature is so very different. Together they create a new reality which has a quality of its own. It demands new competences from the child in a world which has much broader social demands, but it also creates a new type of child, seen from a psychological point of view. They argue that it is important for future research to explore children's lives as a whole, and not to see socialization in the family and socialization in daycare as two separate processes, but as a new life condition.

Parents, however, do not see daycare from that perspective, although they do have a clear idea that daycare is an important experience, and a necessary condition for the child's development.

Daycare traditions

Denmark has a long daycare tradition, a tradition covering more than 175 years. *Kindergarten,* or full-time daycare, goes back to the turn of the century, and the major change which later brought daycare into being as part of the welfare system occurred in 1919. It was in that year, for the first time, that the government allocated funds to all private daycare centres and issued a statement emphasizing the point that there should be unity between care and education.

The Danish daycare system is based on Froebel's ideas, but right from the beginning these were transformed into a uniquely Danish interpretation.

In 1891 one of the pioneers of early childhood education in Denmark, Hedevig Bagger, wrote in her handbook for preschool teachers 'Froebel is too much "institution" – we want a more homelike environment, more free play and more child initiative' (Bagger 1891). Discussions as to the relative merits of structured programmes emphasizing cognitive development and those advocating free play, the development of social skills and the child's personality, continue to the present day. Although there is stress upon the promotion of social interaction and communication skills, independence, and creativity in Danish preschools, there is not, to any great extent, any feeling that this is a choice *against* cognitive development. Danish preschool teachers devise their own programmes, allowing a substantial proportion of time for children to choose their own activities. There is plenty of time for free play, because of a firmly held belief that children learn through play, and that a developmental approach to individual personality and social competence provides a better way of ensuring children are equipped to meet the demands of the later, formal system of schooling.

Planned activities in preschools are mostly organized through themes, to include play, musical activities, excursions, books, storytelling, drawing, painting and so on. Danish preschool teachers work with the concept of 'developmentally appropriate programmes'. Structured cognitive development programmes, and those emphasizing compensatory education have had little impact on provision in Denmark. Discussions concerned with cognitive development have been much more focused on how this can be achieved within current approaches, through a balanced programme with a high standard of planning. The aims of early childhood education and the practices favoured as ways of fulfilling those aims have become, increasingly, the focus of parent-teacher collaboration in Denmark, and this has led to major legislative changes, to be enacted in 1993, following a government Circular about offering daycare facilities in accordance with the recent Social Security Act. Every daycare centre is to have a board of parents who, together with the teachers, will be jointly responsible for the goals and programmes of their centre. Further, the local community will set out the aims and objectives of an early childhood curriculum for services in their area, but the structure is to be loosely framed in order to allow boards of parents and teachers sufficient freedom to work out their own programmes, interpreting the over-arching guidelines. For teachers this is an entirely new experience. For the last hundred years they have had total responsibility, total autonomy for devising programmes. In general, everyone involved is positive about the new development, although naturally there are some anxieties.

Legislation and administration

Daycare centres are established in accordance with the Social Security Act (paragraph 69). The government's policy of decentralization in the 1980s resulted in local communities having responsibility for, and control of, daycare. Further, the responsibility for providing the necessary number of places rests with the local community. This requirement can be fulfilled in different ways:

- by establishing and running day nurseries and daycare centres;
- by entering into a contract with a private kindergarten organization, for example church organizations, Red Cross, Labour kindergarten organizations, etc.;
- a pooling arrangement;
- by running approved family daycare.

The local communities taking up the first option means they can establish their own daycare centres – that is, 'care' for infants and toddlers, kindergarten for three- to six-year-olds (in Denmark the word kindergarten is used for daycare for children between 3 and 6 years).

Also there will be out-of-hours care for children from 6 to 10, most often organized in collaboration with the local schools.

The local community decide for themselves whether they want to run their own daycare, or whether they want to have contracts with private organizations. The difference between a public and a private daycare centre is primarily that the private daycare centre has a governing body consisting of parents and representatives from the organization that originally established the centre. Most communities have a mixture of both types of daycare.

There is no difference in the demands made of community owned daycare and privately owned daycare. All private organizations must have a contract with the local community, and through this contract the local community is in a position to make the same demands of private centres as those made of community-run centres.

A pool arrangement is something new in Denmark. In 1990 the government implemented a new law (the Social Security Act 5.7) that gave the local community the right to give a group of parents or a private organization, for example a business or a factory, the right to run daycare provision for children. The local government then contributes a certain amount of money per child and this sum is decided on an individual basis, case by case. From here on, it is the responsibility of the group setting up the pool arrangement to organize the daycare as they want it. The local community has responsibility for the supervision and inspection of any pool arrangement.

Local communities fulfil a major aspect of their responsibility for infants and toddlers by organizing approved family daycare. The way in which this form of care differs from that offered in daycare centres is that only a few children are cared for together and provision is located in private homes.

The local community has the responsibility for the approval of the person, mostly mothers, and of the home, as being of an adequate standard for family daycare. One 'daycare mother' can care for up to five children, but most mind only two or three. Children up to 14 years old may be found in this form of provision, but in general it caters for children from 0–3 years. Family daycare for children under primary school age is more common than centre-based provision in rural areas (Government Circular – Denmark 1990).

Management

The total decentralization of the provision of daycare is new in Denmark. Before 1973 when an earlier Social Security Act had been passed, there were centralized rules and regulations. Daycare for preschool children has since then become more and more the responsibility of local government. Today only a few rules and regulations established through the central administration and Danish law remain in place. The Ministry of Labour has responsibility for regulations concerning buildings. The Health and Safety at Work Act deals with staff working conditions and, through regulations, with the premises. Health and Safety has central regulations concerned with a number of different aspects of buildings, etc., as well as regulations for kitchens and the preparation of food.

Besides having responsibility for all daycare centres the local community also has a supervisory duty. In larger communities pedagogical consultants are employed as advisers.

The day nurseries, family daycare and daycare centres are administered under the local Social Services Department, the school-related daycare centres are administered under the local Education Department. Some local communities have initiated Departments of Children's Affairs that cover both daycare centres and schools.

Daycare provision: some statistics

Table 3 shows quite clearly the high demand for full-time daycare, and for out-of-hours care for older children.

Table 3   Daycare provision: some statistics

Number of children enrolled in daycare centres in 1991		
	All-day	Part-time
0–2-year-olds:		
Day nurseries	24,217	114
Integrated daycare	7,630	
Family daycare	49,454	
3–7-year-olds:		
Kindergartens	81,648	8,193
Integrated daycare	35,212	
Family daycare	14,417	
7–10-year-olds:		
Recreation centres	30,073	
Integrated daycare	13,144	
Family daycare	951	
Coverage (per 100 enrolled children 1990):		
0–2-year-olds	47.2%	
3–6-year-olds	66.9%	
7–10-year-olds	18.7%	
When school daycare and recreation clubs are added the coverage rises to over 50%.		

(*Source:* Lund 1992)

What these figures do not show is the discrepancy between rural and urban areas. In some districts in the cities the kindergarten coverage is 90 per cent, and in some rural areas only family daycare is available (Lund 1992).

Financing provision for preschool children

Daycare centres are financed by local government, together with contributions from parents. This is because all responsibility for the provision for preschool children is placed on the local authority. The local authority receives a grant from central government, and it is up to each community to decide what proportion of this will be allocated to provision for preschool children. What this means is that central government has the possibility of limiting what happens, through regulation of these grants. Because of the decentralization of responsibility, communities may differ considerably from one another as to how much parents have to pay for a place in a day nursery, daycare centre or for family daycare.

In 1990, the average monthly fee paid by parents on a country wide basis was as shown in Table 4. However, the averages shown in Table 4 mask the considerable variations from one locality to another. For example, in the Greater Copenhagen area payment for day nurseries in 1990 was as low as DKK 852 in Albertslund, but DKK 2,190 in Hedensted in Jutland. For kindergartens payments were DKK 666 in Herlev (Greater Copenhagen area) but DKK 1,380 in Marstal Aero, in the Southern Funen Archipelago (Lund 1992).

Very recently, the government passed a new law stating that parents should pay a maximum of only 32 per cent of the cost in 1991 and 1992, and from 1993 only up to 30 per cent of costs (Lund 1992). It is this percentage that fluctuates from one community to another, thus creating

Table 4 Average fees charged to parents in Denmark for different forms of provision

Type of provision	Cost in DKK
Day nurseries	1,370
Kindergartens	1,003
Integrated daycare centres	991
Recreation centres	657
School daycare	650
Family daycare	1,352

(*Source:* Lund 1992)

the tremendous discrepancies in costs to parents. For parents with low incomes and for children who for special reasons (e.g. social reasons, children with special needs) must attend a daycare centre it is possible for the authorities to make a reduction in fees.

Apart from the differences in charges to parents, there are other differences between the daycare centres from one community to another. For example, the adult : child ratios, and the amount of funding allowed to daycare centres for play materials, excursions, and even food for the children.

However, any pool arrangement is not included in these rules because the local government will consider these case by case, and pool arrangements are not guaranteed funding.

Daycare for infants and toddlers

The local community has the duty to administer home-based daycare staff, and a supervisor visits at least twice a month. The supervisor and worker discuss the development of the children, any practical problems, and the supervisor may bring toys for loan, and materials for the children. The community also supplies food for the children.

Very often supervisors will organize group meetings of 'daycare mothers' once or twice a week, and the children then meet each other in a playgroup/crèche facility. Many of the 'daycare mothers' have their own children to look after, besides those children for whom they are paid.

Although family daycare is less costly for parents than day nursery, the majority of parents want day nursery provision for their infants (Christoffersen 1987). Overall 80 per cent of mothers prefer public daycare and only 20 per cent want private arrangements. Private arrangements are more likely to be preferred in rural areas, whereas most parents in urban areas are reported as wanting public daycare.

The majority of children under 3 years of age are cared for by 'daycare mothers', and around 25,000 are cared for in nurseries. These nurseries are run by the community or by private organizations. Waiting lists for nurseries are very long, partly because of the increased demand over the last fifteen years, which continues to rise.

In the nurseries, infants are placed in small groups of eight children, and toddlers are in groups of between ten and twelve. When children move on from their toddler group they join an age-integrated group, of which they will remain a member until they leave to join the kindergarten. Staff in these nurseries have usually specialized in infant and toddler work during their own education and training, and there is growing co-operation between teachers in the two settings, so that continuity in children's experience is assured when they move on to the kindergarten.

Daycare for three- to six-year-olds

Most children between 3 and 6 years of age are cared for in full-time daycare called *kindergarten*. As stated earlier, the Danish daycare tradition goes back to the turn of the century, and although it has changed with the times, the influences of Froebel and Montessori are still discernible. Children attend daycare centres near their homes, since parents, teachers and local authorities have agreed for the last 30 years that daycare should be part of a neighbourhood network system. It is regarded as important for children to be with peers from their own community, with whom they will move on into the primary school.

Most centres have an outdoor playground, although inner-city groups may sometimes lack this facility, when a playground may be shared with another centre, or children may be taken to a local park. Outdoor life is a very important aspect of early childhood education and care in Denmark, and many centres are open from 7.00 a.m. until 5.00 p.m. in the evening, some even longer.

Children are divided into groups of around twenty, and the groups contain children of varying ages. There is some part-time daycare, but this is rare, since most mothers work full time.

There are many changes currently in progress in the Danish daycare system, because of the growing waiting lists, and because of changes in the structure of the education system. The combination of the nursery (for babies and toddlers) and daycare (for three- to six-year-olds) means that children are able to attend the same centre from birth to school age. Maternity leave is longer, so many babies do not enter the system until they are 1 year old, and with the advent of co-ordinated school start (see below), affecting the five-year-olds, greater continuity is provided during these early years if children can remain at the same centre, with familiar children and teachers. Around 20 per cent of children attend integrated centres from 0–10 years of age. The upper age limit was formerly 14 years, but now most communities run open clubs for children between the ages of 10 and 18 years, as part of the out-of-hours care facilities.

Co-ordinated school start and afternoon care

The way in which children are admitted to, and begin their experience of, primary school has changed recently. In 1989 the Minister of Education passed a law that gave local schools, in close co-operation with parents, the possibility of organizing a 'co-ordinated school start'. This means that the kindergarten class for the five- to six-year-olds and grades 1 and 2 of the primary school work closely together. The intention of this co-ordinated school start is to provide better continuity for the children, and a meaningful, relevant curriculum, one which does not have to be divided according to subjects. The ultimate goal that teachers of grades 1 and 2 should also engage in this development of a holistic, meaningful educational experience for the children takes a slightly different form from that of the past. Co-operative team teaching involving the kindergarten class and the first and second class often consists of focusing on a theme, over a period of time, and the children from the three first classes are divided into small groups, with the primary teachers and the preschool teacher being responsible for the work of the groups. The whole team of teachers has responsibility for the planning.

The reason for this change in policy and practice from the traditional school entry procedures in the early years of primary school was based on practical, observational evidence showing that children were not simultaneously mature and ready for the substantial shift in teaching methods. Additionally, it was noted that the learning processes of children in the five- to nine-year-old age group required far more varied approaches. Varied teaching and learning styles needed to be catered for, including systematic/structured learning, self-elected activities, and concrete experiences as a starting point (Vilien 1990).

Ninety-five per cent of all children aged 5–6 years attend the kindergarten class, and if the number in this class exceeds 28 children, the class will be divided in two. Further, if there are more than 22 children in a class, the teacher is assisted by another teacher. The average number of children in a primary school class is usually around twenty. At present 50 per cent of all schools have moved to the innovative type of co-ordinated school start described above (Danish Teachers' Union 1989).

The length of the children's day is only about three or four hours in the first years of school, so that since more than 90 per cent of all mothers are involved in the labour market, out-of-hours care in the mornings (before school) and afternoons (after school) is vital. More and more communities are establishing this kind of care, in close co-operation with schools and after-school care providers. Often the preschool teachers work at the school in the mornings and at the after-school care in the afternoon. This system gives the children's day a sense of unity, the teachers know them, both at school and in their leisure time. Additionally, there is the advantage that much of the organization and administrative planning will be common to both parts of the day, especially in relation to contact with parents. Moreover, it means that the children do not have to go into the dangerous traffic by themselves to get from school to the necessary afternoon 'leisure home'. Increasing numbers of communities are offering guaranteed places – if a child in any class between kindergarten and grade 3 needs a place in the school's afternoon care provision, then one is made available.

Children with special needs

In Denmark there is a general consensus that all children, irrespective of any special needs or disability, should be integrated into 'ordinary' settings, with other children. It is first and foremost the responsibility of the local community to provide a place in a daycare centre for every child. This means that all centres must be prepared to admit children with difficulties ranging from physical and mental disabilities to allergies, epilepsy, and behaviour problems. When a daycare centre accepts a child with special needs the local community is expected to provide extra staffing, and some teachers are specialized in this work. Other professionals, for example physiotherapists, may come into the daycare centre several times each week, so that the work of a number of agencies must be co-ordinated. The integration of children with learning difficulties is seen as a vital aspect in ensuring the children feel they are part of their own communities, and in helping them learn how to cope in their peer group, with particular support at the start of this integration process. The segregation of children with special needs is unpopular in Danish society, but occasionally a child's disability may be thought to require provision in a special institution or daycare centre, and this will be a county responsibility, usually requiring daily transport for the child concerned.

In a recent evaluation of services Vedel-Petersen (1992) reported that sometimes integration can be difficult, for example, in co-ordinating the work of different professional groups, and ensuring activities in the centre cater fully for children's individual needs. Sometimes only a very small number of children with particular support or treatment requirements attend one centre, so organizing this is less straightforward than it would be if children were grouped together.

Support for children from cultural minorities

Denmark has no legislation at State level concerning the ways in which communities should provide for, or defend the rights of, children from linguistic or cultural minorities. Each community must decide on its own policy. Some offer places in daycare centres with teachers who speak the children's home language, and in some there are playgroups where mothers participate.

Voluntary organizations are active in this field (e.g. Danish OMEP), providing books, tapes, games and play materials.

The development of appropriate provision depends upon the will in each community.

Training of preschool teachers

In May 1991 the Danish government passed a new law concerning a common preschool teacher education and training, which will combine the three existing routes into preschool teaching into one. The new courses, which started in September 1992, will take three-and-a-half years. The education is to B.A. degree level, and will still maintain a broad recruitment base, which means that it is not limited to high school graduates.

The courses are based in special Preschool Teacher Training Colleges. There are two periods, each a half year, of professional practice in daycare centres, and in centres for children with special needs. The term 'pedagogue' (*paedagog*) is used in Denmark for preschool teachers.

After some years of experience in the field, preschool teachers can take one year of advanced studies at the Royal Danish School of Educational Studies or at the School for Advanced Training of Social Pedagogues. The graduate studies programmes at the Royal Danish School of Educational Studies are open for preschool teachers.

At the Royal Danish School of Educational Studies preschool teachers can also undertake further training, as speech therapists and audiologists, or they can take a supplementary course to become specialized teachers of children with disabilities and learning difficulties. Unfortunately, the places available on all these programmes of study are limited, so admission is competitive.

Research

In Denmark the early years field has never attracted a great deal of attention. Until the 1970s most of the research which had been conducted was in the field of developmental psychology and tended to focus on children with specific problems. However, in 1977 the Danish Research Council allocated funds for a five-year project known as the 'Early Childhood Initiative'. When that initiative ended the Ministry of Education funded the setting up of a Department and a Centre of Early Childhood Research in the Royal School of Educational Studies, Copenhagen. The Institute of Education at the University of Copenhagen, and the Psychological Institute at the University of Arhus have a long research tradition. *Socialforskninginstituttet* in Copenhagen is currently engaged in several projects concerning early childhood and the functioning of daycare, for the government. During the last five years the Ministry of Social Affairs has supported research and evaluation work in the field of daycare, especially exploring initiatives leading to development. The pre-school teachers' union, BUPL, supports a number of research projects throughout the country, in order to improve the quality of pedagogy. However, if more research funding could be attracted, more vital work could be carried out than is the present case. Such research as is currently in process is unco-ordinated, based in different institutes throughout Denmark, and no clear picture emerges. However, Kirsten Reisby (1991) has written an interesting and thought-provoking article discussing the status and perspectives of educational research.

Conclusion

The Danish welfare system has created a coherent high quality system for the provision of daycare for young children. Nevertheless, it is a system which has to be protected by repeated reminders to ourselves and our politicians that quality daycare must be constantly discussed and evaluated by parents, teachers and policy-makers, and that it requires money, time and effort, together with ongoing in-service training of teachers, to maintain and improve that quality.

Peter Moss (1992), co-ordinator of the EC Childcare Network has commented:

> Denmark is in every respect exceptional . . . Employment rates for women are the highest in Europe; over 90 per cent are in the labour force . . . Compulsory school begins at seven . . . and Denmark is the only EC country where publicly funded provision accounts for most of the children in this age group (0–6) who attend some form of early childhood service.
>
> (Moss, 1992, p. 33–34)

Further, Moss (ibid) points out that Denmark is the EC member country where integration of services is the most developed and where services are recognized as having both a caring *and* a pedagogical responsibility. The fact that workers in these services are called 'pedagogues' bears witness to this expectation.

4

Preschool Education in France

Madeleine Goutard

In France the Ministry of Social Security and Health (*Ministère de la Solidarité et de la Santé*) administers establishments catering for children aged 0 to 3 years. These are the *pouponnieres* (crèches), the *crèche collectives* (community day nurseries), and family and parental daycare facilities. It is estimated that places offered by these establishments, despite being numerous, are insufficient to cope with demand. Other types of provision, such as *garderies* and *haltes-garderies* (day nurseries), *jardin d'enfants* (kindergartens), centres for children with learning difficulties and special needs, and so on are less prolific. However, since, in this publication, we are considering those forms of provision with a primarily educational focus, and because of its importance as a result of its numerical significance, this chapter will discuss the *Ecole Maternelle Française* (EMF) (French nursery school system).

In fact, almost all children aged 3, 4 and 5 years and more than 36 per cent of all the two-year-olds in France attend a private or a public nursery school, the great majority being the latter, forming 87.8 per cent of the total.

History of the EMF

Since the eighteenth century, feelings of pity at the misery and neglect of young children during their parents' absence were the catalysts of private initiatives, causing benefactors to gather children together for their protection, safety and health and, most importantly, for their education.

Jean-Frederic Oberlin, the French minister, who lived from 1740–1826, set up a model educational establishment, which was to provide further stimulus to the development of daycare facilities in both England and France. In 1770, he founded the first *école à tricoter* (knitting school) in a Vosges valley, which, as well as introducing the technique of knitting to the area, provided the opportunity for children aged 3 and over to learn French (their mother tongue being a regional dialect); to study nature; to understand the rudiments of reading and arithmetic; and to acquire good moral and spiritual precepts. With the help of his wife, he trained young women to work with young children as *conductrices de la tendre enfance*, in order to expand this form of provision throughout all the villages of the valley. He developed teaching materials to make learning more attractive, and less abstract, to the children, and some of the varied and ingenious examples can still be seen in the museum at Strasbourg (*Musée Alsacien*), and some in the Waldersbach presbytery, where Oberlin worked for 59 years.

In 1826 the first *salles d'asile* were founded in Paris, and towards the end of the century, these were to become the *écoles maternelles* (nursery schools). From 1829 to 1881, many official documents were published, encouraging the formation of *salles d'asile* in every region, and at the same time, defining their role. Basically, these were charitable institutions, somewhat like dame schools, run by women dedicated to the wellbeing of children, where both girls and boys up to the age of six could be cared for and appropriately educated. The number of *salles d'asile* increased rapidly as a result of the involvement of religious communities. In 1867, out of 3,572 *salles d'asile*, 2,609 were run by nuns, i.e. 73 per cent, and by 1876 this proportion had grown to 80 per cent.

Following the development of the *salles d'asile*, a mayor of one of the districts of Paris, with the patronage of some wealthy benefactresses, formulated the basis of an education system which was to last for more than a century. The idea was to imitate the system of schooling for older children, ensuring the inculcation of basic knowledge, as well as religious and moral values. Unfortunately, problems arose concerning staff ignorance and inappropriate equipment, so that the question of the education and training of personnel became crucial. In 1845, the first edition of *Conseils sur la direction des salles d'asile* (Advice on management of day nurseries) and *Enseignement pratique dans les salles d'asile* (Teaching in day nurseries), by Marie Pape Carpentier (1815–1878) appeared, and in 1848 she became principal of a training college for heads of nursery establishments.

The inception of the école maternelle

During the period from 1881 to 1887 official regulation ensured the integration of the *salles d'asile* into the French education system, although this had already been set in train as early as 1833. The Third

Republic organized the system of obligatory, free education, and this reinforced the acceptance of the *salles d'asile* as part of that system. In particular, the law passed on 16 June 1881 extended the right to free primary education to the *salles d'asile*. On 2 August 1881, a decree was issued to the effect that young children 'will receive the care demanded by their physical, intellectual and moral development, and that they may be admitted at the age of two and remain until they are seven years old' (IIIrd French Republic, 2.8.1881).

The bye-law of 28 July 1882 defined the role of the *écoles maternelle*, the name which – although proposed way back in 1837, and left for dead – now sprang to life.

In 1884 the training colleges (*école normales d'institutrices*) were given the responsibility for ensuring the recruitment of teaching personnel, not just for the primary schools, but also for the nursery schools (*les écoles maternelles*) and the nursery classes attached to primary schools (*les classes enfantines*). In 1885 the premises, equipment and furniture were all placed in the hands of the local *communes* (parishes), and on 30 October 1886 nursery education became enshrined in law as the first, albeit voluntary, stage of primary education.

The founding influence of Pauline Kergomard

It could be said that Pauline Kergomard (1838–1925) was the real founder of the EMF. When in 1879 she was entrusted with the country's *salles d'asile*, she struggled energetically to combat any premature, inappropriate instruction, not conducive to young children's development, and she was against drill-like activities which, she felt, stifled spontaneity.

For almost 40 years, Madame Kergomard was ahead of her time in working tirelessly, providing the French nursery education system with a strong base. Her thinking and work are akin to that of other great pioneers of early childhood education. She became the self-styled advocate of spontaneity and freedom for young children, and her efforts against formal teaching programmes succeeded in reducing them to almost nothing. She asserted that children needed to play, to be active, to be accepted as people with inner lives and spiritual needs, and a natural propensity to strive for knowledge. Kergomard demonstrated the importance of sensory-motor education and she accorded an important place to music and singing in the French nursery curriculum.

Unlike other educationists of that time, Madame Kergomard did not formulate her ideas into a 'method' of teaching, nor did she advocate the use of particular equipment, arguing that natural resources were more important. However, perhaps what was most distinctive about her was her social work. In one sense because of her constant activities to save children from misery, she acquired personal experience of different social contexts, because she believed that to know the child one must know the family. She became aware of the fact that to satisfy the educational needs of the children, one also had to take account of the educational needs of the adults. Thus, she strove to bring the methods of family education into the *écoles maternelles*, and, inversely, to involve the nursery in the lives of families at home. Her conception of the social role of the *école maternelle* included concern for the children's health, through the provision of improved physical conditions in the schools, and a school health service.

Further, Madame Kergomard feared the over-encouragement of individualism, which she identified in the methods of the younger Maria Montessori, thus she clung to the preservation of a community dimension in the work of the French nurseries. Then, herself a feminist, Kergomard was opposed to the separation of girls and boys during their schooling, because she saw education in the context of social interactions. She believed the *école maternelle* to be the 'cradle of democracy', where, through the fostering of positive habits and an atmosphere of tenderness and affection, the foundation for peace would be laid.

Pauline Kergomard appears to have been advanced for her time, in that she obtained training for early childhood educators equivalent to that of primary school teachers. However, having gained access to the colleges, she realized the dangers inherent in a generalized training, and, before she retired, she advocated specialized training institutions, but without success. This problem of equivalence for specialized training for work with children at different levels or age groups in education, posed by Kergomard in 1917, has never been satisfactorily resolved in France.

Other related developments

In 1905 the separation of the Church and the State meant that nuns were forbidden access to nursery schools. Later, after the 1918 peace treaty with Germany, they were granted entry in those regions which were reintegrated into France (Alsace and Lorraine), but their presence is now almost a thing of the past.

In 1910 an inspectorate was formed, to supervise nursery schools. These inspectors played a crucial role in the development of early childhood pedagogy, right up to their service being completely disbanded in 1990, since when all inspectors have had to cover both the nursery and primary phases.

Earlier, in 1921, a statute had set in place a regulation such that teachers in both primary and nursery sectors had the same conditions of service, in terms of hours and holidays. Additionally, an unqualified auxiliary (*femme de service*) was to be attached to each nursery school and class. As far as recognition for the specialized nature of the work was concerned, in order to obtain a post in a nursery, teachers needed to be qualified in: early childhood pedagogy, child development, hygiene and science related to early childhood, and general hygiene. Later, this requirement for specialized qualifications became more likely to be applied only in the case of the appointment of headteachers, experience in the field being seen as adequate; and since 1990 the demand for specialized, phase qualifications of this kind has been eradicated.

Another event of importance in 1921 was the inception of *l'Association Générale des Institutrices des Ecoles Maternelles* (AGIEM), which, through the enthusiasm and support of the early years inspectorate, organized an annual national conference. This stimulated creativity and the exchange of information, ideas and experiences.

One very special conference, *Congres International de l'Enfance*, was organized in 1931 in Paris by Suzanne Herbinière-Lebert. All the 'great names' of the time – Decroly, Descoeudres, Dottrens, Piaget, Piéron, Simon, Washburn, Montessori and others – were brought together, attracting a tremendous international gathering. After the Second World War, in 1948, Madame Herbinière-Lebert co-operated with Lady Allen of Hurtwood from the UK, and Alva Myrdal of Sweden, in founding *l'Organisation Mondiale pour l'Education Préscolaire* (OMEP), the World Organization for Early Childhood Education devoted to the promotion of early childhood education for children throughout the world. Suzanne Herbinière-Lebert became the president of the French Committee of OMEP. She engaged the *maternelles* in fruitful international exchanges, thus helping the French model of early childhood education to be better known abroad.

The école maternelle: *aims and objectives*

The EMF proved such a great success with families and children, with increasing numbers attending, from all classes of society, that there was a massive expansion in provision after the Second World War. Between 1963 and 1976, the proportion of all children in the age range attending rose from 42.6 to 77 per cent. By 1991/92 this figure had risen to 84.4 per cent, distributed as shown in Table 5.

Studies by, for instance, Jarousse, Mingat and Richard 1991, have shown that at all levels of primary education, and in particular during the first year, school failure decreases according to the length of time attended in the *maternelle*, particularly between the ages of 0 and 3 years.

Table 5 Percentages of children attending EMF, by age

	percentage of whole age group
children aged 4 and 5 years	100.0
children aged 3 years	98.8
children aged 2 years	34.4

(*Source*: adapted from Ministère de l'Education Nationale et de la Culture, 1992)

In fact, this effect has been found to continue into secondary school. However, this effect is more marked for children from disadvantaged families. Thus, attendance at the *école maternelle* appears to be an important factor in reducing inequalities. In this respect, the provision of EMF is recognized as a right for all families with young children, whatever their cultural, social, ethnic or geographical origin.

Priority objectives

During the last fifteen years, recognition for the importance of EMF as a right for all has acted as a spur to the formulation of social and political objectives in official documentation. These include:

- the prevention of impaired development and early detection of handicaps;
- compensation for cultural disadvantage;
- equalizing educational opportunities.

In order to achieve these objectives, policies have been enacted to extend access to provision to groups of children who were hitherto denied this, for example, a) children living in isolated areas, b) children with special educational needs and severe learning difficulties, c) younger children, d) foreign children.

Children living in isolated areas

The law passed on 11 July 1975 favoured the development of nursery classes in rural locations. To take account of the special geographical, demographic and sociological conditions involved, different ways of complying with this law were proposed. Depending on the circumstances, it was possible to:

- transform primary school classrooms into *maternelles*;
- reorganize educational provision through the development of community groupings, with transport available to bring children of the same age groups together, whether nursery or primary phase (this has been the most popular solution);

- the use of mobile classrooms, and peripatetic teachers, a measure which has been interpreted in a variety of ways.

Additionally, whatever solution has been adopted, there is a requirement that resources and teaching methods be satisfactory.

Children with special educational needs/severe learning difficulties
The Ministerial Circular of 9 February 1970 laid the foundations, for the first time, for the provision of special classes for physically handicapped children, or those experiencing developmental, or socio-emotional/ relationship problems. Further, specialized teams were to be set up to work in this field.

However, because any clear definition of the special needs is difficult, and since it was necessary to adopt a global approach taking into account the context and the school itself, more flexible solutions were preferred, avoiding segregating children, wherever possible. The practice adopted was that of continuous observation by EMF staff, followed by timely support from the specialists. As a result of this and subsequent legislation (the law of 30 June 1975, Circulars and Directives in 1982 and 1983), children with motor, sensory or other handicaps are currently integrated into 'ordinary' nursery classes, wherever conditions are favourable and permit this, if necessary, only part-time or only on condition the mothers would help out. In this case the adult : child ratio might be reduced. There is also provision for an extra year to be spent in the *école maternelle*, where it is considered this would be of benefit to the children involved.

The youngest children
All children aged 4 and 5 attend *maternelle*, and this has an effect on the admission of the youngest children. Priority is given to admitting children aged 3, whose parents seek it. In schools where this objective is being reached, efforts are then extended to make places available to the two-year-olds, especially in those areas where children are socially or geographically disadvantaged (see later). In some regions, the fall in the birth rate, with its resultant effects on the uptake of primary school places, has meant that it has been possible to admit all those children aged 2 and 3 whose parents wished them to attend EMF, as long as the premises, etc., have been suitably adapted.

The biggest problems set by the admission of these very young children have been largely related to the need for the conditions outlined in the Circular of December 1982 to have been put in place, these are: premises in which it is possible to satisfy the children's need for naps, tranquillity, space for movement, respect for their physiological rhythms, an emotionally secure and intellectually stimulating atmosphere, good co-operation with families, support from social services and health professionals, extended daycare facilities, proper training for teaching staff and classroom assistants. There has been recognition for the need to co-ordinate the training of different workers, from the various administrative sectors, involved in provision for children between two and three years of age.

Foreign children
Ecoles maternelles have always admitted those children living in their catchment areas, irrespective of their nationality. In fact, it is recommended that children of migrant workers attend *maternelle* from as young an age as possible, so that they can become acclimatized to the French education system. Intercultural education is also seen as important, and is recommended (see later section).

Educational objectives

During the hundred years of its existence, because of the social evolution of French society, the educational objectives of the EMF have become more important than sanitary and social objectives. Health, hygiene, the rhythm of life, and children's safety are, nevertheless, seen to form part of education and other professional services work in conjunction with the school more and more.

Until very recently the EMF managed with a minimally prescribed curriculum, as Pauline Kergomard wished, but after such a long period of time a substantial amount of experience has been accumulated. A Ministerial Circular of August 1977 attempted to synthesize this expertise, to provide aims, objectives and teaching methods and relate these to research findings about children's development. However, this composite text seemed to be practically unusable.

Using a simpler and more direct manner, a Circular of 30 January 1986 defined three over-arching objectives related to approaches in the nurseries:

1. '*Scolariser*' ('to turn children into pupils') – intended to welcome the child into a new and different environment, complementary to the home;
2. '*Socialiser*' (to socialize) – to enlarge and enrich the children's social relations, while fostering enculturation;
3. '*Faire apprendre et exercer*' (to promote learning and allow time for practice) – to develop all the children's capacities.

Although the official documents go on to expand and offer broad interpretations, the choice of these particular objectives, and the way in which they were formulated demonstrate quite clearly that transforming children into pupils is the primary goal. In fact, somewhat tautologously, the first objective makes clear the intention that the EMF should be, first and foremost, a school, in the full sense of the word. What it is always important to ask ourselves, however, is – is the school made for the child, or the child made for the school?

The effect of this pressure to prioritize the transformation of children into pupils can be seen in the gradual integration of the *école maternelle* into the mainstream system. This has resulted from the publication of official documents, released at different times during the last fifteen years, which have eroded the distinctive character of the EMF and its specific pedagogical methods. This has happened in spite of the fact that the specificity of each level has been restated in the official documents.

The Circular of 4 October 1977 proposed that continuity between nursery and primary phases would be enhanced through, among other things, a mixed teaching force, the *maternelle* having been the preserve of women only. This measure was universally applauded, but in reality it resulted in few men joining the early years teaching force, except in more senior appointments.

The Education Act of 10 July 1989, followed by decrees relating to its application (6 September 1990), concerning the organization and running of primary teaching (*l'enseignement élémentaire*) and of the nursery system (now called *pré-élémentaire*, although this name is rarely used in practice), set out 'cycles of apprenticeship' determined according to the psychological and physiological development of each child. The first cycle, or phase, called the *pré-apprentissages* (the prelearning cycle) is concerned with children aged 2, 3 and 4 years, at the nursery. The second cycle, called the *apprentissages fondamentaux* (fundamental, or basic, learning cycle), involves children aged 5 years in the nursery and those aged 6 and 7 years at primary school; the third cycle, called the 'period of consolidation' or *d'approfondissement* covers the last three years of primary school.

The point of all this is to try to prevent the need for some children to repeat years of schooling, or, when it is inevitable, to prolong one period or stage for a particular child, and create better continuity of educational experience.

The inclusion of the last year of *maternelle* in the stage which also includes the first two years of primary school confers on it a linking role between the two types of school, a role facilitated by the creation of teaching teams, doubling the staff board in each school. Consultations,

for which one hour per week has been freed from classroom responsibilities, involve the teaching team in defining together the levels of each
stage, discussing progress and determining the conditions needed for
each pupil to achieve the requirements of the cycle.

The cycle of first apprenticeship, from 2 to 5 years, covers a period of
dramatic developmental change in children. Thanks to careful observational practices, the first indications of any delay or difficulty should
hopefully be detected and appropriate action taken.

A further indication of the integration of the nursery and primary
phases of education can be seen in changes to the inspectoral system. For
fifteen years there have been progressive moves to circumscribe nursery
inspections within those of the primary sector, and in 1990 the generalization of the inspectorate reinforced the subsuming of the *écoles maternelles*. This also implies for the inspectors and their pedagogical advisory
assistants a need to function simultaneously on two levels. Furthermore,
it means that specifically nursery expertise is suppressed, everyone involved needs to be competent in the work of both sectors, if a first-class
education is to be provided.

Funding

Although it is not obligatory, nursery education is provided free of
charge in France. The State pays for the training and the salaries of
teachers in public nursery schools and classes, and even for some of those
working in the private sector, under special contracts (*contrats
d'association*).

The local authorities are responsible for public school buildings, ensuring the finance for construction, maintenance and equipment, with help
from regional subsidies. Local authorities also pay the salaries of unqualified staff (see later). Sometimes local authorities organize complementary services, such as cafeterias, out-of-hours care, holiday centres
and playschemes, etc. They are also the source of funding for educational
supplies and equipment.

Sometimes schools take the initiative for raising funds themselves, organizing co-operatives, fetes, fairs, and so on. Under certain conditions,
they may be able to obtain grants from local or national bodies, by
detailing special educational action projects, intended to create partnership between the school and the community (Circular 6 January
1983), or from an innovation fund (Circular 31 January 1989) if they
plan to implement an innovative venture.

The role of parents

There is an obligation on staff at *maternelle* that they will truly come to know the children with whom they work so, traditionally, contacts with parents are far more frequent and intense than those of the primary school. However, parental roles in the nursery have been very limited.

The requirement for each school to have a committee of elected parents was enshrined in law through the Decree of 28 December 1976, and at least three times a year this committee must meet with the school council, a committee of the school's teachers (such councils have been in existence for many years). This decree, therefore, instituted parents of pupils as partners in the educational establishment, essentially as consultants.

The tendency is to extend the role of the school council (according to the Decree of 13 May 1985, and the Note of 14 March 1986), which gives advice on the teaching organization within a school; the use of resources; effective integration of children with special educational needs; the use of open-air classes, buildings outside school hours; out-of-hours care facilities; extra-curricular activities and clubs; meals services; etc.

Outside these formal consultative duties, parents take part in the life of the school, by accompanying parties on school trips, helping with particular activities such as swimming, preparation for fundraising events such as fetes, improving play facilities, provision of snacks, etc. They may also help with classroom tasks, after seeking the agreement of the appropriate academic authorities. The degree to which the levels of involvement extend, and its effectiveness, depends upon the openness of the teachers, and in some cases may take on great significance, as for example when the youngest children are preparing for the nursery.

Delegates from the federation of parents take part in regional and national academic councils, the State providing funding to cover any costs incurred.

The children

Traditionally the children have been grouped by age in the nursery. Those who are 5 years old form the 'big children's section', the four-year-olds the 'middle section', the two- and three-year-olds the 'little ones' section'. It is rare to find a preference for mixed-age classes, parents are not usually in favour of this arrangement. However, in small schools, rural nursery schools and classes for example, there are often only two or three sections owing to force of circumstances. In large schools too, from time to time one may choose to place children from two age bands in the same class, as a way of grouping them most effectively.

This tradition derives from the fact that a nursery school was often created by admitting children into primary school progressively – one year, then two, then three years earlier. Having the very young children together with many others thus obliged staff to create a protected, appropriate environment for them. This type of organization has allowed the development of a special pedagogy, adapted to the particular needs of the youngest children, and taking account of the differentiated rhythms of life of both the younger and older children.

Mixed-age groupings can have advantages from a social and emotional point of view too, because the presence of older children can both stimulate the younger children and give them a feeling of security, when there is a positive, educationally oriented ethos. In those schools known as 'open-air' establishments, which are very rare these days, groupings will be even more varied, since each member of the teaching team will be in charge of a group containing all ages – a kind of family grouping system.

School hours in the *maternelle* are the same as those for the primary sector – 26 hours for the children, 27 for staff, over four full days (Monday, Tuesday, Thursday and Friday) and usually Saturday morning. Ordinarily, children attend the nursery for three hours in the morning and three in the afternoon, with an interval of two or one-and-a-half hours separating the sessions. For some children, the hours of attendance are prolonged because they use the restaurant facilities during the long lunch-break, and because there is an out-of-hours care service before and after the actual school day. In some of the big cities, there are children who are on the nursery premises for as long as ten hours a day.

Following recent attempts to adjust to children's daily rhythms, some flexibility has been introduced, in special cases, with the agreement of everyone concerned, and bearing in mind the characteristics of the local context (Circular 2 August 1988).

There is one admission date per year, at the beginning of September, the same date as that for the re-opening of the primary schools. This coordination is helpful to administration, and to the gathering of statistics. However, this massed entry of large numbers of children is considered to have an effect on younger children's settling-in to nursery, so that some headteachers take a flexible approach and, in consultation with parents, reduce the number of hours attended early in the school career. By gradually increasing the hours attended over a period of time, the initial group size is diminished, a further benefit to the newcomers. Additionally, parents are invited to stay at the nursery with their children for part of this settling-in period.

Children enter primary school at the beginning of the academic year in which they will be 6. Parents who can prove that it will be beneficial to their child, and that their development warrants it, may apply for them to enter primary school a year early. There is a special procedure, which includes psychological testing. Now that the 'stages of apprenticeship' model has been introduced this should no longer be justified. Nevertheless, with the pressures and difficulties which have arisen, it seems that a new ruling may well be needed.

Activities

In January 1986 a curriculum defined according to four broad 'areas of experience' was summarized as follows:

a) *physical activities* – these are activities which will furnish children with whatever they need to maintain good health and to develop bodily self-awareness. They comprise gross and fine motor activities;

b) *communication activities, oral and written expression* – these take place in a variety of contexts, to encourage understanding of appropriate forms of expression. Voice modulation, sound games, for example, are experienced through singing, speaking and poetry. Early literacy activities are offered through drawing, story and books, without any recourse to formal teaching. Stories and poems feed the imagination;

c) *artistic and aesthetic activities* – these comprise activities involving artistic production through the use of the body, or varied materials or implements. Further, they include aesthetic appreciation, through perception, and through discussions with artists. They provide the basis for the development of aesthetic sensitivity;

d) *scientific and technological activities* – these are activities which offer children opportunities to explore, make, compare, discover relationships, observe everything around them.

While engaging in joint activities with others, children develop their general abilities and their personalities. They participate in social life and acquire the foundations of a moral code.

Premises

The buildings
Regulations laid down in 1927 applied to the building of schools for a great many years, but these were so strict there was little room for creativity. However, the revised rules of 1972 contain directives which are

far more flexible, and allow for architectural creativity, for buildings which can be used in a greater variety of ways, and for different purposes.

These new regulations were the result of research, led by schools of architecture throughout the country. At the national nursery conference in Vichy in 1971, 70 architectural models were exhibited. Their descriptive plans were published by the National Institute for Research and Pedagogical Documentation, under the title *The Architecture of Nursery Schools* (*Cahier de Documentation* 1972). Although no longer applicable, because of decentralization, these regulations and records remain a source of inspiration, a mine of ideas and information, for architects.

Generally, the premises of a nursery school include: nursery classrooms, one for each group/class, of around 64 square metres; depending on the size of the school there is either one or two large exercise/games halls; one or more rest rooms adjoining the youngest children's classrooms, which may be used for other purposes outside 'nap-time'; one or two utility rooms which may be used for water-play as appropriate; an administrative office; staff-rooms – one for auxiliaries, and, more frequently of late, a small one for teaching staff; store-rooms; corridors and other communal spaces, etc., which may be used for different purposes (for example, a reception area, cloakrooms, spaces for exhibitions or for special activities), and if necessary, a refectory, plus rooms for out-of-hours care and leisure centres. Although they exist, nurseries with a heated swimming pool are rare. Children are usually taken to the local swimming baths for organized sessions.

Almost all the contemporary buildings were constructed before 1960. In other words, the immense effort to provide nursery buildings took place over a 30-year period, and although some were newly built, others were established through the thoughtful, aesthetically pleasing adaptation and renovation of old buildings.

Equipment

Indoor equipment has been prioritized in the French nursery system, compared with the attention given to outdoor equipment. This is because the *école maternelle* was seen more as 'school', than as 'kindergarten'. Although some have large outdoor areas at their disposal, the only equipment generally available has been a climbing frame and a sandpit. However, this situation has been considerably improved during the last twenty years, with the provision of a much greater variety of equipment.

Now there are small pets and plants in all the nurseries, both indoors and out, depending on the seasons and the weather. Some have small gardens cultivated by the children, and there is often a shelter of some sort, so that children may play outdoors even when it is raining.

The large indoor areas, originally designed for very large groups of children, have been adapted to provide activity corners of appropriate dimensions for young children, so that they have easy access to the varied experiences and equipment offered.

A number of different types of furniture and teaching apparatus is now available from various manufacturers, since this is a huge market in France, as a result of the extent of nursery provision. However, all equipment used in the *écoles maternelles* must have been approved by the Ministry of Education, and certified as fulfilling safety requirements.

In spite of this apparent abundance, and relatively comfortable financial position, there has not been a habit of spending disproportionate amounts of funds on specially manufactured didactic materials. In fact, natural and waste materials are widely used, since these provide creative opportunities for both children and educators.

Each nursery school, and within each, every class, is generally equipped with a well-stocked book-corner, and, in the towns, children are taken periodically to the local municipal library. Elsewhere, teachers may borrow books listed for them by local government offices (*Centres Regionaux ou Départmentaut de Documentation Pedagogique*), either by visiting or by post.

Human resources

The teaching team

The teaching staff of French nurseries are qualified professionals with the same status, salary, duties and training as those in primary schools. They may teach at either level throughout their careers. In the past they were trained in colleges (*écoles normales d'instituteurs*). Since the academic year 1991/92, they have been educated in university institutes (IUFM – *Instituts Universitaires de Formation des Maîtres*) where parts of the course are common for all levels, whether they will ultimately teach in the nursery, primary or secondary sectors. For the rest, they cover courses specifically geared to work with the primary and nursery age groups. Students are admitted to these courses after a three-year degree course and the length of their teacher education and training is a further two years. They may be awarded grants to help cover their costs, for example, living allowances during their period of study, or reimbursement of travel expenses.

This training is based on three main objectives:

• learning about and understanding learning and teaching, and developing practice;

- acquiring a knowledge of the education system and schools, and how they operate in the economic, social and cultural conditions of the time;
- acquiring competencies in different communication and information handling techniques.

During a career in teaching the continuous availability of in-service training is assured.

The number of teachers on a school staff is dependent upon the size of the school. The ratio is one teacher for thirty pupils, but in reality the national average is closer to 1 : 27 or 28, and this represents an enormous advance on the days when, not too long ago, ratios were far higher, especially among the youngest children.

The headteacher

Headteachers receive a few weeks' extra training for their role (Decree of 9 February 1989), having been selected on the basis of their experience and expertise. As nurseries are usually quite small schools, the head is generally also a class teacher, full-time headship duties being applicable where schools have at least eight classes.

The head is expected to oversee the smooth running of the school, and to ensure that administrative requirements are fulfilled. They are also expected to manage their teaching team and to ensure effective liaison between different members of staff, to maintain a dialogue with the authorities, and positive relations with parents and the whole community, as well as other schools.

Classroom assistants, auxiliaries, etc.

Schools are allowed one auxiliary member of staff for two classes or sometimes one per class. They are appointed by the local authority, with the headteacher's agreement, and their duties are allocated by the latter. No initial training is necessary but auxiliaries are expected to take advantage of the in-service training offered to any worker in France. Their role is generally one of helping teaching staff with the 'care' aspects of the children's day.

Personnel for children with special needs

These are teachers who have completed two extra years of training for educational psychologists, or one year for special teachers of *psychomotricité* (RPM) or *psychopedagogy* (RPP). The inception of these specializations occurred in 1970, but the duties of these special teachers were redefined in April 1990, as follows:

- to carry out clinical and psychometric testing;
- to be involved in subsequent teaching;
- to liaise with other outside agencies, for example, with representatives from the health, social or legal professions;
- to participate in the planning and enactment of a school's projects, studies and teaching.

Special teachers are responsible for work across the nursery/primary sectors.

The school doctor and other health personnel

These representatives from the field of health work in conjunction with services for babies and young children, under the Ministry of Health.

National Education Inspectorate, advisers and advisory teachers

Each inspector is responsible for the administrative and pedagogical aspects of the running of a group of nursery and primary schools, employing around 250 to 350 teachers. Advisers are mainly concerned with supporting new entrants to the profession and take part in their training. They are nursery/primary teachers who have qualified to become 'teacher trainers', and some, because of their particular talents, specialize in PE, music or art.

Teaching

Planning and evaluation

Nursery teachers in France have always planned their work and, to a lesser extent, evaluated their teaching performance, no doubt because their status and training is equivalent to that of primary school staff. This has been demanded by the administration, but in national terms, there is, relatively speaking, some diversity in approaches, firstly, because teachers have always had the choice of teaching methods at their disposal, and secondly, because inspectors may exercise their own influence.

In general, one might say that it has always been the expectation that a nursery teacher will provide details of long-term and medium-term plans for projects, that they will define their short-term objectives, prepare activities and oversee the work in their classroom. This work will be written down, at least in part.

Reflection and evaluation, of which the assessment of the children is a part, even if only implicitly, is the least that can be expected in preparing follow-up work, in order to ensure appropriate learning opportunities. A written account of such evaluations has always been rare, and would be in any case, very succinct. The problem of assessing children in the nursery and the forms that this might take remains a contentious issue. Those activities which are the most 'closed', the most directed/formal, are those which it is easier to assess, but they are not necessarily those which are the most valuable, nor should the development of children be reduced to a checklist of limited tasks.

Now that schools have been opened up, and there is the requirement for greater team collaboration (Act of 10 July 1989) planning is no longer a solitary exercise. Each school must now set out its plan for fulfilling the requirements of the national programmes, having first analysed the particular achievements and needs of their pupils. The whole school plan allows staff to articulate not only their narrowly defined learning objectives, but also to state their wider aims, concerned with the involvement of partners from the community.

Both internal and external evaluations are part of the process, although those external evaluations carried out on a national scale have only taken place in the primary and secondary sector schools since 1989. The external evaluation of work of individual teachers has always been carried out by the inspectorate.

Daily routine

In order to provide young children with a daily routine which provides effectively for learning, it is usual to take account of their rhythms, such as their need for movement and their need for rest; the demands of hygiene and safety; the need for variety, for example, some whole-group, some small-group, and some individual activities, some free and some directed activities, some demanding effort, others being more relaxing, some quiet and some noisy or physical activities, some in the open air and others indoors.

Each morning or afternoon session is divided into two by an outdoor play time, traditionally called 'recreation', a time of free play lasting for half an hour, when children may choose from different gross motor equipment, such as trikes, skates, etc.

Each teacher decides on the way in which sessional time should be organized. For the youngest children, other than the daily nap which occurs after lunch, at the start of the afternoon, there are usually the following kinds of activities on offer: free choice of play from among the equipment or games organized in the different work areas; music and movement, dance or PE; language activities, singing, counting and rhymes; fine motor, sensory and perceptual activities; sound and musical games; the use of picture books, story, puppetry, or other audio-visual equipment, allied to other activities intended to develop the imagination, and foster expression and representation.

Naturally, the quality of the educational experiences lies in the participation by the children themselves, not simply in the activities presented. What is important are the ways in which the experiences provide for the children to grow, to make their mark and establish themselves, to take part in social interactions, to develop independence, and to explore their own creative abilities.

Children in the middle age band are more immersed in the social life of the school, the process of becoming 'a pupil'. For example, they will take part in registration, putting out and tidying up the activities, and so on. There is more emphasis on certain types of pedagogical activities, games of perception, sorting and classification, drawing. Children in this class are usually introduced to making things, and to a wider range of expressive techniques. They take part in gardening, the care of school pets, cooking, and reading picture books.

Through a vast array of different experiences, too numerous to list in entirety, the eldest children take a greater part in the planning and decision-making about projects they will undertake. Their concepts of time and space are becoming more advanced, so they observe the weather, the calendar, the growth of their plants and animals. Further, with the development of their verbal and literacy skills they begin to record events, journeys, images, and invent games involving coding and decoding. They make books, take part in discrimination games, learn about technology, nutrition, engage in dramatic productions and a wider variety of language activities, and their repertoire of physical activity is extended by taking part in swimming sessions at the baths, skating (both roller and ice as available), and so on.

These experiences have value in the nursery curriculum only if they capture the interest and motivate the children, fostering their integration within their community and enriching their lives.

Administrative records
Each school must naturally maintain records of a number of different aspects of the life of the school, such as the details of staff; an admissions register of the children, with their details; inventories of equipment, etc. Other documents relating to classwork include the attendance register, and children's work records.

Equal opportunities policies
Since 1985 some areas, seen as socially disadvantaged, have been designated educational priority areas (*Zone d'Education Prioritaire* – ZEP),

where agencies administered by various ministries are expected to work co-operatively. Extra funding and staff have been placed at the disposal of schools in these areas. The teachers are given special training and there are measures to encourage stability in staff teams. Taking children into nursery at two years old is favoured in these areas.

Another measure put in place by the Ministry of Education in 1975 relates to areas where there is a majority of foreign residents. Special centres, called *Centres de Formation et d'Information pour la Scolarisation des Enfants de Migrants* (CEFISEM), have been founded, where staff organize courses, undertake studies/surveys, and take part in the development of intercultural education, and education to combat prejudice.

In a 1982 Circular, the Ministry of Education set in motion the requirement that nurseries should positively welcome the home culture and language of children from French minority groups. This was followed up by the local authorities concerned, who provided language courses for interested staff.

Sometimes extra staff are involved in schools where children with special educational needs have been integrated into the 'ordinary' classes but require support.

Staff in schools have been required, since the Circular of 24 June 1983, to take part in the protection of children suffering from child abuse and/ or neglect. This Circular detailed the role of the school, with respect to the child concerned, the family, and the other services involved – from the social, medical and legal agencies.

Conclusion

As a result of its total integration into the French education system, the EMF is in a position to take advantage of any school measures which can be taken to influence long-term academic achievement, the objective of the Minister of Education being to have 80 per cent of secondary pupils succeed in the Baccalaureat. However, the problem with this policy is that the nursery is likely to become more and more strictly formalized. In all the circulars disseminated by the Ministry, the schools are referred to as *élémentaire* and *pré-élémentaire*. In the face of the growing number of circulars and documents sent out to schools, it must be said that the French nursery education system has existed for almost a century without a formalized curriculum, but is now, more and more, finding itself in the position experienced by the primary schools. One fears a loss of the creativity which has for so long been its hallmark. In the place of facilitating the flowering of whole children at the same time as fostering academic success, one is being expected to focus, above all else, on measurable, academic success. This narrow view runs the risk of causing school failures, because it places the interests of the school (right until the Baccalaureat!), rather than the spontaneous interests of the children themselves, at the heart of the process.

5

Early Childhood Education and Care in Germany

Hedi Colberg-Schrader and Pamela Oberhuemer

Germany in the 1990s is a unified Germany. An account of early childhood care and education must therefore reflect this new situation. Ongoing changes make it impossible to describe the process of rapprochement between the two parts of Germany in exact statistical terms. However, we shall attempt to pinpoint key issues and developments, being well aware that we do so from a Western viewpoint and that this may influence the description.

Just as the political and ideological development during the last forty years has followed different paths in East and West, so daycare facilities for children have developed different characteristics and organizational forms oriented towards very different views of childhood and education. Access to kindergartens is currently an important issue in German politics, advocated by women of all parties – motivated in the West by the overwhelming demand for places in the face of insufficient provision, and in the East by the fear of losing comprehensive facilities in the course of radical social upheaval.

Common roots and contrary developments

Early developments
Public facilities for the care of young children developed in the context of industrialization in the nineteenth century. Since this time they have been a controversial issue in Germany. When countries are compared, one finds differing blueprints of the relationship between the State and the family, between public and private matters, and different views on the role of women in society. In Germany there is a strong tradition which considers the rearing of children to be a task of the family. Childcare facilities outside the home were deemed necessary only when difficulties

within the family made them unavoidable. The predominant model for German society was the family in which the mother brought up her own children.

It was the German educator Friedrich Froebel (born in 1782) who created the kindergarten as an establishment complementary to life at home. His demand to set up kindergartens, i.e. to create special areas for children where they could develop freely, was a revolutionary idea at that time. Froebel attached great importance to gardening, creative activities and the use of natural materials such as clay, sand and wood. He developed a 'Theory of Play' and a series of play materials which became known as the 'Gifts' and 'Occupations' (*Spielgaben*). His idea was to enrich the shared experiences of children and adults. Kindergartens were set up in rapid succession in many places in Germany after 1840. In 1848 Froebel's proposal to establish the kindergarten as the first stage of the educational system for all children was discussed at a large teacher's convention (Erning, Neumann and Reyer 1987). In 1851 these progressive ideas became a victim of Restoration policies in Prussia.

The next initiative to secure universal education in kindergartens followed in 1920 at the *Reichsschulkonferenz*. This attempt also failed to get the necessary political and public support. However, educational ideas developed in the 1920s (*Reformpädagogik*), coupled with the aims of the early women's movement, had a decisive influence on preschool institutions. Within this tradition kindergartens were seen as qualified pedagogical institutions as well as a means of supporting working mothers. During the Nazi regime these ideas and innovations were brought to an abrupt halt. Many eminent educators and scientists emigrated and during this time the majority of kindergartens integrated ideas of the Nazi ideology into their programmes.

Post-war developments in West Germany

During the post-war years, West Germany carried on the old tradition of the family-oriented policy. Until well into the 1960s the provision of daycare facilities for children was only considered justifiable for families with special needs. The employment of mothers was seen as a social problem because it endangered the usual childcare resources. Post-war politicians rejected the idea of expanding childcare facilities, arguing that these would undermine the family. Since the 1970s this position has changed with regard to kindergartens, which cater for children aged between 3 and 6 years. At a time of comprehensive educational reform, kindergartens were given the status of the first stage of the education system. Today they are seen as institutions which should be available for all children. Nearly all families wish to send their child to a kindergarten.

The level of provision, measured as approximately 67 per cent in 1990 (Deutsches Jugendinstitut, 1993), is therefore not sufficient, and in many regions there are complaints about the lack of available places. The controversial discussion as to whether caring for children outside the home damages the child and undermines the family is now focused on the under-threes – and in this respect West Germany, with only a minimal number of daycare places available to this day, is a special case amongst the modern industrial nations. In 1990 only 2.6 per cent of one- and two-year-old children attended a publicly funded daycare centre or a crèche and there were places available for roughly the same number in publicly supported family daycare (Deutsches Jugendinstitut, 1992).

Post-war developments in East Germany

Developments in the former German Democratic Republic (GDR) as a Socialist society based on the Soviet model were completely different. The economic necessity of employing women accelerated the provision of state subsidized facilities for the care of very young children. Preschool education was seen as part of the State education system and as a contribution towards achieving equal education for all. Social aims included the basic right of all members of society to work, equal rights for men and women, the priority of collective education, and the early training of the Socialist personality. The State decided many questions relating to childrearing, and parents were not consulted. In this context, public preschool education had high priority. The development of comprehensive facilities was geared to releasing the mother to take her place in the workforce and to binding the children to the state ideology. The result of this policy was that no other country in the world had such well-developed crèche facilities as did the former GDR. In 1989 there were places available for 80 per cent of one- to three-year-olds, and 95 per cent of all children between the age of three and starting school attended a kindergarten (Boeckmann, Neumann and Sebastia 1991).

The rationale for childcare provision

New patterns of family life and the changing face of childhood

Demographic and social changes in the Federal Republic of Germany call for a rethinking of policies for children, families, and the public education system. Sociologists in Western Germany refer to the plurality of family life-styles and to the growing diversity of needs (Bertram, 1991). Structural transformations in society and the changed life histories of women are resulting in new directions in the patterns of family life. Families are smaller in size; it has become unusual for more than two generations to live together. The number of children per family has decreased. In 1989, 53 per cent of families with children under 18 had only one child, 36 per cent had two children. Families with three or more children have become a minority. Today a third of all children grow up in single child families (Statistisches Bundesamt 1990). Consequently, these children have little opportunity for peer interaction in their home environment or for developing stable friendship groups in the immediate neighbourhood. It is not only that children have become scarce, but also that the street is no longer a safe place to play.

This situation has resulted in changed living patterns for children and their parents. Facilities and organized activities aimed specifically at children have increased in number. Children's activities no longer arise in an unplanned and spontaneous way in their immediate environment but instead have to be arranged in different settings. This development has been called 'islandization' (Zeiher 1983), implying that children – especially those living in cities where processes of functionalization and specialization of different areas are particularly apparent – no longer live in one homogeneous undivided area but on numerous 'islands' (home, kindergarten, leisure activities, etc.) scattered over a greater area. For parents, the changed face of childhood means that they increasingly have to plan their children's 'timetable', to establish contacts with other families, and to transport the children to the various meeting places. Organizing peer group experiences for children of preschool age has become a time-consuming part of parent education, a task which in most cases is left up to the mother. As a consequence there is no equality of opportunity concerning the social contacts of preschool children – different living standards, access to social networks, and the working conditions of the parents determine the opportunity to organize children's lives and their social contacts (Herlth and Schleimer 1982). This is one important reason for having good kindergartens available for all children.

At the moment we are faced with a contradictory situation. The time needed for organizing children's lives has increased, due partly to modern life-styles and partly to changed parental expectations concerning their children's education (Beck-Gernsheim 1987). On the other hand, time spent together within the family has diminished. Today's generation of mothers who have profited from the educational reform of the 1970s and as a result are better qualified, want to combine having a family and going to work. The number of mothers in employment in Western Germany is relatively low in international comparison; however, the labour market participation of women has increased over the last few years and is expected to increase further during the next decade. The number of mothers in employment increased from 37 per cent in 1972 to 45 per cent in 1987. Labour market participation varies according to the age of the children. In 1987, 39 per cent of married women with the youngest child under three years, 44 per cent with the youngest child between 3 and 6 years and 50 per cent with the youngest child between 6 and 15 years were in employment (Statistisches Bundesamt, 1990). Results of a representative polling study carried out in the 'old' Federal Republic and West Berlin indicate that most adults – men and women – would prefer one parent to be at home during the child's first years of life (Deutsches Jugendinstitut, 1990a).

Families are very different, and not only with regard to the employment of mothers. There are, for example, great regional disparities in family life and also considerable differences in the lifestyles of various ethnic groups. A large number of children today grow up with just one parent. This type of family structure need not necessarily be a burden – many women have deliberately chosen this form of living with children – but often it does coincide with a drop in social and economic status, with many single-parent families consequently dependent on social security. Unemployment, illness and drug problems in families are factors which have a stressful impact on children's lives. In recent years the problem of child abuse has been given more public attention. All these different contexts in which children grow up have implications for the necessary policies for children. New demands have arisen for more differentiated types of public daycare able to support children with different backgrounds as well as parents with varying expectations in a way which will capacitate children and families to cope with their individual life situation.

In most regions in Western Germany there is a mismatch between parental wishes and needs and current forms and capacity of provision. According to local admissions criteria, eligibility for places in effect often starts at age 4, although there are many families who need or would like a place for younger children. The short kindergarten day means that one parent always has to be available at home, and there are families who need full-time daycare places. Efforts are under way to develop more flexible kindergartens which can respond to the changed needs of families. Such measures need to account for regional differences because what is considered an unquestioned right to a social service in one area may be seen as interference in private matters, to be solved informally, in another.

Childhood in East and West
The situation for children and families in Eastern Germany is quite different. In the former GDR uniform patterns used to determine life. For adults, both men and women, full-time employment was the rule. The

availability of State childcare facilities was taken for granted as a component of everyday life. Almost all children spent a considerable number of hours daily in institutions from their second year on (Boeckmann, Neumann and Sebastian 1991; Deutsches Jugendinstitut, 1990b).

During the past forty years the different educational aims and ideologies of childhood have led to adults and children interacting in different ways in the two parts of Germany. In the West since the 1970s there has been a change in the way children are brought up. Today's model is the child as an individual. Parents increasingly place emphasis on individual development and the autonomy of the child. The wish to fashion a phase of childhood and to enrich it with a variety of different opportunities has led to a wide range of activities being on offer to children. These include playgroups, musical activities, ballet classes and many other forms of provision which, apart from kindergarten, occupy the children's time (and arranging children's activities occupies their mother's time). We speak of a children's culture geared towards children and their wishes – and which is available for those children whose parents are able to organize and to pay for it. Former East Germany was cut off from this development. There it was the task of uniform State institutions to organize the children's life. Within the family there was not much time left over for family life after a nine-hour working day and the efforts needed to acquire the necessary things for the household. But working mothers – single, married or divorced – were supported in a comprehensive way which permitted them to combine having children and working.

How children and families in Eastern Germany live today cannot yet be described in statistical terms. However, it is possible to outline some ongoing developments. The radical change of system has provided new possibilities and chances for those able to cope, but it is also destroying the life concept and breaking the identity of many people. Unemployment has risen due to economic collapse. The profound social upheaval is having an incisive effect on the living conditions of families. It is largely the women who have lost their jobs and who are thus being forced to reorient themselves in relation to work and family. Statistics in the new *Bundesländer* show that in 1991 the birth rate had decreased by 40–50 per cent in many regions. Many families are moving away to Western Germany to find employment. In this situation the need for public childcare facilities is changing. The demand has decreased due to the decreasing numbers of children, due to unemployment, due also to the fact that a place must now be paid for. At the same time, needs have become more diverse due to the social problems in the families during this time of change. Generally the Western system requires an understanding of public and private responsibility for education very different to that which people in the past have been used to, and as a result of this mismatch families need to find new ways of living with children.

The administrative framework

Level of administration: federal, regional, local
According to the German Constitution (Basic Law, 1949) educational matters in the Federal Republic are the responsibility of each of the (now sixteen) constituent states (*Länder*). Although the kindergarten was in 1973 officially recognized as the first stage of the education system, kindergartens are neither legally nor administratively a part of the statutory education system. Whereas compulsory schooling in each *Land* comes under the jurisdiction of the Ministry of Education and Cultural Affairs, kindergartens and day nurseries are in most *Länder* the administrative responsibility of the Ministry of Social Affairs.

Within this framework of federalism national legislation on early childhood education and care is skeletal. It provides a basic frame of reference within which the individual *Länder* and local authorities and agencies are obliged to operate. According to the Child and Youth Services Act, which came into force on 1 January 1991, 'programmes and services shall orient themselves educationally and organizationally towards the needs of the children and their families'. (Federal Law Gazette, 1990, Segment Three, Section 22).

Nearly all federal states have their own kindergarten laws, most of which are at present under review as a consequence of the Child and Youth Services Act. These laws provide the regulative framework for funding, buildings and equipment, space allocation per child, sanitary conditions, staffing, parent participation, etc. The local authorities (youth offices) are responsible for the overall provision in a specific region. However, youth offices are required to set up facilities only if independent child welfare organizations are not in a position to do so. Voluntary agencies have legal precedence.

The basic principle of subsidiarity means in effect that church welfare organizations operate the majority of kindergartens in the Western *Länder* (about 65 per cent). In contrast, almost all preschool institutions in the five 'new' states are administratively affiliated to the regional youth office, a consequence of the still sparse network of voluntary organizations in former East Germany. According to the principle of subsidiarity, the operating agencies have a great deal of autonomy: they determine their own educational goals and philosophies, employ personnel, supervise the running of the institution, provide in-service training, and employ educational advisers.

Funding procedures

Regulations concerning the financing of kindergartens and daycare facilities differ from *Land* to *Land*. Basically, kindergartens are funded from four sources: the particular organizing body, parental contributions, local authority funds and state subsidies. Parental contributions vary in accordance with their own income and the number of siblings attending the kindergarten. They also vary from agency to agency, from region to region, and according to the length of time the child spends in kindergarten each day. Parents generally finance between 10 per cent and 15 per cent of operating costs.

At the end of the 1970s attempts were made in some of the Western federal states to abolish parental contributions. These failed due to increasing financial restrictions during the early 1980s. However, this could be an issue for renewed public debate in the near future, since in the Eastern part of Germany parents are not used to having to pay for daycare services, which were free of charge under the Socialist system.

Preschool provision: a place for every child?

Forms of provision

Children up to compulsory school age (the September following their sixth birthday, provided the birthday falls on or before 30 June) may experience one or more of the following forms of registered provision: a daycare centre or crèche (*Kinderkrippe*, four months to 2 years), a kindergarten (3–6 years), or family daycare (four months to 6 years). Some federal states (mainly Hesse, Berlin, Hamburg, and Lower Saxony) operate preparatory classes for five-year-olds which fall under the school system and are free of charge. About 5 per cent of five-year-olds in the western *Länder* attend this kind of provision. Children who prove to have or are expected to have difficulties in adjusting to school may attend a one-year remedial class (*Schulkindergarten*). For handicapped children there are a number of special kindergartens (*Sonderkindergarten*). Recently there has been a move towards extending the 'traditional' age groups in the respective forms of provision, in particular in kindergartens. For children living in the federal state of North-Rhine Westphalia, for example, it is possible to attend a daycare centre where infants as young as four months are in a group alongside other children up to compulsory school age.

Besides these State subsidized forms of provision there are self-help groups run by parents, especially for the under-three age group, as well as private kindergartens. Grandparents or other relatives or neighbours are also a frequent form of care for many working mothers, especially during 'in-between' times (e.g. before and after opening and closing times, or if the kindergarten shuts down over midday) (Tietze and Roßbach, 1991).

As a result of historically different lines of development the extent of State subsidized provision in the Western and Eastern federal states differs considerably. Whereas the new *Länder* have a well-developed network of daycare institutions for the under-3s and almost universal provision for the three- to six-year-olds (see page 58), the Western part of Germany has only very few *Kinderkrippen* (in 1990 there were places for only 2.6 per cent of one- and two-year-old children) and an insufficient level of provision at the kindergarten stage. According to official statistics there were kindergarten places available for 80 per cent of the three- to five-year-olds in 1990. However, a large number of six-year-olds also attend kindergarten. Consequently only about 67 per cent of children from age 3 up to school age have in fact access to a kindergarten place (Deutsches Jugendinstitut, 1992).

'A place for every child in kindergarten' as his or her legal right was a major issue during the debate preceding the Child and Youth Services Act of 1990. Although this claim was not in the end endorsed by law, it has since been reiterated in connection with the current debate on abortion law reform. As a supportive measure to a new legislation on abortion, kindergarten places are to be created for all children wishing to attend by 1996. Considerable regional disparities in the extent of provision mean that some authorities will be harder hit than others. The continuing pressure for places in recent years is already in some cases leading to a deterioration of agreed standards, such as enrolling more than 25 children per group, or admitting different groups of children in the mornings and the afternoons.

Education and integrated services

During the early 1970s research and innovation in and around the kindergarten focused predominantly on educational issues. This was a major breakthrough towards achieving recognition of the importance of preschool education and upgrading the public status of the kindergarten. In recent years there has been a move away from emphasizing the purely educational side of the kindergarten's task towards stressing the potentially integrative quality of kindergarten programmes. This broader concept which embraces education and socialization, care and health, child-related and family-oriented provision, represents what could be called the 'second wave of reform' in the field of early years education and care (Tietze and Uferman, 1989; Zimmer, 1991). At present, however, this discussion is still largely programmatic. Research and provision-based innovatory projects are needed in order to translate this concept into policies and programmes tailored to meet the needs and characteristics of particular children as well as the circumstances and expectations of specific families and communities.

What goes on in kindergartens?

The changing curriculum

The end of the 1960s and the early 1970s in former West Germany witnessed the beginning of a widespread debate on preschool education. A combination of factors had contributed to this situation: research findings which stressed the importance of the early years in children's development; a political commitment to the concept of equality of educational opportunity; and a desire among post-war German parents to rethink the whole process of education along anti-authoritarian and emancipatory lines.

In 1970 the German Education Council, a national advisory body, made a seemingly radical proposal which marked the beginning of an unprecedented reform movement within the history of early childhood education in Germany. The proposal was to reduce the compulsory school starting age from 6 to 5 years. This triggered off a series of research projects throughout the country aimed at identifying optimal learning situations for five-year-olds, accompanied by intense public and professional debate about what and how young children should be learning.

The first wave of curriculum development that followed was aimed at operationalizing instruction in such fundamental areas as perception, language and cognitive skills. This concept of learning became known in Germany as the function-oriented approach. A whole range of didactic games and vast batteries of worksheets flooded the market and these found their way into kindergartens.

This one-sided approach towards the fostering of cognitive skills soon became a target of criticism from early childhood educationists concerned about a more comprehensive understanding of children's learning and development. The need for a stronger link between children's real-life situations and the preschool programme became a central issue.

New curricula were developed, in particular by Jürgen Zimmer and his co-workers at the German Youth Institute in Munich (cf. Zimmer 1985, for a retrospective analysis). This *situation-oriented approach* focuses on real-life situations and the materials developed at the time approached them through a variety of didactic measures which combined the development of personal and social competence and the mastery of skills and knowledge.

During the late 1970s various pilot projects and curriculum models that had been developed at the height of the reform movement were evaluated in a nationwide implementation programme. About 15,000 children were included in this attempt to transfer curriculum research and development into everyday contexts in regular kindergartens. It was during this phase that the situation-oriented approach met with widespread acceptance among the participating kindergarten educators.

However, the economic recession which set in during the early 1980s and a change of government put an end to the reform movement. So, although the situation-oriented approach met with general acceptance both among practitioners and at the administrative level, the funding needed to ensure transfer through initial and in-service training was no longer available. Despite this, many of the basic characteristics of the situation-oriented approach have become part of everyday practice in kindergartens.

Main approach today: social learning

Taking the real-life situations of children and their families into account, attributing greater importance to everyday experiences than to artificial learning situations, the precedence of mixed-age groups, parent participation, and the integration of the kindergarten into community life are characteristics of the educational approach which has influenced everyday practice in kindergartens since the reform movement (Colberg-Schrader, Krug and Pelzer, 1991). The aims of this approach are to counteract the general processes in society that separate children from adults by placing them into specialized institutions.

During the last two decades expectations directed towards kindergartens have changed. Parents today value the kindergarten as a place where their children can meet other children and develop social relationships in a rich and stimulating environment. The quality of time spent in kindergarten has become an important factor. Kindergartens today are places where children can develop their individual abilities and play together, where they can generate and negotiate social rules – experiences former generations had in street play and neighbourhood groups. Kindergartens in this sense have to compensate for the disappearance of public spaces for children.

It is the task of the educator to create a communicative milieu which enables the children to negotiate their contacts and conflicting interests, abilities necessary in later life. This entails providing varied activities for small groups according to the children's interests and levels of development. The educator is thus able to give individual attention to children who need help while other children manage their activities independently. Opening up the kindergartens and going with the children to places where 'real life' takes place is a further strategy to enrich the children's impressions and experiences and to enable them to participate in public life.

Planning, assessment, evaluation

It is generally accepted that educational work of this kind must be based on an open curriculum and cannot be planned and dictated from outside but instead developed according to the needs of children, families and local communities.

This requires high professional competence. Open planning demands a reflexive and flexible approach on the part of the educator. This kind of pedagogical work needs a continuous support and evaluation system which includes teamwork in the institution, educational advisers and regional groups where educators can exchange their everyday experiences and problems. This informal approach also depends to a large extent on the given working conditions. If there are too many children in a group it is virtually impossible to respect their wishes and to create a communicative milieu for choice and independent action. If the educator is alone with the children she cannot leave the kindergarten for excursions or develop interesting projects with the children. There are therefore considerable differences in the quality of pedagogical work taking place in (Western) German kindergartens today.

The nationwide evaluation programme in the late 1970s demonstrated that situation-oriented work under acceptable working conditions (e.g. group size, number of staff, support system) enables educators to work in a reflexive and independent way in pursuing the aim of respecting the children's individuality and connecting the children's world with life in the family and community. There was, however, no systematic evaluation of the effects of the pedagogical work on the children (Krappmann, 1985).

Philosophies and methods in former East Germany

In the former GDR the task of preschool facilities, which generally provided full-time daycare, was tightly bound to the Socialist view of man and society, and was closely linked with the school system. The State educational plan described play as the most important educational activity through which children's physical and mental faculties are developed. In addition, the children were gradually directed towards a kind of systematic learning, which was considered to be a mental activity to be guided by the educator (Das Bildungswesen der DDR, 1989). The role of educators in preschool institutions was predominantly directive and was geared towards specified aims which were to be achieved through structured educational procedures. Even the children's games and independent activities were to be guided along the right lines by the educators (Christensen and Launer, 1989). The centrally prescribed education programme had a pervading influence on all activities in the kindergartens and crèches. Although in 1985 new guidelines assigned greater freedom to the educators and represented a move away from the very rigid forms of 'leadership', a strongly directive type of educational style geared towards cognitive stimulation and discipline remained the norm. According to socialist convictions childhood is a phase of preparation. The 'here and now' of the children, their everyday experiences, are considered only in so far as they can be used to further that stated aims for the educational process. According to this 'teach-and-learn' idea children were grouped together in same-age groups.

There was almost no awareness for unintentional results in the educational process (hidden curriculum). The educators were embedded in a system of educational programme, control and inspection. Even though many educators did their best to inject some life into the prescribed framework, there was very little freedom for individual initiative or creativity, or for regional or local differences to develop.

Since the political changes in 1990 there have also been great changes in the work of kindergartens. There are discussions that the changing life situations of children and families and democratic values require a new conceptual and methodological orientation in the pedagogical work. This, it is argued, does not mean copying Western ideas but developing new lines which reflect the different traditions in Eastern Germany. It could well be that the process of unification will engender a fresh discussion about learning in kindergartens in both the East and the West.

Towards equality of opportunity

Children with a migrant family background

Living alongside children with different linguistic and cultural backgrounds is becoming a part of life for more and more German children. Among children of preschool age one child in nine in the Western part of Germany has a non-German family background. Many migrant families from Turkey, Italy and former Yugoslavia originally came to West Germany during post-war labour migration movements – beginning in the 1950s and reaching a peak in the early 1970s – and have now been living in Germany for over twenty or even for more than thirty years. In recent years increasing numbers of ethnic German families from Poland, the former Soviet Union, and Romania have migrated to Western Germany, and further waves of economically and politically motivated migration are to be expected during the 1990s. According to present figures, five million foreigners live in unified Germany. Eighty-five per cent are from European countries, and about 30 per cent of these are from EC states (Winkler, 1992). Fifty-four per cent of children with a migrant family background attend a kindergarten (Statistisches Bundesamt, 1989). In 1975 this was the case for only 29 per cent of non-German children. Despite this rise, however, children of foreign origin are still under-represented in public care and education facilities in comparison with their German counterparts. During the 1970s and early 1980s a number of projects were launched in kindergartens which aimed to promote the integration of migrant children. Programmes tended to focus on the differences between cultures, on the problems of migrant children and their families, and on informing educators about social, economic and cultural phenomena in the countries of origin. In recent years an intercultural approach has become more common, with an emphasis on the acceptance of cultural pluralism, and on attempting to raise awareness of other cultures through shared experiences in everyday settings. A recently developed approach along these lines focuses on children's literature and childlore from different countries (Ulich, Oberhuemer and Reidelhuber, 1992). The aim is to make 'other' cultures attractive for German children as members of the dominant culture, to strengthen a positive bicultural identity amongst minority children, and generally to promote intercultural exchange in educational, community and family settings. Sharing stories and games in everyday situations may help to combat negative stereotyping and to create a more differentiated picture of individual cultures.

Children with handicaps
Nowhere within the education system has the joint education of handicapped and non-handicapped children been propagated to the extent that it has in the preschool sector. This was largely due to groups of parents committed to the idea of integration, and who found the general educational principles in preschool settings (e.g. the importance of social learning in mixed-age groups) to be a viable framework for promoting integration processes. The philosophy of 'together from the start' not only helps to promote the handicapped child's individual development and to combat the threat of social isolation but also has an important signal effect for school education, since parents of handicapped children become less and less willing to sacrifice in school what they have achieved in kindergarten.

In 1988/89 in Western Germany there were 263 preschool facilities with specially designed integrative groups with an average size of twelve to fifteen children, three to five of whom were handicapped. Approximately 2,100 places were available for handicapped children in integrative groups. At the same time about 21,000 handicapped children were enrolled in special facilities. Roughly the same number of handicapped children attend standard kindergartens (Lipski, 1989).

The enrolment of handicapped children in neighbourhood kindergartens was common in Western Germany long before the integration discussion began. The main advantage is proximity to the child's home. However, regular kindergartens at present are only suitable for individual children receiving therapy outside the kindergarten, for those who can be in a group of children without special treatment, and for those whose parents are prepared to accept the lack of individual support in comparison with that offered by special facilities.

In spite of the progress which has taken place concerning the integration of handicapped children in kindergartens, it has not become an established fact in all areas. Two goals in particular are important for future developments. One is to establish a decentralized and flexible care network within which both the integration of individual children into the standard kindergarten as well as specially designed integrative groups complement each other (Hössl, 1988; Staatsinstitut, 1991). Another goal is to promote the concept of integration in the Eastern federal states, where there is no tradition of jointly educating handicapped and non-handicapped children.

Kindergartens: the physical setting

The immediate environment is of basic importance for children's group experiences. Kindergartens are subject to State inspection which mandates and checks the demanded minimal standards like space available to each child, the equipment of group and ancillary rooms, sanitary conditions for children and for staff, rooms for staff and parent consultation, store rooms, facilities for physical education, etc. The requirements laid down by the supervisory authorities are of special importance because they are the basis for subsidies for the building and running costs of kindergartens.

Room arrangement
Architecture, room arrangements and equipment reflect the generally accepted educational philosophy that kindergartens should be an environment for stimulating and rich learning experiences and many-sided

social relations. Rooms in kindergartens today are divided into diverse areas which structure activities within the group, e.g. there are zones for playing and experimenting with different materials, for relaxing or looking at books, for being alone for a time or for rough and tumble play. This structured room arrangement provides the children with a communicative milieu and gives them freedom of choice and the chance to plan their activities in an independent way. Reorganizing the room arrangement with the children and respecting their ideas and wishes is a concern of projects in kindergartens pursuing the idea of creating an individual environment which reflects individual and local needs. Children need to be able to create their own unique 'house' in which they enjoy spending time and in which they can leave their own traces.

Rooms in East German kindergartens were formerly more standardized and uniform, responding to the organized teaching of skills and knowledge. For example, corners with mattresses or curtains for children to withdraw behind were neither commonplace nor desired. Rooms were arranged to give educators an overall view. Concerning room arrangements educators in Eastern Germany have changed quickly; almost everywhere now the rooms are more colourful and offer possibilities for varied experiences.

Garden and outdoor play area
Generous garden space is desirable but not possible in all kindergartens. Facilities in town centres especially often lack adequate outdoor play space and are forced to use public playgrounds in the neighbourhood. Concerning the design of outdoor play areas there is move away from providing mainly standard equipment (e.g. climbing frames) towards creating interesting and stimulating environments with different levels and niches, with areas for ball play and for hide and seek, with trees and bushes, with water and sand, etc. Growing vegetables and fruit is also an activity which has increased during recent years.

Whereas a garden and enough space to play outside is needed in all kindergartens, there is at the same time a trend towards looking for interesting places to play, meeting up with people in the neighbourhood and sharing experiences in the immediate environment.

Size of kindergartens and group size
The size of the kindergarten depends on the locality: urban kindergartens occasionally provide groups for children under three, from three to six and for school-age children. But the majority of kindergartens in Western Germany have three or four groups of three- to six-year-olds. In former East Germany the typical institutions for children (*Kinderkombination*)

had crèche groups and kindergarten groups combined under one roof. Meanwhile, the number of crèche groups is decreasing.

With regard to the size of groups there are no general statistics which account for the diverse forms of group provision. The following information is based on particulars of the *Länder* and on common knowledge about the conditions in everyday practice. In crèches there are ten to fifteen children in a group with two adults. The maximum number of children permitted in a kindergarten group is regulated in the *Land* kindergarten acts. Average group size is twenty-five children with two adults or one full-time and one part-time adult. There are some variations: full-day groups are usually smaller (twenty children). In Eastern Germany where the full-time kindergarten is the rule groups have about eighteen to twenty children. Mixed-age groups with children from 1 to 6 years (one of the current innovations in kindergartens) are required to provide better conditions concerning the number of children, the number of staff and room space. There are also variations due to the huge lack of places and the interest of communities and welfare organizations to economize on kindergartens. Some *Länder* make allowances in their guidelines for enrolling more than twenty-five children per group if there is great demand, and in some institutions there are not two adults per group during the whole day due to personnel costs or a lack of available educators in some regions.

Early years personnel

Staff employed in kindergartens and other early years settings are almost exclusively female. The largest group of trained staff in kindergartens are *Erzieher* (educators/childcare workers). *Erzieher* are responsible for a group of children or – after a number of years' experience – may be appointed head of a kindergarten. Childcare assistants (*Kinderpfleger*) are employed as auxiliary staff. Childcare workers trained at a higher level (*Sozialpädagogen*) (and therefore more expensive to employ), are only occasionally to be found in kindergartens. About one fifth of staff employed full time in kindergartens are non-qualified.

Initial training
Erzieher are not trained exclusively for work in kindergartens or other forms of preschool provision. Their initial training is aimed at preparing them for work in a variety of childcare facilities covering a wide age range, e.g. kindergartens, daycare centres, afternoon provision for school-age children, open-door youth centres, children's homes. In contrast, training in former East Germany focused on specific institutions,

predominantly kindergartens for the three- to six-year-olds and daycare centres for the under-3s.

Despite a federal regulation in 1982 which attempted to define common criteria for the training of preschool educators, there are still considerable differences between the constituent states in the Western part of Germany as far as entry requirements, course structure and course content are concerned. Generally speaking, training takes place at a vocational college (*Fachschule, Fachakademie*) specializing in so-called 'social pedagogy'. Entry requirements are an intermediate school certificate and two years' practical experience in an appropriate setting, or, alternatively, a completed course at a vocational school.

In most federal states the length of training is three years. Two years are spent at training college, interspersed with short periods of practical work in different professional settings. The final year is spent in a daycare institution (e.g. kindergarten) and is interspersed with 'theory days' at the training college.

The two-year theoretical part of the training course is organized along the lines of the traditional school system, with subject-oriented timetables, an average class size of twenty-five pupils, and regular achievement tests and assessment profiles. Critical debate in recent years has centred on the lack of interchange between theory and practice, the lack of interdisciplinary and project-oriented approaches towards learning, and the inadequate role of training in professional socialization as a whole (von Derschau, 1984). The present structure and content of courses, it is argued, do not provide appropriate opportunities for developing the required stability in personal and professional identity (Ebert, 1988).

In view of the development towards a single European market and the need for mutual recognition of national professional qualifications within the member states, a renewed attempt is being made towards defining a unified system of initial training in this field. For many critics this is proving a welcome chance to initiate a long overdue reform debate, and the structure and content of initial training courses are at present under review.

Compared with primary school teachers, who are university-trained civil servants, kindergarten educators have a significantly lower social status. This is not only apparent at the salary level; professionalism is altogether low profile. One of the many reasons is that until recently the length of professional life was very short, on average a mere five years. However, since more and more young women – including childcare workers – now prefer not to give up their jobs but to combine working and having a family, the number of years spent in the profession is on the increase. It remains to be seen whether time spent 'on the job' will have a noticeable impact on (women's) involvement in politically relevant issues and organizations.

In-service training

In-service training is generally provided by the organizing bodies responsible for kindergartens, i.e. church and other welfare organizations, or the local authorities. Courses are subsidized through Federal State funds. There are a few non-affiliated central in-service training centres (e.g. in Berlin and Frankfurt), but these can cater for only a relatively small number of childcare workers.

In-service training operates on a voluntary basis. Educators are granted a certain number of days per year to attend such courses, generally up to eight days, although this may vary from employer to employer.

Recent analyses of the situation concerning the professionalization of staff working with young children describe the need for a more coherent and co-ordinated approach towards initial and in-service education and training (Fthenakis, Lehner and Oberhuemer, 1990; Oberhuemer, 1991). In particular, childcare workers need a more comprehensive range of further education courses which qualify them for special posts within kindergartens, e.g. counselling students in training and newly qualified staff, or networking with relevant organizations and groups within the local community. Apart from the chance of becoming head of a kindergarten, there are very few other openings for career advancement and promotion.

Advisory services

Support services for personnel in preschool institutions are closely aligned to the operating agencies, i.e. to the educator's employer. Advisers focus on educational and managerial problems and tasks; some are also responsible for ensuring that State regulations concerning standards are adhered to (inspection). Educational advisers collaborate with the staff in kindergartens (on-site visits, regional meetings), co-operate with the kindergarten sponsors and associations at different levels (committee work), and – where necessary – initiate and maintain contacts with other organizations concerned with children and families, e.g. youth and social service offices, health department (networking).

Each adviser is responsible for a certain number of kindergartens, daycare centres and out-of-school care facilities. The present situation is such, however, that this number far exceeds that which is needed to ensure an adequate advisory network. Some advisers are responsible for between 80 and 100 kindergartens, whereas the optimum number proposed by a national committee of experts is twenty-five (Arbeitsgemeinschaft für Jugendhilfe, 1988).

Parent participation

Parental involvement in kindergartens

Kindergartens are regarded as a complementary experience to the child's family upbringing. Close co-operation with parents is central to this concept. In practice, ways of working with parents vary a great deal. Participation in the sense of electing a board of parents is anchored in the relevant federal State laws and regulations regarding kindergarten provision. Parent committees advise on organizational matters, such as the opening times of the kindergarten, and also on educational and personnel issues. They often initiate fund-raising activities.

Most kindergartens have a general policy of inviting parents to sit in on sessions in order to become familiar with their way of working. However, the extent to which this in fact takes place has not been documented. Common forms of co-operation with parents include parents' evenings focusing on educational topics, informal and formal talks on the child's well-being and progress, joint organization of festivities and outings, and social evenings. However, these 'traditional' forms of co-operation between parents and kindergartens do not always meet the many and various needs of families. Although there is a growing recognition that families even in one particular region live very different lives and have, accordingly, different sets of expectations concerning daycare and educational facilities, there is still a tendency among educators to talk of 'parents' in general. One reason may be that until now initial training courses – in both the Western and Eastern parts of Germany – focused almost exclusively on preparation for work with children and tended to ignore the fact that today's childcare workers also need the appropriate attitudes and skills for working with adults.

In the eastern *Länder* in particular, educators are aware of the need to develop new ways of involving parents in their children's education. Former role models, which assigned families and institutions generally accepted, clear-cut functions, are no longer valid. This is one of the many challenges currently facing educators in the Eastern part of Germany.

Strengthening links with non-conventional forms of provision

Groups run by parents can be traced back to the student movement in the late 1960s, when the first *Kinderläden* were founded in Berlin. These parents' co-operatives were based on socio-political motives and an anti-authoritarian approach towards education. In recent years a new set of self-help groups has developed, initiated in particular by parents (generally mothers) with infants and toddlers. A major reason for this phenomenon is the thoroughly inadequate extent of provision for children under three years of age. A further reason is that some parents wish to play a more active role in the day-to-day running of preschool groups and in determining educational and organizational policies than is normally possible within the conventional kindergartens and other daycare establishments (Hopf, 1988).

Until now these two strands of childcare and education – professional and informal – have tended to work alongside, or to a certain extent even in competition with, one another. In a way, neither system reflects reality; both have been geared to a single type of life and family concept. In former East Germany family life was pushed onto the periphery and the idea of an 'educational childhood' in institutions prevailed.

The new Child and Youth Welfare Act (KJHG) demands that facilities must be geared to meeting the needs of children and families. The idea of the kindergarten as a kind of neighbourhood centre open to all children in the area regardless of their age or the preferred times of attendance is gradually gaining recognition as being one way of dealing with the changing demand and with existing regional disparities. The aim is to have facilities which are able to react flexibly to meet the particular needs of the area, which provide children with education as well as care, which offer the children extended play facilities, and which provide a meeting place for parents, helping them to develop their own social networks (Colberg-Schrader and von Derschau, 1991; Colberg-Schrader and Oberhuemer, 1989).

The development of this sort of facility in Western Germany is at present the focus of a comprehensive action research project in different parts of the country (Deutsches Jugendinstitut, 1991). The aim of the project is to encourage each individual organization or institution to tailor their own particular group policy to cater for the specific situation in that region. The goal of opening institutions for all children in the catchment area will involve redefining the age groups by broadening the intake to include under-threes and school-age children. It will also involve changing present opening times. A further goal is to strengthen links between conventional forms of provision and the varied kinds of informal and private initiatives (e.g. mother-and-toddler groups, family centres, meeting places for mothers) which have sprung up over the past few years in Western Germany. In this sense kindergartens could become places where parents meet and are helped to develop strategies to increase their influence in campaigning for a policy for children in their locality. Regional social and cultural policies for children not only require high quality institutions for children, they also need to include a 'child-friendly' environment (less traffic, attractive meeting places in the community for children and adults) as well as working conditions for the parents which allow them to spend more time with their children. In Western Germany the sponsoring of childcare by industry is under discussion (Busch, Dörfler and Seehausen, 1991).

The further development of facilities for early childhood education and care implies different things in East and West. In the West, concern is centred on providing more places and full-time facilities to match the diverse needs of families; in the East it is focused on offering more differentiated types of public daycare, respecting the individuality of children and families, and with retaining as many public facilities as families want and need. A matter of common concern for experts in both East and West is that the interests of families and children shall not be submerged by the radical economic changes taking place. Even if unification means for the coming years that a great deal of public money is needed for developments in the Eastern part of Germany, it must not be forgotten that a high quality of social infrastructure for children and their families is an investment in a secure social future.

6

Preprimary Education in Italy

Lucio Pusci

Introduction

The Italian education system can be seen as a composite structure, with different agencies contributing to its functioning, each with different historical, legal, administrative, philosophical and pedagogical backgrounds, as well as with different organizational and managerial criteria.

The essential connecting element of this structure is, today, one of the basic principles of the Italian Constitution, according to which each and every citizen is, on one hand, accorded the right to benefit from education and school and, on the other hand, to provide education and schooling. This means that everyone – institutions or private agencies or individuals – may in principle run schools as well as education, care and training centres, at any level and in any educational field. The Constitution does not allow for any kind of monopoly in this area, neither by the State nor by local authorities nor by private institutions or individuals.

The Italian education system has always, even in its pre-Republican history, been characterized by the diversification of provision, in the sense that in some cases, as for example in the preschool field, it fostered a multiplicity of private initiatives. These were further encouraged by the fact that the State explicitly renounced any responsibility for that educational field; while in other sectors, for example primary education, the reverse was the case, since Government policies had the effect of engendering a sort of competition between the public and the private agencies, which often resulted in fruitful outcomes, both quantitatively, in terms of an increase in educational provision, and qualitatively.

An historical outline of the Italian education system must take into account this basic and characterizing trait of the beneficial nature of this inter-agency friction. The whole development and refining process of the system has been marked, little by little, by this interaction – be it spontaneous or forced, conscious or not – between the different educational agencies, with their different philosophies, policies, strategies, aims and interests.

Philosophy/politics and management

Historical outline

As in many other countries, formal recognition for a need to set up any systematic organization of educational provision in Italy, particularly with respect to its legislative and legal coverage, is much more recent than the actual existence of education institutions, at any level.

The prehistory of school provision in Italy could be said to have ended in 1859, when the so-called Legge Casati[1] was promulgated, as the Kingdom of Italy was born. Before that year, there really was no school system in a strict sense, at least so far as preprimary and primary schools were concerned. Indeed, such schools, where any of them did in fact exist, were more or less the results of spontaneous ventures by enlightened individuals or social groups, the first being religious institutions. At that time they could work in a completely free way, without any binding rules with regard to content and methods of education, nor with respect to qualifications, professional competence and responsibility of the teachers and their institutions.

However, even if we trace the historical background of the Italian primary school, or secondary education, back to 1859, we have to wait until well into this century to find preprimary education included rationally in the general framework of an educational provision open to all children, regardless of their ethnic, religious and language groups, their gender, class and special needs.

One of the typical traits of Italian educational policy up to the beginning of this century was the almost complete lack of interest in early childhood education, i.e. both preprimary *and* primary education. Facilities for this age range were traditionally provided by religious institutions and private organizations and, as regards primary education, by the municipalities. Furthermore, the situation did not change substantially until 1968 as far as preprimary education was concerned. It was not until 1968 that the State preprimary school (*scuola materna statale*) was finally established, and there is still, today, no public (State) educational provision for 0–3-year-old children.

This delay could be explained by lack of awareness, on the part of policy-makers, of the very important role of education in the growth and the development of society, and, on the other hand, by the lack of interest or lobby groups. The problem was, however, clearly realized by a small proportion of aristocratic and middle-class families, who let their children be educated by private tutors or by religious institutions. They felt that the education of their children would be seen as a manifestation of their superior social image and, especially in the case of middle-class families, to improve their economic chances.

The very first steps towards a modern understanding of early childhood education were made only at the beginning of this century. Following the re-organization of compulsory and secondary education,[2] a significant body of opinion began to be focused on this issue. At the same time the pioneering theories and practices of Rosa and Carolina Agazzi on the one hand, and of Maria Montessori on the other, made decisive contributions which attracted the attention of opinion leaders and, at least to some extent, policy-makers, on the crucial role of early childhood education.[3]

But the turning-point in the history of the Italian preschool education can be pinpointed as occurring during the 1960s, concurrently with a high point in events concerning nearly every aspect of social life: in the economy, politics, moral concepts, employment, family structure, etc. Throughout that decade, as a result of very hard political, ideological and social struggles, a design for a public, State-run preprimary school system was worked out. This was to be an institution which would be open to all three- to six-year-olds, and aimed at providing an educational setting able to fit the actual rights and needs of children.

This process resulted in the Education Act of 1968,[4] which was followed, in 1969, by the enactment of the *Guidelines for the Educational Activities in the State-run Preprimary schools* (*Orientamenti dell'attività educativa nelle scuole materne statali*). In the history of Italian preschool education, this law represents the final, formal ratification of children's right to the benefit of an educational institution in a strict sense, the quality of which is assured not only by theoretical principles and the content afforded through educational activities, but also by the requirement that educators be professionally qualified, and institutions supervised and controlled by the State administration.

Nowadays there is general recognition for the emergence of State-run preprimary schools, positively assuring real and equal opportunities for all children to benefit from a reliable educational setting. Moving from a situation where religious and private institutions had a monopoly and were challenged by municipalities coming on the scene, especially during the 1950s and 1960s, diversified provision was created. Forms of provision were to be various and differentiated both in terms of quantity and quality. Within the span of a very few years, the State-run preprimary schools succeeded in spreading throughout the national territory, first by filling in the gaps where no facilities were provided by other agencies, and then by competing directly, especially through the quality of the provision, with the existing local, religious and private institutions.

Indeed, quality has been the most marked feature in the recent developments in early childhood education. In fact the struggle for quality was the catalyst to significant progress in research and innovation, particularly with regard to the concept of the function of preschool education and, therefore, the definition of methods and content of provision. Perhaps the most remarkable outcome of this process has been the recent enactment of the new *Guidelines for the Educational Activities in the State-run Preprimary schools* (*'nuovi' Orientamenti dell'attività educativa nelle scuole materne statali*), passed on 3 June, 1991, by the Ministry of Education.

Although they are compulsory only for the State-run preprimary schools, it is obvious that the 'new' Guidelines are likely to yield significant changes and improvements in privately run schools as well, because of the ongoing competition between State, municipal and private institutions.

The guidelines of preschool education

Early childhood education has traditionally been conceived, at least until the middle of this century, as a chiefly social facility for the benefit of families, and in the first place that of working mothers, rather than of the children themselves. Hence the character of 'day nurseries' (*asili infantili*) and more recently – and still nowadays, at least as far as the official name is concerned – *scuole materne*.

Until the beginning of this century, the charitable motive on the side of the providers seems to have been the salient feature. In fact they – religious institutions, but also private groups and individuals – were urged on by their wish to help families, as well as being attracted by the prospect of receiving subsidies for this work. There were no rules governing their supply either relating to premises and equipment or to staff qualifications, recruitment and evaluation, teaching methods or content. Since there was no supervision of the public school administration, both the quantity and quality of the education provided depended entirely upon the provider's goodwill. In fact, in most cases, it is hard to speak of *educational* institutions when referring to that period, since they were quite clearly daycare centres, lacking even the basic prerequisites for genuinely educational provision (i.e. educational staff, specially trained for such a task, with a planned educational orientation to the children's experiences).

At the very beginning of this century, following in the footsteps of the Agazzis and Montessori, an innovatory concept of early childhood education bloomed and began to expand. According to this precept, provision for young children was to be explicitly educational, with its own pedagogic and didactic content and methods, overtly focused on children's personality development. This idea has been a favourite topic of research and debate during several decades. Immediately after the Second World War, as the material and social reconstruction of the country was initiated, the idea began to be put into action, chiefly by a number of municipalities. In fact these municipalities could benefit from almost complete autonomy as regards the organization of social facilities as well as educational preschool provision. And many of them relied, among other things, on nurseries and infant schools in order to prove themselves to be beneficial and efficient. Accordingly such initiatives were also seen as a weighty contribution to the image promotion of the local ruling class. Suffice it to recall the prestige accorded the model of early schooling initiated in the Region Emilia-Romagna during the 1950s, in some *Scuole dell'Infanzia* in Reggio Emilia, which are now recognized to be among the best institutions in Italy, and are even well-known abroad.

This trend has been supported by a body of research and experiments carried out, in particular following Bruno Ciari's 'new course' (*nuovo indirizzo*) (Ciari, 1969; 1972; 1975). Such initiatives essentially helped educational decision-makers as well as opinion-leaders and policy-makers in general, in realizing the great social, cultural, and especially political impact of early childhood education.

The final result of this process has been, as mentioned above, the law of 1968 and the subsequent issue of the Guidelines. But the country had to experience a long period of struggle to reach this result. There was a fierce confrontation between the devotees of different philosophies of education, ideologies, political parties, all of whom were fully aware of the implications – not only economically, but also socially and culturally – that the establishment of a State-run preprimary school would have. That is, this was to be a genuinely *educational* institution, not explicitly relying upon a particular religious confession nor on the promotional campaign of a particular political party or local administration.

The 1969 Guidelines were, of course, the result of a compromise, which, in the final analysis, was highly fruitful. By combining the Agazzian and the Montessorian formulae on the one side and, on the other, hints coming from advanced research and experiments both in Italy (in particular the 'new course' infant schools) and abroad, the legislature gave the newborn State-run preprimary school a flexible enough structure – certainly not a stiff or narrow one – to result in a soft impact in the field, one which did not run the risk of confirming widespread fears that there would be unfair competition, and resulting bitterness, between State-run and private institutions.

The leitmotif of the new preprimary school still remains, essentially, that of the traditional nursery schools, that is the integration of family and childcare. But a new element is added: the character of preschool – the aim and objective of preparing children to attend primary schools. An interactive system has been established, in which the child's personality, family and school can each express their own original and typical traits without dominating one another and, over all, without deadening the originality and diversity evident in both educational supply and demand. This means that the new preprimary school distinguishes itself by its school-like or 'pre'-school role, while taking into due account its traditional function of completing and complementing the child's education and care by the family.

The Guidelines mark, for preschool education, therefore, a definite movement away from the concept of social facilities: the image of a 'daycare centre' is dropped and the sector has become recognized as a part of the school system.

But the years 1968–1969 were only the starting point of this process, which has been brought to its current conclusion with the 'new' Guidelines in 1991. Here we really find the outline of a curriculum-like structure as a basis for educational activities. Six so-called 'fields of experience' have been isolated and thoroughly defined as curricular sections of the provision. Within their framework, aims and objectives, content and methods, teaching instruments and equipment have been described according to the age of the children and to the pace of their physical, as well as psychological, development. The 'fields of experience' are, obviously, not clearly defined school 'disciplines' or 'subjects'. Nevertheless, simply reviewing the curriculum articulation by fields, or areas, of experience one can make out the explicit goal of the legislators: that education provided by the preprimary schools should cover each and all of the traits of a child's personality; each and every one of the fields of experience should be cultivated by means of appropriate methods and instruments, as if they were school subjects.

Although it has finally cast off the typical traits of the former 'day nursery', the preprimary school designed by the 'new' Guidelines retains its own particular characteristics in comparison with primary education or any other level of schooling. In fact the experience fields encompass not only the preacademic skills in the accepted sense, as for example, in emergent literacy and numeracy and the like, but also in developmental areas such as personal care, motor skills, social competence etc. Although

there is general recognition for the importance of out-of-school experience, first of all family life, it is obvious that the educational methods
adopted in the preprimary school differ from those used by any other
agency, so that this extension of children's experience alone provides
justification for the specific contribution of the preprimary sector.

Attendance and costs of preprimary schools

The establishment of State-run preprimary schools brought about a
remarkable rise in the quality of early childhood education. At the same
time it marked the beginning of a process aimed at a substantial ame-
lioration in the self-evident inequalities which had previously existed as
far as the opportunity to benefit from preschool education was concerned. Many children, indeed most children, were previously excluded
from any possibility of enjoying preschool education facilities, either
because of lack of provision, or for economic reasons.

From this point of view the State-run preprimary school has undoubt-
edly been successful. Briefly, during the school year 1951–1952, only 35
per cent of the age group attended a preschool setting; but, by 1971–
1972, just a few years after State-run preprimary schools had been
established, this figure had risen to 59.4 per cent; and the reports for
1991–1992 state that more than 92 per cent of three- to six-year-old
children were attending a preschool setting, with about half being catered
for in State-run preprimary schools. This means that the basic aim of the
political design which led to the inception of State-run preprimary
schools has been essentially achieved. Within the span of less than 25
years nearly all three- to six-year-old children in Italy have been given the
real opportunity to attend a preschool educational setting.

This success also seems to be evident from another point of view – from
that of equal opportunities for families and, principally, for mothers, who
are no longer forced to choose between their own opportunity to continue
in employment, especially that outside the home, and the duty laid on them
by society of bringing up and educating their children.

As the 'new' Guidelines were enhanced in 1991, the goal of ensuring
all the children equal opportunities and, at the same time, social equity
for families and mothers, was virtually fulfilled. In particular the gap
between equality of opportunity in Northern–Central Italy and the
South–Islands had been closed, although problems still persist to some
extent, due, in some regions, to various reasons, chiefly of a social and
cultural nature, which seem to be somewhat difficult to overcome, at
least in the short term.

As for funding, the variation in forms of preschool provision as a
whole has to be taken into account. As mentioned, educational provision

is assured by different agencies: State, regions, provinces, municipalities, religious and private institutions. While this differentiation is unfailingly reflected in the quality of provision, there is an obvious parallel in the functioning of groups, as well as in the proportion of financial income contributed by the parents.

From this point of view, the most homogeneous situation is presented by the State-run schools and, to a certain extent, the schools run by the so-called 'Special Statute Regions' (Valle d'Aosta, Friuli-Venezia Giulia, Sicily, Sardina) and the autonomous Provinces of Trento and Bolzano as well. In these cases, the free provision – there are no fees for tuition, transportation and meals – involves total funding by the State. It can be direct (staff salaries and functioning of the settings) or indirect, through the regions and the municipalities (buildings, equipment, support staff, transportation, meals). Funding by the State covers almost all the costs of the provision, so that parents are relieved of any significant contribution. They make only a contribution (about 50–80,000 Italian Lire per child per month) towards the cost of children's meals.

The situation as regards non-State preprimary schools is, on the contrary, very different. This involves around 60 per cent of all provision (900,000 children in 1991). Here, parents have to contribute directly to funding the school. Such contributions are required under different headings: entrance and tuition fees, transportation of the children home–school–home, meals, materials and equipment, excursions, etc.

Although these schools are subject to common rules with regard to licensing as well as the requirements concerning the qualification of the education staff, they are in no way forced to offer provision free of charge, nor is there a maximum threshold for fees. However, the State administration grants each non-State institution a yearly contribution, for which they must apply explicitly, certifying that a proportion of the children attending are exempted from tuition and/or lunch fees. (The amount of the contribution is usually dependent upon the number of children exempted.) Nevertheless they are not compelled to adopt reduced or 'social' fees for other children on the roll.

The amount of the parents' financial contribution varies according to the particular type of setting (e.g. municipal, private) as well as to different regions and towns. A recent survey[4] gave the following averages on a national scale: about 45,000 Italian Lire per child per month as tuition fee (with a minimum of 5,000, maximum of 100,000); and around 50–80,000 Italian Lire per child per month as contributions for meals. It is difficult to quantify the costs of transportation, since only around 7 per cent of all children attending non-State-run schools use a transportation service provided by the institution (with an average cost of 22,000 Italian Lire per child per month). Most children reach their setting on foot or by private car.

Parent involvement

Whatever the type of agency offering the provision, preprimary schools enrol their educational as well as support staff in an autonomous way, without the involvement of parents. And in the same way – autonomously – they plan, organize and carry out the educational activities. Nevertheless, parents have always played an active role in their children's preschool education.

For State-run preprimary schools, two different levels of formal parent involvement are regulated by law.

The first level lies in the 'Parents' Assembly', which includes the parents of all the children enrolled in a particular class, or a number of classes, or sometimes in a school as a whole. Formal meetings of the assembly are regulated by law. Such meetings represent a real opportunity for parents to discuss the content and methods of the educational provision. But they also provide the forum where parents can air possible criticisms, or proposals to be entrusted to their representatives in the Elective Collegial Bodies of the school.

The second level lies in those Elective Collegial Bodies (*organi collegiali elettivi*), which are twofold: the Interclass Council (*consiglio di intersezione*) and the School Council (*consiglio di circolo*). As far as the Interclass Council is concerned, the parents of each class elect one of their number to be their representative. In addition to the parents, the school director and all the teachers are also full members of the Council. This kind of council deals chiefly with formulating proposals as regards the educational activities in general and possible experiments or innovations aimed at improving the quality of the school provision. In the second case – the School Council – six to eight parents (according to the school size, whether less or more than 500 children are on the roll) are elected by the parents of all children enrolled in the school. They represent all the parents in the Council, in which the school director and the elected representatives of the teaching, as well as non-teaching, staff are also full members. By law, the chairperson of this Council should be one of the parent representatives. The School Council is responsible for a wide range of matters: in-school regulations, especially as regards supervision of the children; enactment criteria of the Guidelines; purchase, preservation and renewal of equipment, teaching and play materials; aid initiatives; co-operation with other schools; participation in play and recreational activities, which are considered to be relevant to the educational provision of the school, etc.

Unfortunately, the law has not yet been fully put into practice, especially as far as the establishment of autonomous management of preprimary schools is concerned. This fact has, indeed, drastically reduced the impact and benefits of the regulations mentioned above. State-run preprimary schools are, therefore, still under the jurisdiction of primary school directors, so that even the Collegial Bodies are unified, with only one or two representatives for preprimary schools, who naturally have little influence.

Parent participation seems to be, in general, stronger in the 'communal' schools, particularly in some regions where they boast a longer tradition from this point of view. Parent committees, classroom and interclass councils are not regulated by law, as in the State-run schools, but simply by local practice or in-school regulations, according to which parents co-operate in planning activities and methods and, to some extent, in supervising them as well.

It is worthwhile noting, however, that the autonomy of communal and most non-State schools lends itself to two divergent trends: on the one hand, the active involvement of parents is likely to lead to advanced and innovative policies, to experimentation with new education models and methods, and to a deeper interaction between school, families and community; on the other hand, it may result in fossilization, with traditional models, and hence the inhibition of any experimental endeavour, and a closed attitude on the part of teachers towards any kind of innovative work.

What children actually experience

Functioning of preprimary schools

According to the law, preprimary school is open to all three- to six-year-old children. Younger children, 0–3 years old, attend nurseries, and at 6 years of age children enter primary school.

This is the situation in principle, but there are institutions, namely municipal and private institutions, where the boundary line between nursery and preprimary school is nominal rather than real. Indeed, they may provide both types of facilities, and the educational staff involved in them usually hold similar, if not the same, professional qualifications and initial training. As a result, the kind and quality of provision for three- to six-year-olds may not differ significantly from that available for the youngest children, except that curriculum content and approaches will be adapted to their needs.

According to the official calendar, preprimary schools function from the third or fourth week of September (the opening day is fixed year by

year by the regional authorities) until 30 June. Teachers, however, are on
duty from 1 September onwards, and they use the early part of the school
year for planning activities and for professional updating.

As for the weekly and daily timetable, different standards are allowed
and adopted. They vary from four hours a day for six days a week
(Monday to Saturday) to ten hours a day for five days a week (Monday
to Friday). Most of the State-run preprimary schools follow the standard
of eight hours a day for six days a week, while non-State-run schools
share two modules (eight hours for six days per week and five to six
hours for six days per week) in nearly equal proportions. Very few
schools function for less than five hours a day.

Children are assigned to classrooms (*sezioni*) usually by age groups: 3,
4, and 5 years old. In small towns and villages, however, given the small
number of preschool children, mixed-age groups are possible. In some
cases, especially in experimental schools, class groupings may follow
different criteria, grouping according to both the age and the type of
activity or only the type of activity.

The number of children assigned to a classroom may vary from a
minimum of 15 to a maximum of 30 children.

When the module of 8-10 hours per day is adopted, the school day is
divided into two periods: morning and afternoon, with each classroom
entrusted to two different teachers. During one or two hours a day,
usually corresponding to lunch time, the two teachers are both responsible for the children.

In Italy any kind of discrimination (race, ethnicity, religion, language,
gender, class, special needs) is not allowed and all children may enrol in
and attend educational institutions appropriate for their age. Since the
1975–76 academic year, 'special' classes for children with disabilities and
learning difficulties have no longer existed. Children with severe learning
difficulties, as well as those with milder special educational needs, are
fully integrated within the preprimary schools. (The same happens at
primary and secondary school levels.) For this purpose, specialized staff
(called support teachers – *insegnanti di sostegno*) are available to schools.
They co-operate with classroom teachers while having particular responsibility for the children with special needs. One support teacher is allocated for around four to five children with special needs.

The preprimary school curriculum

Planning, organization and implementation of educational activities are
carried out according to the model provided in the 'new' Guidelines
(1991). However, these apply directly to only the State-run preprimary

schools, although non-State schools generally also choose to conform to the same model.

The most typical characteristic of these Guidelines is the sharing of time among a number of activities which cover the child's experience as a whole. The activities are condensed within the so-called fields of experience (*campi di esperienza*), which are defined as:

> Ambits of child's doing and acting, and then (they are) specific and identifiable competence areas, where the child gives meaning to his/her manifold activities, develops his/her learning, achieves language and process instrumentation, and pursues his/her goals. This happens in the solid framework of an experience which develops within well defined boundaries and with the child steadily and actively involved
> (Italian Ministry of Education 1991)

Six experience fields have been identified and thoroughly defined, and for each of them aims, objectives, and the pace and methods of teaching and learning have been described. They are outlined briefly below:

The body and motor skills, where the proposed activities include physical activities (gross and fine motor skills) and play in particular;

Language and literacy – practice with communicative capacities with regard to oral language as well as to a first contact with the written language (emergent reading and writing). This practice is encouraged by an intensive interaction with peers and by planned teaching activities as well as, for example playing with structured materials, exploring, listening to and telling stories, etc.;

Space, order, measure. This field includes the child's first experiences with logical functions. Activities include grouping, ordering, ranking, quantifying, measuring, and hence special relations, classifying, etc.

Objects, time, nature – knowledge about natural and artificial objects, developing scientific attitudes and abilities, basic ecological or environmental education;

Messages, shapes, and the media – activities connected with communication and any other kind of expressive activities such as manipulation–visual, sound–music, dramatic–imaginative play, audio-visual and mass media, arts and crafts, and their inter-connections;

The self and others – experiences and activities which help the child develop consciousness of his/her own individuality as well as positive relationships with other people, children or adults, and the ability to acknowledge and follow moral and social rules and values.

The planning of educational activities is the main task of every teacher, for his/her class. However, this planning should be harmonized right from the beginning of the school year within the whole-school plan, in order to provide all the children with a co-ordinated and coherent curriculum. School directors, who also bear a guiding and controlling function at institutional level, are entrusted with the co-ordination and supervision of this.

Assessment of children's achievements and evaluation of classroom teaching approaches is committed to the teachers themselves, who use methods and instruments suggested by current practice, as well as those afforded by relevant research. Very few standardized instruments are available at this school level for monitoring achievement. A complete set of assessment instruments is currently being piloted, and should be available for teachers within a few years.[5]

Assessment and evaluation are generally of a formative nature. Their principal aims are not really the classification and ranking of children according to the quantity and quality of their achievement, but rather the identification of possible problems, or recognition of talents, so that a more individualized educational approach can be adopted. This applies in particular to children with special educational needs.

The final assessment at the end of every school year concerns both the individual children and the classroom as a whole. In the first case it is a detailed description of the quality and pace of each child's development, as shown during the school year. This assessment is conveyed, in a formal way, often by means of standardized report forms, to both parents and the school director. Classroom evaluation, on the other hand, consists of an outline of the educational activities carried out during the school year: these are compared with the educational plans devised at the beginning of the year, and also with the actual achievement of the children.

Staff training and qualifications

At present the minimum qualification required for teaching in preprimary schools is a vocational certificate achieved by completing a three-year course of study in the Preprimary School Teacher Training College (*Scuola Magistrale*). These colleges provide three-year post-compulsory courses which are, like any other vocational courses, specially designed for the particular professional demands which may be made of students on qualifying.

Preprimary school teacher candidates usually enter the college at fourteen years of age, i.e. after completing compulsory school, and obtain their vocational certificate at the age of seventeen. Their school

curriculum includes the following subjects: Italian language and literature; history and geography; pedagogy; mathematics, computing and
natural sciences; hygiene and child rearing; music and singing; domestic
economy and housework; modelling and drawing, physical education
and sports. Moreover the curriculum involves a practical training in the
preprimary schools (two or four hours a week, every school year) and
reporting on it.

Besides the initial training and qualification, in order to get a post as a
teacher the candidate has to pass a public examination (*concorso*) to
achieve a qualification (*abilitazione all'insegnamento*) that is formally
recognized as such for teaching in the preprimary schools.

In several regions, experimental five-year courses are currently provided for preprimary school teacher candidates. These have retained the
minimum qualification after the first three years, but add two more years
in order to ensure the students a full (five years) upper secondary course
as well as the possibility of passing a school-leaving examination (*esame
di maturità*) with the corresponding upper secondary school leaving certificate (*diploma di istruzione secondaria di secondo grado*), which is
required for entry to a university course.

Meanwhile a plan to radically reform initial training for preprimary
school teachers is under consideration within the framework of a thor-
ough reform of upper secondary education. According to this project, the
current *Scuolo Magistrale* would disappear, and preprimary school
trainees would attend a four-year university course, after completing a
normal five-year upper secondary school. The first two years of the new
teacher education is aimed at providing them with basic competences,
and the last two years at offering them a specific professional training.
Such courses would be to graduate level. This was the intention of the
1974 Education Act, but it has not yet been enacted.

Endnotes

1. The Education Act of 13 November 1859 was devised by Gabrio
   Casati, the Minister of Education at that time. It acknowledged the
   role of education in improved development of the individual personality, and established the principle of a compulsory elementary
   education.
2. Two laws (Daneo-Credaro, 1911, and no. 517/1913) thoroughly re-
   organized school provision. As for compulsory education, it was extended to six years of attendance. Preprimary education is not yet
   explicitly taken into account, but the principle that basic education is
   a matter of public interest is strongly stated. Moreover, the first of

these laws established the *Patronati Scolastici* (public institutions responsible for nurseries and nursery schools), while the other set up the preschool teacher colleges (*Scuole Pratiche Magistrali*). Ten years later, the *Riforma Gentile* (Education Act of 1923) included preprimary education within the general framework of basic education, although it did not make it compulsory, and established the so-called *Scuola di Metodo* for the initial training of preschool teachers. Finally, in 1940, the first syllabus of preschool education was published.

3. Among several initiatives, a National Association of Childhood Educators (UNEI – *Unione Nazionale delle Educatrici dell'Infanzia*) was established (1904).

4. IEA Preprimary Project – Italy. Phase I, co-ordinated by CEDE, Frascati, 1988.

5. The initiative, which is co-ordinated by Lucio Pusci, is currently being carried out by the Centro Europeo dell'Educazione (CEDE), Frascati in the framework of the IEA Preprimary Project (International Co-ordinating Centre). It covers a set of development measures (cognitive development, language, motor skills, pre-academic skills, social competence, social thinking) as well as a number of observation instruments (child activities, adult behaviour, time management, affective climate).

7

Provision for Preschool Children in Spain

Teresa Aguado Odina

Educational Philosophy and Policy

In Spain, education for 0–6-year-olds prior to starting compulsory schooling is currently undergoing a major reform process, as is the rest of the educational system. First of all, this chapter briefly looks at the social and legislative background which immediately preceded and justified this process and also the general guidelines of the reform project currently being put into general use. Significant information is also provided on the organization and field of action of preschool education. The second section describes the features of the education received by preschool children – the educational model, curriculum, criteria and the steps taken to cater for children and groups with specific educational requirements.

The background to the present situation

The organization and structure of the Spanish educational system prior to the current educational reform were ruled by the General Law on Education (LGE) of 1970, which was the most important such law since the Moyano Law of 1875. In spite of emerging from the political framework of the previous régime, this Law modified to a great extent the educational model established after the Civil War (1936–39), and the 1965 Primary Education Law.

The economic and social changes which took place in the 1960s led to a new, predominantly urban and industrialized social structure. The General Law on Education attempted to cater to its requirements, as did the financing of the Educational Reform Law (4 August 1970), in response to the 'existence of strong social pressure to create nursery and infant schools' (Ministry of Education and Science, 1969), and for the first time a preschool level was set up within the Spanish educational system. The Law acknowledged the State's duty to cater for this level and the possibility of providing such education free of charge in public teaching institutions. However, in spite of recognizing its educational role, the General Law on Education did consider preschool education a priority. It was to be voluntary, non-compulsory and for children aged from birth to 5 years old, inclusive. It was divided into two stages: kindergarten (two- and three-year-olds), and infant school (four- and five-year-olds).

Later on, a Ministerial Order of 27 July, 1973 established specific Educational Guidelines for this level which ended the supposedly educational role of the whole of this stage by relegating the kindergarten level to situations in which 'mothers or maternal substitutes are unable to take care of the child' (MEC, 1973). More recently, the organization of preschool education was modified by the Royal Decree 69/1981 of 9 January, which repealed the previous Educational Guidelines of 1973. These rules emphasize the importance of co-ordination between preschool and the first cycle of General Basic Education (EGB – compulsory primary education), and they establish the need to develop language, psychomotricity and logical thought syllabuses which prepare for school, particularly for children not attending preschool. The Ministerial Order of 17 January 1981 established 'Renewed Syllabuses' which did not recognize any difference between the preschool stage and the first stage of EGB and proposed globalized education in structured blocks of subjects, and activities focused on subjects aimed at acquiring skills and habits which would prepare children for primary school.

All these rules recognized the importance of infant education in children's development and in preventing subsequent school problems. In spite of all this, preschool education was still mainly focused on the role of custodian for which it was originally conceived and its original, somewhat chaotic, development was apparent.

With the proclamation of the Constitutional Law on the Right to Education (LODE) (3 July 1985), an attempt was made to ensure that educational requirements were met, making a suitable number of school places available. This gave public schooling some dignity and encouraged equal opportunities at all levels of the school system and particularly in the level before primary school.

Finally, the Constitutional Law on General Organization of the Educational System (LOGSE) (3 October 1990), has set out the new structure of the Spanish educational system. The Law describes the components of the curriculum. Taking into account that the Spanish State is made up of various autonomous Communities, with varying degrees of political autonomy, the central government will establish the minimum of schooling and the basic curricular aspects – introduced and discussed in this chapter – whereas the autonomous Communities, with full authority as regards educational material, will set out the curricula for the various levels, stages, cycles, grades etc., of the educational system.

According to the new structure established by the LOGSE, infant education – a name which replaces that of preschool education – is the first stage of the educational system and is not compulsory. It is aimed at 0–6-year-old children and is divided into two cycles according to the age of the child: the first cycle is for under-three-year-olds and the second cycle for children between 3 and 6 years of age.

Infant education reform

Over the last decade there has been a gradual awareness in Spain of the need to carry out an overall reform of non-university education, for the two following main reasons: on the one hand, the urgent need to adapt the educational system to the real economic, political, social and legal situation which has arisen as a result of the major changes which have taken place in Spanish society since the arrival of democracy and, on the other hand, the need to correct the numerous disorders within the educational system which are mostly apparent in the high percentage of 'school failures'. Thus, for example, some data provided by the MEC (1986) show that approximately 20 per cent of pupils are behind in their schooling at the beginning of the higher cycle of EGB.

It has also been acknowledged that proper attention during a child's early years ensures better personal development and balance. Early education, which we understand as the intentional actions of a community on the developmental process of small children, is aimed at providing conditions which enable them all to develop. One of the purposes of the Preschool Education Reform Project is 'To compensate as much as possible for the inequalities which arise from children's environment, in order to ensure the equal opportunities that every democratic society requires' (MEC, 1987a: 20).

Traditionally, educational responsibility covered the family in the widest sense: parents, siblings, uncles and aunts, neighbours, etc., who lived and worked together. The historical transformation process of this family medium has made it necessary for other institutions to co-operate with the family, sharing, completing and making its educational function easier. Modern living conditions (work, distances, schedules, room, etc.) require different ways of attending to, caring for and educating small children.

The infant education reform in Spain, while taking into account the close relationship between the last cycle of preschool and the first cycle of primary education, conceives infant education as a level with its own purposes and targets, conditioned by the evolution of the child prior to (primary) education (MEC, 1989).

The reform process of the 0–6-year-old stage began with a Ministerial Order from the General Under-Office of Preschool Education (O.M. 26/4/85), which required public institutions of General Basic Education (primary) or preschool institutions to take part in an experimental infant educational programme which would provide information which could be used for reforming the educational system.

The second stage involved developing and putting into practice selected infant education projects (O.M. 1/4/86), during the period covering the academic years from 1986 to 1989. During the 1989–90 school year, these experimental projects began to be put into circulation and are currently in general use in all institutions.

The reform project emphasizes its wish to consider the period between 0 and 6 years old as having its own identity and to find the particular conditions which make any institution educational which caters for children of this age, based on the children's characteristics and the socio-historical circumstances in which their childhood is spent. As theoretical assumptions of the proposal included in the project for the reform of infant education, some general principles are to be taken into account in any educational proposal aimed at the 0–6-year-old stage, such as valuing the development of the child as a whole person. This implies according the same values to each aspect of the child's development: intellectual, physical, artistic, etc. A child's experience arises from and tends towards integration. In other words, any childhood experience contains, in an integral and condensed form, multiple different aspects. These should not be separate but, instead, an attempt should be made to find the integration and complex unity which has always existed in childhood experience and which is their natural way of learning and growing up (MEC, 1986). The environment should be carefully prepared, providing experiences which can compensate for living conditions and enhancing children's opportunities and abilities. Education should be decentralized away from the classroom and placed within the child's living environment. Both in school (dining rooms, kitchens, corridors), and outside (home, neighbourhood), we can find a much more lively medium, full of significant experience for the child. Moreover, individual children are the agents of their own development. One basic element in building up knowledge is for children to be able to trust themselves and their own experience as a source of knowledge: this means that first of all adults must trust them and consider them able to learn and modify their perceptions, opinions, beliefs and attitudes according to their progress and constant interaction with reality (Ausubel, Novack and Hanesian, 1989).

Rules, values, attitudes, procedures and ways of approaching new situations are all built up through learning. As in systems derived from the constructivist-Piagetian theory (Kamii and De Vries, 1982; Saunders and Bingham-Newman, 1987; De Vries and Kohlberg, 1987), the project recommends the following:

- Educators should take advantage of real-life stimuli and experiences, respect this natural learning process, observe these processes and intervene or not as deemed appropriate in order to encourage the constructivist mechanism.
- They should take the child's interest into account when joining in a game or making a suggestion. What is learnt is just as important as the way in which it is learnt.
- The child should be placed in situations which are appropriate to individual abilities, so that cognitive challenges will arise enabling the young learner to create new resources.
- Mistakes are highly positive for learning and are natural intermediate steps in building up knowledge.
- The important thing is to achieve 'meaningful learning', i.e. connected to the child's previous culture.
- The final purpose is for the child to learn how to learn, in other words, to learn meaningfully and autonomously.
- The relationship among equals has a decisive effect on socializing and independence and on learning in general.
- It must be remembered that, most of the time, changes in behaviour and learning do not occur quickly, suddenly and visibly: instead learning is a slow and, sometimes, imperceptible process.

The analysis and evaluation of the conditions and results obtained from some of the programmes carried out in the experimental scheme for reforming infant education, when compared with non-experimental programmes, have shown that, in the programmes belonging to the experimental scheme (Aguado, 1991):

- Pupils show a higher school attendance rate at three years of age. Parents show a more positive attitude to school, greater reading about and knowledge of educational subjects, a higher participation in training activities and a closer connection between what they consider priority targets in education and those proposed in the programme followed by their child.
- Teaching staff show greater professional satisfaction and constant participation in further training activities focused on subjects related to the purposes of the programme.

- Classroom processes correspond to various educational models, amongst which can be found the maturationist, pre-academic and cognitive development approaches; they also show a higher degree of suitability to the organization and teaching principles of basic curricular design proposed by the Ministry of Education (MEC).
- Pupils achieve better results in general and academic intellectual skills and interests – science and maths – assessed by direct observation in class, and complexity and diversity of thought in activities related to physical knowledge, logical-mathematical knowledge and plastic expression skills.
- Pupils of the programme most suited to basic curricular design obtain higher results in complexity and diversity of thought, mathematical, musical and creative skills, independent habits and attitudes, initiative, autonomy and concentration.

On the other hand, we must point out some areas which have not been sufficiently dealt with by the experimental process. These include amongst others, and taking into account the research/development/ circulation model (Stenhouse, 1981), adopted by the MEC for carrying out the reform process:

- Efficient strategies for the permanent training of teaching staff which would enable them to reflect on previous practice, by providing them with material and personal resources such as written matter, time, opportunities and techniques for consideration and debate without becoming overloaded with work.
- Means of ensuring the integration and stability of active, critical teaching teams involved in the project.
- Financial and human resources to provide for swapping experiences and knowledge of experiments in other contexts.
- Improvement of the substructure of institutions in order to adapt them to the new organization and teaching proposals.
- Training assessment throughout the project, both internal (teaching staff) and external (technical inspection, co-ordinators, people in charge of the Teacher Training Centres).
- Paying attention both to fulfilling the social demands for schooling from three years of age upwards and developing and improving the design and practice of specific educational programmes.

Organization and area of action

As we have already said, infant education in Spain is the first stage of the educational system, it is non-compulsory, aimed at children between 0 and 6 years of age and is divided into two cycles according to children's age: the first cycle for children under 3 and the second cycle for those between 3 and 6 years old.

The diversity of institutions and the great variety of educational attention they provide have been the characteristic features of preschool education to date – since the infant education reform. This diversity is apparent both from their organization and owners, and in the names of the institutions (nursery school, kindergarten, preschool, infant school), or the age and characteristics of the pupils and the qualifications of teaching staff. Basically, three types of institution can be found, catering for under-six-year-olds.

- Public or private preschools for the three- to six-year-old stage, run according to MEC regulations and aimed at preparing for compulsory schooling. In these institutions, children are admitted at the beginning of the school year – which runs from September to June – of the year of their fourth birthday.
- Nursery schools dependent on non-profit-making institutions, regulated by the Ministry of Labour, whose functions are related to social work and/or education.
- Institutions run on private initiative under various names, for children of different ages and with the most diverse concepts regarding development and education. In many cases these institutions have had no supervision whatsoever from the educational administration, as the only stipulations for setting them up are those required for any other commercial enterprise. The timetable for attendance of these institutions is flexible and is usually adapted to work requirements.

The State and other official organizations are responsible for financing preschool units in public EGB institutions and those which depend on other public administrative bodies. Preschools in private institutions are also free of charge in those subsidized by the MEC. In institutions which depend on provincial and town councils, parents pay a fee in proportion to their income. Along with this, in order to support the generalization of preschool education, grants are awarded at this level – approximately 14,000 during the 91–92 academic year – as well as food subsidies or grants for attending 'home schools' (institutions where children from isolated rural areas live for the five school days of the week).

The problems involved in regulating this stage of education are also apparent from the wide variety of qualifications of those in charge of education. Article 102 of the General Law on Education established the minimum qualifications required for preschool teachers, which are identical to those required in primary education. However, these rules were only applicable to the infant stage (4-5 years), and not to nursery schools (2-3 years). Currently, teaching staff in the second cycle (3-6 years) have to be university graduates, preferably specializing in infant education. In view of this, the MEC has started up initiatives aimed at achieving the specialization of teaching staff via specific courses and distance teaching. However, provision for children under 3 years of age is still in the hands of unqualified professionals.

Since the LGE was passed, preschool education has continued to expand until reaching its current rate of school attendance. From 819,914 pupils enrolled in the 1970–71 academic year, school attendance reached 1,197,897 pupils in the 1981–1982 school. The decrease in the birth rate caused these figures to drop to 1,084,752 in 1986–87 and to 967,692 in 91–92.

Since the mid-1970s, pupil numbers in public sector provision have doubled. However, private education enrolment has moved in the opposite direction during the same period.

Of the 2,756 preschool institutions, 1,291 are public and 1,465 are private. Sixty-six per cent of the 39,326 preschools are public. In the private sector, most are non-confessional (secular), although there is a considerable percentage of institutions which depend on the Catholic Church (27.95 per cent of nursery schools and 14.84 per cent of infant schools). During the 91–92 academic year, public institutions were attended by 609,322 pupils (64 per cent), and private ones by 348,369 (36 per cent). School attendance for four- to five-year-olds is 96.92 per cent of this age group in Spain.

The number of pupils per unit varies greatly according to the ownership of the institution and the age of the children. During the first cycle, the recommended ratio is around ten children per teacher, diminishing with the age of the child. In schools which depend on the public sector, for children between three and six years old the average PTR (pupil : teacher ratio) in 1986–87 was 26.2, while in the private sector this increased to 30.3 and reached 33.1 in schools which depend on the Catholic Church. During the 1991–92 academic year, the ratio in public institutions was 22.1 per cent and 26.5 per cent in private ones (MEC, 1992).

Having achieved full school attendance of five-year-olds in 1986–87, four-year-old attendance is now 96.2 per cent (MEC, 1992). Places for three-year-olds are currently being created. The total number of places made available in public or member institutions in the 1991–92 academic year was 9.060. Currently places in public institutions for the first cycle of infant education make up only 9.5 per cent of the whole child population, while the remaining 90.5 per cent is made up of second-cycle pupils.

One of the educational authorities' priority tasks is to cater for the need for public school places for the ages included in the first cycle of infant education, up until now mostly catered for by private initiative in institutions not always ruled by suitable educational criteria as regards aims, substructure, staff, ratio, materials, etc.

Preschool experience

The educational function of the infant education phase is understood to be complementary to that of the family, offering children the chance to interact with other adults and their peers and offering them experience and learning opportunities.

This stage of education is arranged in two cycles according to children's age – 0–3 and 3–6. Access to primary education takes place during the academic year which begins the year of the child's sixth birthday. The cycle is the curricular period of programming and assessment, and team work between teachers of the same cycle is encouraged. A sequence is established which enables the child to transfer from one cycle to the other and from infant to primary school without trauma. In order for this to occur, both purposes and content must be planned and developed without losing sight of the overall concept of this stage, and paying attention to the aims and methodology of the first year of primary school.

During the first cycle, children are encouraged to identify their needs and take steps to fulfil them on a more independent basis. The arrival of a small child at school for the first time is planned so as to allow a period of positive adaptation, so avoiding school admission being a traumatic experience. Amongst other precautions, parents are present during some parts of school activity or during the child's arrival and greeting period, until their presence becomes unnecessary.

The educational model

In the 'Project for the Curricular Framework of Infant Education' (MEC, 1986), the educational model for this stage is defined as the combination of fundamental ideas, criteria, guidelines etc. which define a particular educational proposal: 'The attitudes and actions that adults intentionally perform in order to encourage the maximum development of under-six-year-olds' potentials, in order to enable each child to achieve the fullest possible personal development' (MEC, 1986:19).

In Spain at present there are a number of different forms of early childhood education. On the one hand, there are numerous preschool programmes, particularly in the 0–3-year-old stage, which belong to the model which could be described as maturationist/developmental, or non-directive, derived from organic theories of childhood development. This is the model proposed in the 1954 Law on Primary Education (Art. 18/19), when it recommended the creation of affectionate, playful and intuitive atmospheres in order for children to develop in harmony, and also in the General Law on Education of 1970, which defined preschool education as a bridge between the family and school, recommending an atmosphere similar to home.

Along with this, particularly in the age groups towards the end of this stage, we encounter what is known as the pre-academic model, established by the General Law on Education of 1970, which was aimed at achieving academic preparation for primary school. The renewed preschool syllabuses, to which we have already referred, proposed this educational model because, while acknowledging certain features of the cognitive-developmental approach – such as development stages and curricular areas to be considered – it fixed operative targets focused on acquiring skills and habits which prepare children for compulsory schooling.

Finally, the model for this level proposed in the Infant Education Reform in the Basic Curricular Design (MEC, 1989), belongs mainly to the transactional or cognitive development model and, more particularly, to a constructivist approach derived from the Piagetian theories. Along with this, it also includes the objectives belonging to the pre-academic model, while at the same time proposing materials, resources and activities from the most maturationalist model (Kamii and De Vries, 1982; Saunders and Bingham-Newman, 1987; De Vries and Kohlberg, 1987).

Two of the major purposes of the 0–6-year-old stage are defined: making the most of children's possibilities for development, both cognitive and affective and psychomotor; and providing them with skills, habits and attitudes which will enable them subsequently to adapt to primary education (MEC, 1986/89). It is emphasized that the latter purpose should always depend upon the former, i.e. encouraging and increasing development is a priority, which in order to take place must be carried out in such a way as to simplify adaptation to future requirements (MEC, 1989).

This dual objective is specified in the following general purposes (MEC, 1986/89):

1. Motor development: knowledge and control of the body, gradually picturing the shape of the body, use of spatial–temporal co-ordinates.
2. Cognitive–linguistic development:
   - Encouraging the move from sensory–motor to symbolic and from intuitive and pre-categoric to logical and categoric thought.
   - The use of sufficiently correct oral language to understand and be

understood by others, to express ideas and opinions, feelings, experiences and wishes.
- Development of observation skills and exploration of surroundings.
- Acquiring abilities and skills which simplify adaptation to primary school (perception, memory, conceptual development, numeracy, pre-academic skills).
- Appreciation of musical and plastic representational forms and using their basic techniques.
- Reproducing original and varied aspects of reality or products of the imagination.
- Knowing and understanding the cultural features and rules of the community.
3. Affective development:
- Development of co-operative habits and attitudes.
- Encouraging a sense of belonging to and chances of participation in various social groups.
- Achieving personal balance by developing self-esteem, a positive approach to school, confidence, security and independence.

Curricular development

The purpose of educational reform in Spain has been not only, or even mainly, the organization or structure of education. It is mostly about content and the availability of and opportunities for learning experience that schools offer pupils. A teaching reform always involves curricular reform, i.e. educational intentions and the conditions under which they will be put into practice (MEC, 1989). The curricular approach adopted by the Ministry of Education is an open and flexible Basic Curricular Design (DCB), which must ultimately be defined and variously specified by those autonomous Communities with educational authority, by educational institutions and by teachers themselves.

The proposed curriculum design is laid out in three levels, in three degrees of specification, ranging from the most general and unspecific – DCB – to teachers' timetables, via the Teaching Institutions' Curricular Project (PCC). In the DCB, such educational intentions are expressed as the social and moral education of pupils, educating to achieve certain attitudes and values which allow pupils to make responsible choices in the pluralism of modern society, achieving non-discriminatory education aimed at equality both for people and their chances of fulfilment; and opening up school to the environment. The DCB described the common framework within which, in very general terms, a number of instructions, suggestions and guidelines are formulated regarding the purposes of schooling and the most appropriate educational strategies for achieving such purposes. The MEC is responsible for compiling the DCB, which teaching institutions use as standard regulations.

The PCC is part of the educational project that, according to the LODE, schools themselves are responsible for putting together. It is a bigger project and includes priority and basic aims, methods of organization and co-ordination, organizational structure, operational rules and links with the community. It involves defining the general purposes of the cycle, or phase, selecting content, sequencing content according to cycle, establishing assessment criteria at the end of the cycle, defining the criteria for spatial and temporal organization, deciding on the main teaching materials to be used, etc. Finally, teachers make up the syllabuses, the planned experiences, in a more or less explicit way to make their pupils' teaching/learning process operate.

The DCB is carried out in two dimensions. The vertical dimension is composed of the two cycles into which it is divided: 0–3 and 3–6 years old. The horizontal dimension is composed of the various areas or fields of experience in which each cycle is arranged. In each curricular area, various specific aims are made explicit, along with the appropriate blocks of content aimed at providing teachers with information concerning work considered appropriate to each stage. These plans should include facts, concepts, procedures and approaches. The selection criteria is that they should be well-suited to achieving the general targets.

The areas of experience and blocks of contents are as follows (MEC, 1989):

1. Identity and personal independence:
   - Knowledge of the body and the shape of one's own image.
   - Perceptive/motor skills required for solving various tasks.
   - Cognitive, affective, relationship aspects of everyday activities.
   - Health: basic abilities for caring for oneself and one's surroundings.
2. Discovery of the physical and social medium: social relationships and human activity, objects, animals and plants, the landscape.
3. Communication and representation: oral language, approaching written language, plastic, musical and corporal expression, relationships, measuring and representing space.

Organizational and educational principles

Consistent with the proposed educational model of cognitive development, the educational process attempts to improve the extent and depth of development by structured experiences and by confident exploration. The areas of experience – cognitive structures, inner schemes, physical, logical, mathematical and social knowledge – are globalized by setting up learning institutions which stimulate the child's interest and provoke curiosity and the desire to learn. The learning process is planned according to Piaget's evolutionary stages and includes spontaneous activities, free play, active construction of reality and encouraging assimilation and adaptation processes (suggesting hypotheses, experimenting, verification, using mistakes).

The principles by which the organization and development of learning processes are ruled are as follows (MEC, 1986/92):

- Parents are an integral part of school and the link between the outside and the inside of the institution. School must share the task of education with the family. There are two angles to parents' participation in school: one, which is regulated by LODE, involves their participation in the operation and management of teaching institutions; the other, under the LOGSE, has to do with the importance of parents' participation in school activity, which can be channelled in various different ways, such as meetings which create an atmosphere of mutual trust and enable information to be exchanged, periodical contacts to be made in general or classroom meetings, activities to be organized by or for parents (workshops, parties, school plays, excursions, etc.), and parents to collaborate in school structure and compiling teaching materials, discussion groups, parents' courses, talks, etc.
- Pupils must be able to make meaningful connections between their previous experience, what they already know and what they are finding out anew. This involves intense mental activity motivated by interest and the desire to become involved in the process of building up meanings. In the same way, an atmosphere must be created in which the child's participation is encouraged, in order that individual children's methods of observation and exploration, trial and error and discovery are set up and improved (Bruner, 1984).
- Teaching and learning situations must be globalized, as learning does not occur through the accumulation of new knowledge, but rather as the result of making numerous connections and establishing relationships between what is new and what was already known, past experience and living. Projects should be set up with purposes which are clear and mean something to children, activities which involve the use of various expressive languages and fields of experience. All this does not mean that specific non-global activities should be suppressed (explaining a story, singing, workshops), but they should only focus on globalization and meaning.

- For activities, experiences and procedures, the use of processes which are known to have been used in various situations must be encouraged, along with knowledge and testing of new strategies, discovery and use of new methods which enable reality to be understood and modified. All this is possible via spontaneous play, manipulative and mental performance and experiment.
- As regards relationships and affection, it is essential to build up an atmosphere of security in which a child's autonomy and self-confidence is stimulated. Rules, challenges and demands must be consistent and flexible. The child will participate in establishing and modifying these.
- The organization of space, materials and time must be systematic, but varied and flexible enough to adapt to children's different rhythms and interests, supplying room in which to relax or act, to be alone or work with others; time to transfer from one activity to another, for routines and surprises, for planning and assessment; conventional and unfamiliar materials in differing degrees of structure and complexity.
- As regards the sub-structure of the institution, infant school is an institution purposely designed and conceived for following the proposed educational model and to act as the background for providing and encouraging education; each and every one of its components is responsible for and has a commitment to the end result. Thus the school building, close to children's homes, must be situated somewhere which has adequate hygienic and safety conditions, designed according to the defined system. Its size must combine the need for room with the need for a child to be able to use it. Both indoor and outdoor spaces must be carefully designed. Material supplies will be the result of careful selection in order to achieve the proposed purposes. It must be a whole, open space.
- The adults who take part in an infant school are the team composed of teaching staff, other adults and parents and the technical team. The team is made up of all those who, with various functions, work in the school. This team must adjust the educational scheme to children's needs and those of their environment, by gradually adapting it as the result of analysis and a common search for creative solutions and on a scientific basis. The technical team is an inter-disciplinary team composed of professionals – a psychologist, a paediatrician, a social worker – whose role is to provide reflection and analysis, to work together with the educational team and to attend to children's special needs.
- One of the educator's functions is to encourage and motivate children's interests and to listen to their proposals; to plan and put into

practice global projects and activities: to observe and interact with pupils; to take part in the process, modifying it wherever necessary; to join the educational team in putting together the project, organizing the school, setting up timetables and sequences, planning activities, establishing methods of action, assessment and project readjustment, relations with other members of the school community and with other institutions in the area. Among its tasks are observing, assessing and arranging the surroundings according to children's interests, asking questions and guiding the learning process. Most of the time the teacher watches and enquires, collecting information for guidance in the choice of materials and additional activities which will increase children's interests and skills. The teacher acts as a companion, minimizing the use of authority and control over the children, guides them and encourages their initiative, games, experiments, reasoning and social co-operation (Weil and Murphy, 1982; De Vries, 1987).

• Assessment is global, constant and formative; it is not a judgement on children and their performance, but a collection of information in order to appreciate and adjust efficiently the effect of education. It is carried out by initial diagnosis – an interview with parents in order to obtain information on each child's background, routines, preferences, habits, customs, relationships, etc. – daily observation of the child in various different situations – in the playground, corridors, dining room, during games, drawing, teacher–pupil interaction – and work specifically aimed at observing, such as tests arranged by an adult. Among the tools used are teachers' logs, observation and conversation with pupils. Parents are informed periodically of their child's progress. Written reports are usually supplied at the end of each term in the second cycle and at the end of the year in the first cycle.

Space, materials and time

Although learning can occur anywhere, using any materials and at any time during school activity, the surroundings in which a child moves stimulate, simplify or encourage certain types of behaviour and condition the kind of relationship with and interaction between people and objects (Evans, 1987; De Vries, 1978). There is no such thing as organized surroundings which would serve as a model for all infant classrooms, the criteria being that they should favour development and enable the pre-set educational targets to be achieved. In general, an attempt is made to create an aggreeable, warm environment, close to home, as personal and flexible as possible and large enough for working with the available materials. In general, teaching is carried out in classrooms which are focused upon the child and designed for self-teaching and learning by discovery. Materials and areas are varied and flexible in use, as they must encourage exploration, experimentation and independent discovery. Organization depends on the characteristics of the group and the activity (Saunders and Bingham-Newman, 1987). As a general rule, each age group, with its own teacher, occupies one classroom on a permanent basis. Spaces outside the classroom are used – corridors, toilets, workshops, kitchen, gym room, playground – and trips to the surrounding area – the neighbourhood or village – and brief one-day excursions – the countryside, a farm, etc. – are encouraged.

The recommendations of OMEP suggest encouraging children to enjoy the open air, in large outdoor spaces with areas of sun and shade, some trees, areas with mounds, sand pits, see-saws, covered areas, plants and small animals. When the school structure permits, some activities such as painting, collages, modelling, sand and water games or gym are carried out in rooms or areas specifically intended for such a purpose, with wooden structures, games, mats, tunnels, cushions, fabrics, hoops, slides, steps and ramps, meccano sets, giant constructions, etc.

Materials are considered a primary tool for educational activity as a means for providing action, mental creation and cognitive structural processes. The variety and organization of materials and their accessibility and visibility should be taken into account in order for children to be able to use them more independently as they grow, and to encourage experiments and active participation. Usually, materials are kept in activity areas known as 'workshops' or 'corners', which allow children to behave independently when choosing their activity according to their interests or to progress in their learning, developing content knowledge and skills around one point of interest. Frequent corners are those offering engagement in activities which are either symbolic – home corners, shops, hairdressers – natural – plants, animals or materials for experiments – painting, resting, reading, etc. (Vigy, 1988). In general, these areas or corners are fixed and change according to children's interests, contexts and educational planning requirements.

During the first cycle of early childhood education (0–3 years old), plastic, multisensory and resistant materials are used, large objects in attractive colours and shapes. For example: carpets, baby-walkers, rocking toys, carpentry benches, musical boxes, trampolines, carts, home corners, cushions, swings, construction games, slotting games, threading cards, mirrors, counters, hammocks, games for opening things, closing things, putting things in or taking them out, mobiles, picture books, sand and water games, rattles, roller skates, telephones, tricycles, tunnels, rubber and rag dolls, lottery games, photos, murals, puppets, fabrics, balls, etc.

During the second cycle (3–6 years old), and according to the characteristics of each institution, many of the above materials are used along with others, such as abacuses, wooden alphabets, self-dictation, jumping blocks, logical blocks, classification boxes, slides, records and cassettes, dominoes, jigsaws, musical instruments, weighing games, calendars, clocks, magnifying glasses, Pictionary, written books, illustrations, clay, different kinds of paints and paper, fabrics, costumes, etc. As pointed out above, these are made accessible to children, in activity areas or corners as planned.

As far as the planning of the use of time is concerned, the rhythms and frequencies of the daytime routine are ruled by children's biological needs during the first few years: feeding, resting, hygiene, activity, going outdoors. During the second cycle, they are arranged according to adults' social criteria. As the child grows, participation in timetables and activity planning increases.

However, timetables vary according to the type of institution and the age of the children. Thus, in schools for under-three-year-olds, the day is usually adapted to parents' work schedules. The day is a succession of events: arrival and greetings, organizing activities, games, cleanliness and washing, activities for acquiring hygienic habits, group activities, a meal, a nap, outdoor games, tidying up and saying goodbye.

A typical timetable for daily activities for 3-6 year olds might be as follows:

9.00–9.10	Arrival and free playtime.
9.10–9.30	Assembly. Children decide on the work for the day. Teachers point out options, new corners or materials.
9.30–10.30	Planned projects. Children go voluntarily to art, science, music, maths, or games corners or areas, etc. to carry out activities of interest or guided activities (making a salad, putting together a model, practising consonants, etc.). They record their activities.
10.30–11.00	Outside to the playground. Mid-morning snack.
11.00–11.45	Assessment in working groups. Sharing activities and tasks, discussing plans. The surroundings are examined to see what items can be kept.
11.45–12.00	Tidying-up time.
12.00–15.00	Lunch and a nap.
15.00–15.30	Return to schoolroom. Reminder of activities planned.
15.30–16.30	Activities started in the morning. Play-acting, games, songs. Using shared spaces: gym room, audio-visual room, kitchen. Activities with other groups.
16.30–17.00	Tidying-up time and saying goodbye.

A teacher or educator is in charge of each group of children of the same age the whole day. Some activities may be carried out together with other groups, or tasks may be shared out among teachers and assistant teachers according to the time of day – lunchtime, rest period, outdoor playtime, gym activities, games, painting, music, etc. – or parents might help in some corners, workshops, or trips to the surrounding area, etc.

Adaptation to specific educational needs

One of the main purposes of the preschool phase, now known as infant education, is to compensate for any insufficiencies, disorders or inequalities (MEC, 1989). Due to the need to adapt the curriculum to pupils' requirements, the following explanation analyses the attention to three major groups with special needs and for which particular steps have been taken. These are pupils with learning difficulties, underprivileged groups and minorities and pupils in rural schools. Finally, some proposals for overcoming sexual discrimination and inequality are analysed.

The Ministerial answer to the needs of children with learning problems has been the School Integration Scheme for Backward Children, i.e. children who, for whatever reason, have greater learning difficulties than other pupils in the learning areas appropriate for their age, and require forms of access or more than one area of the syllabus to be adapted (CNREE/MEC, 1992).

This scheme is intended to integrate these pupils into normal life by encouraging their relationship with other adults and children. They are taught in ordinary classrooms rather than in special institutions during most of the school activity. In schools attended by pupils included in this scheme, support teams are provided composed of psychologists and paediatricians, as well as specialized support teaching staff who collaborate with teachers in applying suitable individualized curricula. Moreover, if one of these pupils is included in a classroom the number of 'ordinary' pupils attended by one teacher is reduced by five.

As regards schooling for under-privileged groups, some specific procedures have been included in the Compensatory Education Scheme (Royal Decree 1174/83), the purpose of which is to benefit any areas or parts of the population whose particular features require priority educational action. Amongst other tasks, an attempt has been made to provide preschool experience to all those children whose living conditions – e.g. life in city outskirts, usually the gypsy ethnic minority – or geographic isolation in rural areas, meant they had no access to schools.

In a country whose intricate geography has meant the proliferation of very isolated, small urban settlements (many with fewer than a thousand inhabitants), it has been necessary to find methods for improving the insufficiencies of school staff and materials in rural areas. Amongst the most interesting projects are the schemes called 'Preschool at Home' and 'Travelling Preschool'. Basically, these consist of an educational project aimed at preschool children, who do not attend school, from various villages in a certain area. They are designed and carried out by a team of preschool teachers co-ordinated by an area inspector and with the support of a psychologist, paediatrician and a social worker. These teachers guide and train mothers in activities to carry out with their children and supply them with suitable material in periodic meetings, either weekly or every fortnight, throughout the school year. During their visit, teachers also get together with children and analyse their progress, pointing out possible individualized syllabuses.

The so-called area teams work alongside these. They are made up of the teaching staff from several villages and are grouped around a resource centre, which supplies teaching material and training and has the substructure for holding meetings, providing publications, etc. These teams plan and apply the Area Education Project adapted to pupils' characteristics and environment. One of their activities is to organize seminars and working groups on the 0–6-year-old stage, co-ordinated by an experienced teacher specially trained in preschool education.

As regards equal opportunities for both sexes, official documents point out the need to eradicate all inequality in the educational system in order to contribute to greater social equality (MEC, 1992). Sexual discrimination and differential treatment of boys and girls begins in the family and reflects social values and usage. Mixed education has existed in Spain for two decades and yet, although boys and girls are taught together in the same classroom, often a teacher or other adult in the school, perhaps unconsciously or without thinking, may behave in a discriminatory way, attributing or expecting different behaviour and attitudes in boys and girls (Browne and France, 1988; MEC, 1992).

School must play an active role in this sense, using direct and positive methods aimed at achieving equal opportunities for boys and girls as well as for different groups or minorities. With this in mind, the educational guidelines for the 0–6-year-old level must aim for the following targets: to help children to discover and form a positive image of themselves, to value their sexual and cultural identity, encourage independent behaviour, establish positive links with both adults and their peers and to allow them to express themselves through play and other forms of expression in diverse activities and without prejudice derived from cultural or sexual stereotypes.

8

Early Childhood Care and Education in Sweden

Monica Bergman

Introduction

This chapter attempts to provide an overview of the education and care of the youngest (i.e. preprimary phase, 0–6 years) children in Swedish society. In discussing the quantity and quality of provision, development is traced from its beginning to the present, focusing in particular on events during recent decades and concluding with ongoing changes. Crucial documents and decisions are explored in order to elucidate on the development of services.

Women's work and family policy have been dominating factors in the framework of care and education of young children in Sweden, and they have been more influential than ideas concerned with early education in decisions to extend provision. Therefore, the chapter will also deal with this crucial perspective in discussing service development.

Some definitions

Unambiguous definitions of early childhood care and education, especially when making comparisons between countries, are difficult, not least because of variations in structure and policies. In Sweden, the term childcare is used for both preschools and family daycare in official documents. Preschool (*förskola*) is the general term used to denote daycare centres, part-time groups, and open preschools. Daycare centres (*daghem*) care for children aged 0–6 years, whose parents are gainfully employed or studying. (In Sweden, more than 80 per cent of women with children under 7 are employed, a large number work part time.) Part-time groups (*deltidsgrupper*) are common for six-year-olds, and are usually for three hours daily during the school year. (Primary school is compulsory from age 7, but the age of admission will be reduced to 6 within a few years.) The open pre-school (*öppen förskola*) is targeted at preschool children without any other form of preschool service, and they may attend for a few hours a week accompanied by a parent or family childminder. Family daycare (*familjedaghem*) is the system by which the municipalities employ family childminders to care for children aged 0–12 years whose parents are employed. All these are included in the complex term *childcare* and constitute a mixture of pedagogical activity and pure childminding. This double aim makes any debate on departmental responsibilities and the development of childcare difficult, since it involves social welfare and family policy as well as education and labour market policies (Bergman 1991). In this chapter, therefore, I will concentrate mainly on the services which include education, i.e. daycare centres and part-time group provision. Both these forms of provision are distinguished by the fact that a trained teacher manages each group of children throughout the time attended.

Administration

Society's responsibility and organization of educational provision for children is administered by two different government departments – the Ministry of Health and Social Affairs, and the Ministry of Education. The former has the responsibility for all provision labelled childcare, the latter for compulsory schooling (currently relating to children aged 7–16).

Childcare is regulated by the Social Services Act. It is looked upon as part of social policy, but a major sector could just as easily be placed under education, and if this were so, preschool provision would then be likely to possess a different legitimacy, as part of the country's education system. The (former) Social Democratic Government directed the Commission for the National Curriculum to set up common aims for education at all levels, from preschool to secondary. However, these directives were changed following the election of a non-Socialist Central Government to office in 1991, and the early childhood phase was excluded.

The National Board of Health and Welfare, together with each county administration, is responsible for supervising childcare at local level in the municipalities. There are 289 municipalities, with populations varying from 3,000 to 70,000. Constitutionally they are a strong form of self-government, and they have the right to levy income tax and to charge fees for certain types of services. As a result of this self-government, there is a considerable ability to influence the level and quality of provision and, in fact, in some areas the decision has been made that childcare and

compulsory schooling be governed by the same local authority administration.

Historical and philosophical perspectives

The first hundred years
Educational provision for the youngest children in Sweden has its roots in the mid-nineteenth century, and derives mainly from two different traditions which continue to exercise an influence more than a hundred years later. On the one hand there have been institutions whose origins lie in the fact of women's employment outside the home, and on the other, those set up for educational reasons (Hultquist 1990).

In 1854 the first crèche (*barnkrubba*) started in Stockholm, intended for children whose mothers had to work, because they were poor and breadwinners. The purpose was philanthropic, and such crèches were organized by private foundations or the Church.

Meanwhile, during the last decade of the nineteenth century, kindergartens (*barnträdgårdar*) were established for purely pedagogical reasons, and were largely intended for children of more affluent families. The first of these is recorded as having been in Stockholm in 1896 (Ds U 1985:5), but some were founded as charitable institutions for workers' families around the same time. Infant schools similar to those in England had been established since 1836, with the aim of raising and educating poor children, in the expectation that such teaching would prevent later criminal behaviour (Johansson 1992). The infant schools were later transformed into crèches or folk-kindergartens.

The significant pedagogical tradition underpinning the kindergartens in Sweden, as in many other countries, was based on the work of Friedrich Froebel (1782–1852), and the further development of his ideas by his niece, Henriette Schrader-Breymann (1827–1899). Her influence on Swedish kindergartens is fundamental, since the Swedish pioneers were trained at her Pestalozzi-Fröbelhaus in Berlin at the beginning of this century. In 1918, when the Swedish Froebel Foundation, an organization for preschool teachers, was initiated by Anna Warburg, the social aspects of kindergartens were stressed, but the framework of Froebelian thought still remained.

Education and training for preschool teachers began around the same time, at the end of the last century. The sisters Ellen and Maria Moberg were the most influential figures in that field, being responsible for both the Froebel Institute in Norrköping, founded early this century, and the Swedish Froebel Foundation, together with its journal, over a period of decades. Thus Froebel's ideas were predominant until the 1930s, which was the period when the reforms behind the modern welfare society began in Sweden.

Child psychology became more important and the philanthropic, paternalistic philosophy of the kindergartens was criticized. Carin Ulin and Alva Myrdal were two of the ideologists in that debate, and they were the founders of the YWCA Institute in 1934 and the Social-Pedagogical Seminar in 1936 respectively, both in Stockholm. However, Johansson (1992) demonstrates that the Froebel tradition still maintained its position, despite the stance of these new institutes.

Another key figure during this period was Elsa Köhler (1879–1940). Köhler was a reforming educationalist from Austria, but she was active in Sweden. She succeeded in combining the ideas of Froebel with modern psychology, thus strengthening its dominance (Johansson 1983). The pedagogical approaches of Maria Montessori never became a threat to the Froebelian tradition in Sweden, because her theories and methods were questioned by the Froebel movement and by Köhler in particular (Johansson 1983; Balke 1988).

As stated earlier, many of the reforms constituting the modern Sweden began in the 1930s. Alva and her partner, Gunnar Myrdal, influenced family welfare policy during the 1930s and 1940s with their book about the falling birth rate, which was published in 1934, and Alva herself contributed further, through her publications on the organization of provision for young children (Johansson 1992).

During this time there were several parliamentary commissions working on the issue of family policy, women's employment, and care and education in the early years (Hatje 1973). Official terminology now shifted from *barnkrubba* (crèche) to *daghem* (daycare centre) for provision related to social need, and from *barnträdgard* (kindergarten) to *lekskola* (nursery school) for provision involving educational objectives (Ds U 1985:5). Although many of the official reports of this period dealt with the need for expansion of provision for preschool children, politicians argued that children should be mothers' concern. Early childhood services were regarded as a threat to the family. The sole reason for granting subsidies was as a strategy for enabling the employment of single parents.

As a result, a State grant to day nurseries was introduced in 1943. Prior to this, all early years funding came from private sources. Although there were ambitious proposals for increased provision during the following decade, no further changes ensued. Now the issue focused on the controversial question of women's position in the family and employment, rather than children's education (Hatje 1973; Hultquist 1990; Johansson

1992). During the 1950s all planned reforms related to provision for children with working mothers were halted, despite the continuous parliamentary investigations indicating growing demand (SOU 1955:29). There was even a small reduction in the 10,000 places in day nurseries, in one year during the 1950s, while the number of places in nursery school doubled. This points to the fact that the latter form was less crucial in the prevailing political climate (Simmons-Christenson 1977).

Three decades of expansion
After a decade of no reforms in the field of early childhood education in the 1950s, a time during which far-reaching amendments in compulsory schooling and in the field of social insurance were decided upon and implemented, the issue of provision for small children reappeared on the agenda in 1962, and it has remained there ever since. Women in both the blue-collar and white-collar trade unions, together with the Swedish Employers' Federation, roused public opinion in favour of extended daycare. In consequence, a parliamentary investigation was set up, and the so-called Family Commission was directed to conduct a survey of society's services for families with children, to analyse the issues involved, with particular reference to the proportions of State grant to day nurseries and potential need for future expansion. By 1963 far-reaching measures to encourage an increase in provision had been enacted by parliament, and additional policy initiatives were taken in 1966. Here one witnesses the close connection between the expansion of preschool facilities and the need for women's participation in the labour market, and this relationship has continued to exercise its influence.

In its final report, the Commission made a number of important recommendations, such as the development of research in behavioural sciences; the integration of children with mild learning disabilities into 'ordinary' groups; and collaboration between preschool and the primary sector (SOU 1967:8).

1968 can be seen as a watershed for early childhood services in Sweden, for this was the year when the 68 Commission on Nursery Provision was set up.

The 1970s
During the 1970s the Commission's work resulted in several reports, all of vital importance for future developments in the field of early childhood. The directive of the Commission stressed the objectives, pedagogical content and formulation, and plans for extension of provision. The main report, published in 1972, became the document used as a guide during the phase of expansion in the 1970s.

The first part of this report deals with theories of child development – substantially those of Erik Homburger Erikson and Jean Piaget – related to the content of preschool educational programmes, the interaction of the people involved (i.e. children, parents, staff) and the methods of working (SOU 1972:26). The second section of the report contains a broad range of topics, such as the objectives of preschool provision, group organization, parents' working hours, the physical and mental health care of children, co-operation between early childhood services and primary schools, family daycare/childminding, the preschool environment, the expansion of preschool facilities, provision for all six-year-olds, for children with special needs, for migrant or bilingual children, children in rural areas, the education of staff, local authorities' planning for expansion, and costing aspects.

As a result of the work of the Commission, parliament took the decision that nursery places should be provided for all six-year-olds during school termtime, and this became a legal requirement of the local authorities under the 1975 Public Preschool Act, although it was not mandatory for children to attend.

Additionally, municipal councils were required under this legislation to produce rolling, five-year plans, indicating annually any need for expansion and the means by which such needs would be met. Nineteen seventy-five can therefore be seen as the starting point for current early childhood service provision in Sweden.

Nineteen seventy-five was also an important year in relation to staff education and training, since the Commission on Nursery Provision also published the report which led to an extension in this field, the intention being to safeguard quality, especially at a time of planned expansion. The dramatic increase in women's participation in the labour market, peaking in the 1970s and early 1980s, underlay the need for rapid expansion (SCB 1989). The government made a pact with the Swedish Association of Local Authorities to increase the number of places available by 100,000, in less than five years, between 1976 and 1980. An important contributory measure was an increase in the State grant (Prop. 1975/76:92), but the local authorities failed to reach their target, providing an extra 63,000 (not 100,000) places during the stipulated period.

The debate was at that time largely dominated by quantitative concerns, with some employed mothers lacking places for their children. The Public Preschool Act was replaced by the Childcare Act of 1977. This strengthened the responsibility of local authorities to plan and expand provision (Simmons-Christensen 1977). It was also decided that the National Board of Health and Welfare should be the authority with responsibility for supervision, and also that required to control criteria relating to day nurseries, and other factors linked to the State grant (Henckel 1990).

The 1980s

Around 1980 the parliamentary debate began to concentrate more and more on issues related to pedagogical aspects of provision, and as a result the National Board of Health and Welfare presented a policy document on the aim and direction of preschools, intended for politicians in the local communities. The document was to be used as the basis of a central educational programme, or curriculum, for preschools, and as a guide to the management, quality and development of childcare services. Another contribution to this debate was the report from the Commission on Family Support (SOU 1981:25), which presented a survey of the requirements for good quality care for children under three. A further important step in this progress was the government's delegation to the Board of Health and Welfare of the task of forecasting future childcare requirements. This document (Socialstyrelsen 1982) included a checklist of measures which should be taken to safeguard the quality of early years services. It highlights the importance of developing an educational programme and, in part, this is considered to be related to the fact that a new national curriculum had been implemented for the compulsory years of schooling. A comparable document became vital for early years teachers, in order to improve their status. Other aspects stressed by this report include management, in-service training, and research and development – all fields which became especially significant during the 1980s. The report can be seen as an attempt to maintain the professional credibility of early childhood services during a time of rapid growth and change. In 1982 the Child Care Act was constitutionally incorporated into the Social Services Act. This Act typifies a new type of legislation, being less concerned about State control and regulation of local authority responsibilities than an expression of target orientation and intent. A further document pertaining to the curriculum (Socialstyrelsen 1987) was eagerly awaited by preschool staff, but unfortunately it was not supported by parliament. Although the publication was primarily aimed at municipal politicians and administrators, it proved to be of vital importance for the professional ambitions of preschool teachers.

Another feature of this progress was a 1985 government Bill proposing the provision of services for every child in the one-and-a-half to six-year-old age range by 1991 (Prop. 1984/85: 209). This was once again a serious attempt to meet the growing demand with a bold venture of expansion, and it was passed in that same year. The proposal included possibilities for parents who were not employed outside the home, and for childminders, to visit open preschools (parent-and-toddler clubs) for some hours each week, and for nursery schools to be opened for the four- and five-year-olds who had not been granted a daycare centre place. The government also suggested that parental leave be extended to eighteen months, but this remains to be implemented.

In 1990, when the government realized that its objectives probably would not be attained, a commission was set up to analyse the possibilities for bringing about a speedy expansion of childcare facilities, and to investigate the communities' ambitions to reach the goal of full supply. The commission was also directed to explore opinion as to the likely effect of introducing a legal right to a place for each child, in other words, a measure to tighten up the duty of local authorities. A report (SOU 1990:80) was published in the same year, stating that demand had outstripped even planned supply, since the need for facilities had increased above the predicted levels. This can be explained by the rise in the birth rate, the increase in women's participation in the labour market, and for many an extension of hours worked, together with an increase in the number of immigrant children. However, the commission went on to suggest that there was evidence of reluctance on the part of some local authorities – a lack of will to expand early childhood services.

The policies and context of childcare expansion

The context
The expansion of early childhood services in Sweden during the last two decades has been mainly related to women's greater visibility in the labour market, and not come about primarily as a result of attention to the early educational needs of children. Thus it may seem more appropriate to use the term 'childcare' to denote provision, especially that for the youngest children. National objectives of family policy, such as parental leave, have been initiated to support equal opportunities for women and men, and the possibility of combining motherhood with gainful employment.

Women's work
Swedish women constitute a considerable proportion of the labour force, with 80 per cent of all women and 82 per cent of the total population aged 16 to 64 gainfully employed at the end of the 1980s. As far back as 1970 Sweden had the highest rate (59 per cent) of female employment for women aged 15–64, when compared with the USA, Canada, Japan, and all the other Western European countries (Arbetsmarknadsstyrelsen 1974). This figure was probably accentuated by the rejection, at that time, of joint taxation for husband and wife. The demand for more women to

participate in the workforce was, therefore, one of the driving factors which has guided the development of public childcare provision in Sweden.

In 1988 the total number of children aged 0–6 was 697,767, and 84.1 per cent of those children had mothers who were employed outside the home in varying degrees. Of these, 4.8 per cent had mothers who were employed outside the home for between one and fifteen hours per week, and one can assume that the majority of this group had organized their own childcare arrangements and were not drawing on the resources of the municipalities. A further 41 per cent had mothers who were employed for 16–34 hours per week, and 37.7 per cent had mothers in paid work for 35 hours or more. From these statistics one can see that the majority of the mothers are employed part-time, and there is now a legal requirement that parents shall have a reduced working day of six hours (75 per cent duty) until their child is eight years old (SoS-rapport 1991: 28).

Maternity leave and parental leave

Maternity leave in Sweden is for 50 days before the birth, with 90 per cent pay, if work conditions are too heavy. Fathers are entitled to ten days paid leave at the time of the birth. Parental leave following the birth constitutes twelve months leave at 90 per cent pay, and three months at a low flat rate. Parents themselves may decide how they will use this leave, since they are entitled to 450 days between them from the time of their child's birth until age 8 is attained. Further benefits include the right to 60 days per year when the child is ill, or needs treatment, and the right to two 'contact' days per year of paid leave to visit preschool or school, when children are aged between 4 and 12 years old.

Fluctuations in the birth rate

In recent years the birth rates have changed dramatically in most European countries (Statistics Sweden 1992a). Many different reasons may

Table 6 Employment rates for women 1950–1992

Year	% employed women	% employed women with children aged 0–6
1950	34	*
1969	53	47
1988	80.4	84
1992	78	82.6

* Data not available

Source: A compilation from AKN (1970); Arbetsmarknadsstyrelsen (1974); SOU 1972:27; Statistiska meddelanden Am 10 SM 9212

underlie such changes, for example, the legalization of abortion, and the availability of contraception. Statistics indicate that the cumulative fertility in Sweden actually increased to 2.1 in 1990, whereas in 1970 Sweden had the lowest birth rate (1.9), compared with EC countries. At that time the birth rate in Ireland was the highest in the EC at 3.9, but by 1989 Ireland's figure had fallen to 2.0. In other words, over the same period in which Ireland's birth rate fell by almost 50 per cent, Sweden's had remained fairly stable.

Expanding early childhood services

As a result of the concentration on expansion of early childhood services during the last twenty years, the percentage of children under 6 registered in day nurseries alone has risen from 7 per cent of all children in the 0–6 age range in 1973, to 36 per cent in 1991 (Statistiska meddelanden S 10 SM 9201). The majority of this provision has been publicly funded, but in more recent years there have been some changes in the rules applying to State grants, and attitudes have altered, so that alternative solutions to funding are on the increase. Nowadays 6.5 per cent of the total number of institutions are private, or are run by co-operatives subsidized by a State grant.

Table 7 provides the statistics indicating the ways in which publicly funded provision has expanded over the last 40 years (1950–1990).

One can see from Table 7 that childcare in organized daycare centres has grown rapidly since the middle of the 1960s when policy was

Table 7 Publicly funded provision in Sweden

	Daycare centre Day nursery	Part-time group Kindergarten Nursery school	Family daycare Childminder
1950	9708	18743	–
1955	10015	27769	1696*
1960	10270	38373	–
1965	11924	52114	6900
1970	32626	80580	30000
1975	65962	112030	49811
1980	129101	104702	90156
1985	184392	78025	113466
1990	256349	63111	110356
1991	283367	65509**	104988

Source: A compilation from AKN, 1970; Statistiska meddelanden S 10 SM 9201, 1992 and SOU 1955:29.
*In 1954
**One third of this group is also registered in care centres or at a childminder.

changed. It was also intended that family daycare should act as a provisional complement during the expansion period, to be replaced later by centres. This has not happened, and there has been stagnation, possibly even decline, since 1985. The underlying reason is the increased demand. Further, it is important to draw attention to the displacement of provision in part-time centres and groups, to the full-time daycare centres, reflecting women's need for full-time childcare during their hours of outside employment.

Breaking down the figures for 1991 in Table 7, 36 per cent of the children attend daycare centres (21 per cent of the 0–2 age range, and 48 per cent of the three- to six-year-olds); 13 per cent of all under-6s are in family daycare (i.e. with childminders); 65 per cent of six-year-olds and 13 per cent of five-year-olds have places in part-time preschool provision, combining this with family daycare (Statistiska meddelanden S 10 SM 9201, 1992).

The demand for childcare in 1992

According to official Swedish statistics, despite the expansions, there was a shortfall of 50,000 places in 1992. One explanation for this is the increase in the birth rate, which has been attributed to the improvements in parental leave and benefits (Demografiska rapporter 1992:1). Forty-nine per cent of all under-6s had childcare facilities provided by municipal authorities in January 1992. Of these, 73 per cent had a place in a day nursery, and the rest with a childminder. A further 8 per cent had private arrangements, these included provision by: a private childminder or nanny (2.5 per cent); private day nursery or co-operative care (3 per cent); friends or relatives (2 per cent). Nursery schools could be used as a form of childcare by only 5 per cent of the age group, since sessions last for only three hours, and parents' working hours are rarely so short each day.

The remaining 36 per cent of the age group are cared for by their own parents (Statistiska meddelanden S 11, 1992), and this figure could appear confusing when comparing it with the fact that almost 90 per cent of women with children under primary school age go out to work or are studying. Many parents in Sweden have different hours of employment, so that childcare can be shared, some work as childminders so that they look after their own children as well as those of others (4 per cent). A further 24 per cent of parents were taking parental leave at the time in which the statistics were gathered.

Childcare for school-age children

Although children of primary and secondary school age are not really in the remit of this chapter, it is important to point out that decisions were

Early childhood care and education in Sweden

made to offer care for these children, whose mothers are employed outside the home. In 1991 38 per cent of the seven- to nine-year-old age group and six per cent of the 10–12 age group had a place in an after-school centre or in family daycare.

The size of institutions
Centres are most frequently organized in two or three units, for example, one centre may provide daycare for preschool children, part-time group sessions, and after-school care. The structure of such groups could be: toddlers, from 1–3 years, in a group of ten to twelve children with two full-time members of staff per five children; or in sibling groups aged 3–6 years, or extended sibling groups from 1-12 years old, so that fifteen to eighteen children will be placed according to a staffing ratio of one adult per five children.

In recent years there has been a movement towards age-related grouping, which ties in with the tendency for strengthening the pedagogical aspects of the provision.

The educational programme for Swedish preschools
Although in no way regarded as a National Curriculum for preschools, the programme/curriculum mentioned earlier was implemented to improve the quality of experiences for children in Swedish preschools. The aims of the curriculum are based in the democratic values expressed in the Social Services Act, and require attention to be paid to the whole development of children and their interactions with their environment, so fostering learning through work and play. The areas of experience are divided under the titles: 'nature'; 'culture'; 'society'. They are intended to support children's growing sense of identity, comprehension of the environment, and ability to communicate with others (Socialstyrelsen 1987).

The influence of party politics
Provision per 100 children in those communities where a Socialist local authority is in power are higher than those in non-Socialist authorities. To some extent the differences reflect the type of area in which they are situated, with the rural communities tending to be non-Socialist. Here the levels of provision are lowest and expansion slowest (Svenska Kommunförbundet 1992).

Differences in the socio-economic backgrounds of children enrolled in daycare centres are also apparent from the available statistics. For example, children from families with parents in white-collar employment are found to represent 76 per cent of children in the 1984–85 figures.

Children of blue-collar parents tend to be found more frequently in family daycare. This may be due to the hours worked by parents in the different trades and professions, but it may also reflect differences in views about educational orientation of certain forms of provision, and the importance of this to certain parents. However, for working-class parents whose hours of employment are too long for them to use the centres, there is no choice, even if they sought more educationally oriented provision for their children.

Differences in levels of provision between authorities range from 72 per cent in Nykoping, to only 31 per cent in Grums and Tanum (Statistiska meddelanden S 10 1992), indicating decisions made by politicians at local level.

Children with special educational needs
In accordance with the Social Services Act, children in need of special support for their development should be given priority in the allocation of places in preschool. The objective of this is to facilitate the integration of children with hearing and speech impairment, as well as children with a physical or mental disability, or those with psychological or behavioural problems. State funding is available for increasing the staff : child ratios in such circumstances.

Children from ethnic and linguistic minorities
Children whose home language is other than Swedish have priority for places in day nurseries and nursery schools, as a result of the Social Services Act. There are facilities for the children to receive instruction in their home language. In 1992, 33,919 children from linguistic minorities were registered, of whom 13,032 received some instruction in their home language, 92 per cent for at least four hours per week. The largest linguistic minorities in Sweden are from Finnish, Arabic, and Spanish backgrounds, but teaching is also provided in Assyrian/Syriac, Greek, the eight languages of the former Yugoslavia, Pharsee, Polish, Turkish, and occasionally other languages. The majority of children from linguistic minorities live in the Stockholm, Goteborg, and Malmo metropolitan areas (Statistiska meddelanden S 10 1992).

Children of refugees
Roughly half the local authorities in Sweden have made special arrangements for preschool facilities for refugee children. In most cases the children attend while their parents learn Swedish, and after about one year they are prepared to join the ordinary provision for children living in their area (SoS-rapport 1991:22).

The cost of early childhood education and care

Childcare is an important economic phenomenon. According to the Swedish Association of Local Authorities, the cost of childcare (including facilities for school-age children) was 25 billion Swedish Kroner in 1989, which amounts to 2 per cent of the GNP, making childcare more extensive than agriculture. Today it is financed by State subsidies amounting to one third of costs, and this is levied by way of a special childcare tax of 2.2 per cent from every wage-earner. The local authorities cover around half the costs, and parents contribute the remainder of the fees (Bergman 1991). Parental contributions in the form of fees are dependent upon the municipality and family income. Overall, the cost of a childcare place for one hour is less than that for one lesson in primary school (Svenska Kommunförbundet 1992). Expenditure on the education (i.e. schooling) system tends to be regarded as an investment in the future, while childcare is discussed purely in terms of expense. Profitability studies (Rudebeck 1989) have shown, however, that childcare can become a benefit for the societal economy.

Transition to primary school

Admission to primary school in Sweden occurs in August the year of the child's seventh birthday. However, a progressive reform will change this. The new School Act, implemented as of July 1991, states that children have the right to start school at age 6, if the municipality has the capacity to provide such opportunities. Until 1997 there is an intermediate stage, during which the Act will be phased in, but after that date it will be binding for municipalities to offer places to all children whose parents wish them to start their primary education. This issue of school entry has been on the agenda in Sweden for many years, and thus the question of co-operation between early childhood provision and compulsory schooling, and children's transition, has been the subject of quite a number of parliamentary commissions. The latest, the Preschool-School Commission, did not suggest any definite change in their final report (SOU 1985:22). Instead, three alternatives were put forward. The first was that the school admission age should be unchanged, but that the final year of preschool should be more adapted to the methods of primary school, and primary school adapted similarly, to the methods of preschool, to enable smooth transition. Another alternative suggested was that the length of compulsory schooling be extended, to take in children from age 6, or even age 5. The final suggestion was that there should be a gradual, or flexible, school admission.

Neither the politicians and management, nor personnel in the two sectors involved could agree to one solution, and the decision was postponed until 1991. Parents have now been given the decisive influence, rather than the professionals and politicians.

At present this reform is a matter of national interest, and aims and guiding principles for both schools and childcare were in preparation. But due to a change in government, only a curriculum for schools has been prepared. The directive given to the committee appointed to deal with this development stresses that their resulting document should lead to a more efficient and higher quality education system. The moves towards closer collaboration between schools and early childhood services hold meaningful implications for both sectors. Early childhood services could see their educational element strengthened, and schools develop their caring activities. Both perspectives are essential in both fields, for the social and pedagogical aspects cannot be separated in early childhood (Bergman 1991).

As Karrby (1992) has pointed out, the Swedish preschool system was not intended to prepare children for compulsory schooling, and different teaching and learning traditions have been developed in the two sectors. The styles of the preschool could enrich the school. Closer liaison between the sectors has been initiated in many municipalities where there is now common management.

Staff and staff training

The staff who work in the centres with young children constitute two different occupational groups – preschool teachers, and nursery nurses. In daycare centres about 45 per cent of staff are trained teachers, who have undertaken higher education courses, while another 50 per cent are nursery nurses who have been trained for two years during their upper secondary school education (this will be extended to three years in Autumn 1993). The other (approximately) 5 per cent have no specialist training for this work. Only 2,000 out of the 70,000 employed in preschools are men.

In the part-time groups, 60 per cent are qualified preschool teachers and the rest are nursery nurses. Fifty staff out of the 6,000 total in this form of provision are male. At managerial level the proportion of men is much higher, around ten per cent (Statistiska meddelanden S10 1992).

In a part-time setting a teacher may work alone with a group or be assisted by a nursery nurse. The group size varies between fifteen and twenty children. The adult : child ratio is set by the local authority, who also make decisions about training. There is no requirement for preschool teachers to be qualified, comparable to the requirement on primary teachers.

A further issue for early childhood services in Sweden is the length of training for preschool teachers. Currently it is two-and-a-half years, which corresponds to 100 weeks/100 points of full-time study. In comparison, courses for teachers of the first seven years of compulsory schooling have recently been extended to three-and-a-half years. There are several motives for this development. Firstly, there is the raised status accorded to longer training; secondly, the European Community requires courses to be of three years' duration to count as academic, and thirdly, lengthening the course gives it a better chance of leading to a degree.

Moving on to research degrees and to training for research posts is difficult for those who have studied only short courses, entailing study for extensive bridging courses in order to qualify. Thus, a more systematic education, making it possible to proceed to master's, licentiate or doctoral levels, without detours, needs to be created (Bergman 1991; Bergman 1992a).

Policies for research and development

Since 1984 the National Board of Social Welfare has allocated funds to support the development of projects within the field of childcare, by municipalities. More than two-thirds of the 289 municipalities have been involved in around 650 projects, and special priority has been given to enabling co-operation between preschool and primary school, co-operation with parents, and work within the facilities themselves. The Board has also set up a computerized database detailing information about research and development relevant to early childhood services.

Currently there are some 135,000 persons occupied in the field, and more than 700,000 children are enrolled in childcare subsidized by the State, that is, more than half of all children aged up to 10 years old. (Sweden's total population is around eight million.) Consequently there are strong economic reasons why a more purposeful concentration on research and evaluation, from different perspectives, including the search for new knowledge, is demanded. This is a field whose costs and quality have received much public attention during the last few years.

Such major reforms as the massive expansion which has been achieved in Sweden should be accompanied by equivalent developments and achievements in higher education, most notably, in teacher education. It is in this way that high quality can be guaranteed. Such a development has long been an ambition of people in Sweden, but it has not been implemented (Bergman 1991). Three important parliamentary commissions of inquiry during the 1980s emphasized the significance of developing childcare research and teacher education: they were the Investigation of Family

Support (SOU 1981:25); the Committee of Leisure Time Centres (SOU 1985:12); and the Committee for Preschools and Schools (SOU 1985:22). In its 1982 report on childcare to the government, the Board of Health and Welfare, the government's own authority on childcare, stressed the same requirements (Socialstyrelsen 1982), and in fact a government research bill of the early 1980s (Prop. 1981/82:106) pointed out the need for more exploration of this area, and for this reason childcare has been noted as one of the most urgent priorities for research attention.

There has been a century-long discussion concerning the influence of research on various types of teacher education, and on the relationship with research and universities. No co-ordinated body of research has been built up around early childhood provision, in contrast to institutions, or fields, of comparable size and importance, whether public or private. Further, despite the fact that pedagogical-psychological research, particularly that on child development, has for a long time played a significant role in the theoretical aspects of the curriculum for the education and training of preschool teachers, there has never been a special research organization connected with this. Although there is a positive attitude towards strengthening childcare research, few decisions have been made in that direction. For example, when Riksdag decided to allocate 30 million Swedish Kroner to the development of the childcare system in 1984, the major proportion of this was used for practical development work in childcare activity. Part of this money could have been earmarked for courses leading to postgraduate studies and research projects directly connected to teacher education. The 30 million has now shrunk to far less than 20 million. Meanwhile, in 1991, parliament granted 118 million for research and development within the compulsory education system during the coming fiscal year. (Research and development funding for social care, which includes childcare, and for education are negligible when compared to those funds granted to R&D for defence, e.g. central government budget for the fiscal year 1987–88 shows: defence 26.9 per cent; education 0.7 per cent; social welfare, social environment and social security 0.4 per cent.) Not even the newly established Social Research Council, organized directly under the Ministry of Health and Social Affairs, has highlighted childcare. At the time of its inception there was some discussion about whether the new council should be placed under the Ministry of Education and Cultural Affairs, and this might have proved a more advantageous outcome, since it could have strengthened the links between teacher education and research.

Having made these comparisons, it is consistent to ask upon what this inertia depends. Is it the fact that childcare as a whole has low status, that education in this field has low status, that the principal interest groups –

women and small children – have low status in society, and that all this leads to low status for childcare research? Is this why, despite all the talk and rhetoric, this field of research has low priority when decisions about funding are made? During the last ten years there have been numerous possibilities to consolidate and elucidate the knowledge base in this field (Bergman 1991). Not until the latest government research bill (Prop. 1989/90: 90) was the first research appointment created, but this was still not at professorial level. In the same bill, however, one can read that nine chairs in sports research have been created over the last few years. Presumably we are to conclude that this is an important field, and one with higher status than childcare (Bergman 1991).

Research training as an equal opportunities issue

Research training in Sweden currently has a somewhat restricted intake, and this is particularly marked in relation to childcare research, a field which would benefit from progress and enlargement, since this would stimulate the formation of more research groups. The first step would be to create more chairs; more students need to be enrolled for higher degrees, especially doctorates, where a doubling of the current figures is vital. This should hopefully lead to an increase in the number of women doctoral students, because more than 95 per cent of personnel in this field are female. The government has recently declared its interest in the important equal opportunities issue of increasing the proportion of women taking PhDs. Around 60 per cent of Swedish first degree students are women, compared with only 31 per cent of those embarking on research degree programmes (Prop. 1989/90: 90).

The situation is not helped by the fact that two ministries are involved – the Ministry of Health and Social Affairs being responsible for early childhood services – so that there is a lack of co-ordination at national level, and there are no programmes concerning the two aspects together, care and education.

The current change of system

Many of the values which have underpinned the Swedish welfare society are now being questioned and are in a state of far-reaching change. For several years, the cost of the social security system and public sector facilities have been constantly debated. This debate has come to a head with the election of a non-Socialist coalition, comprising four different parties, to power in the Autumn of 1991, after several decades of Socialist government. This reshaping of the Swedish model of government has been accelerated for financial reasons, to enable a·reduction in both taxation and in public sector spending. In addition, there have been gradual reforms over the last few years, reducing the power of the State over the activities of the municipal authorities. There have also been decisions concerning political unity, aimed at strengthening local democracy and self-government. This pressure for decentralization has arisen as a result of increasing objections from the municipalities to central control and bureaucracy. The fundamental principle underpinning these reforms is a transition to government by goals instead of government by rules. Many municipal authorities have improved organization in their areas by developing co-ordination between preschool and primary provision, and this has been enabled by the local authorities taking over responsibility for the education system from the State.

In parallel with the reforms outlined above, there has been a continuing discussion about the possibility of privatization of municipal activities. The new government presented a Bill related to this issue, making it possible for State grants to be available to private childcare providers, shortly after taking office (Prop. 1991/92: 65). A similar process is under way in relation to schools. An evaluation has indicated that there has been a slow response, and that the municipalities may have miscalculated in expecting short-term economic gains (Ds 1992: 108).

The most radical reform is that relating to changes in funding earmarked for State subsidies to childcare, schools and care of the elderly. This funding will now be placed in one 'pot' and reduced from 1993 (Svenska Kommunförbundet 1993a). Local authority politicians will have the responsibility for deciding on priorities. Naturally one becomes apprehensive that childcare will ultimately lose out in this competition. Already municipalities are increasing parental contributions by an average of 7.4 per cent for 1993 (Svenska Kommunförbundet 1993b). One economics professor (Schwarz 1992) has predicted that women's participation in the labour market will decline, the consequence of this will be compensation to the local authorities, for loss of tax revenue. In other words, it will be more profitable to the municipalities if more women are encouraged to stay at home. Coincidentally, this is occurring at a time when unemployment is rising in Sweden, and of course the loss of jobs will strike women as well as men. Forecasts indicate that there will be a substantial reduction in municipalities' budgets, leading to a diminution in personnel, starting with a 7 per cent cut during the 1992–94 period. Most of the cuts will affect women's work, since they are mainly in the fields of childcare and compulsory schooling, sectors where a large proportion of the staff is female. At the same time, the number of children in the preschool and school age ranges will increase.

Summary and conclusions

The overview of early childhood services in Sweden provided by this chapter shows that there have been two lines of development, one with mainly social objectives, in the full-time daycare centres, the other in part-time groups as educational provision for children. There have been attempts to unite the two during this century, but the two systems still remain. Only 40 per cent of children aged 1–6 have a place in a full-time centre, and their mothers should be studying or working. A further 21.5 per cent have to accept family daycare with childminders. Thus the expectations of the system are twofold – childminding while a parent (i.e. mother) is employed, and the pedagogical task of ensuring children's full development during this important period of growth.

Swedish reforms relating to family policy during the 1970s and 1980s, with concentration on extended parental benefit, child allowances (with a supplement for three or more children), and childcare provision, seem to have stimulated women to give birth to more children and to try to combine motherhood with a working life (Bergman 1992b; Statistics Sweden 1992b).

In Sweden, women's work and family policy have been more important factors than an educational rationale, in the development of services. Here, there is not the tradition of general nursery *education* as in, say, France, or countries where admission to primary school occurs at an earlier age. However, the function of childcare is still expected to be twofold, to provide childminding facilities for children of parents (i.e. mothers) who are employed or studying outside the home, and, at the same time, to fulfil a pedagogical responsibility to children during the most marked period of their development.

If one explores the philosophies underpinning early childhood services in Sweden, one can see a shift from the focus on the development of the individual child, which was a salient feature of the 68 Commission on Nursery Provision, to a concentration on the group in documents during the 1980s. This is evident, for example, in the Educational Programme for Swedish Preschools. There was a definite, increased awareness of pedagogics in the 1980s and this can principally be seen in the creation of programmes/curricula for preschools during this period (Walch 1988). This also indicates that Sweden is moving from a non-textbook tradition (Froebelian) towards one where more written documentation is demanded (Dahlberg and Asen 1986; Dahlberg *et al.* 1991). However, this is not a guarantee of an educationally oriented system in the future. Ongoing cuts constitute a real threat to the development of high quality provision. The paradox is that if a country like Sweden has a system of early childhood provision so closely linked to the immediate needs of the labour market, children will lose educational opportunities, women their position in the labour market.

This points up the subordinate position of women and young children in society – when the economic climate becomes harsher, they are the losers. Childcare has been an important factor in improving equality of opportunity between women and men, and although such egalitarian principles have been part of the social policies of the 1960s, 1970s and 1980s, some non-Socialist groups have been pushing for care allowances for women to remain at home ever since the mid-1970s, and it seems likely that there will be a decision for care allowance until the child is 3 years old. This more than fifteen-year-long debate has progressed in parallel with the development of facilities, indicating an ideology which questions women's right to gainful employment. Increasingly, politicians want women to go back to being housewives. A further ominous signal is that of the government in cutting down the number of places for pre-school teacher training, which could result in a lessening of the educational aspects of services.

One positive feature of Sweden's current situation, however, is the Minister of Health and Social Affairs' wish to strengthen the Social Services Act, making it statutory for local authorities to offer childcare facilities according to demand.

9

Educating Children under 5 in the UK

Tricia David

> Fragmentation, lack of resources and lack of vision persist in preventing all children having access to the start in life they so richly deserve.
>
> (Pugh 1992a p. 28)

No UK government to date has acted on a policy to provide comprehensive nursery education for all children under statutory school age, which in Britain, in law and in theory, is 5 years old. The recent substantial increase in the number of children entering primary school at the start of the academic year in which they are 5, has meant that the already muddled provision detailed in Pugh's earlier work (1988), is further complicated by the presence of many young four-year-olds in the reception classes of the primary sector. In the EC report (European Commission 1990) the stark reality of the paucity of any kind of provision for children under 2 was another clearly demonstrated feature of this fragmentation. Add to this the fact that more three- and four-year-olds attend playgroups than public nursery schools and classes (see Table 8), and that since the publication of the 'Rumbold Report' (DES 1990) these have been deemed, by the government, to be educational provision, despite being administered by local Departments of Social Services, and one begins to have a sense of some of the difficulty and confusion arising in this country when attempting to describe and analyse education for our youngest children.

Further, this is complicated by the fact that, traditionally, some forms of provision have been seen as 'care' and others as 'education', and this is discussed in the historical section of the chapter. However, early childhood educators find it anathema to separate out these aspects of work with young children, for children are whole people, and surely they have opportunities to learn in settings labelled 'care', and workers in settings labelled 'education' care for and about the children in their charge.

In this chapter, I will first give an historical overview of early childhood provision in the UK, and through this describe the emergence and characteristics of some of the main forms on offer. I will then discuss the philosophies underpinning those types of provision, the curricula they offer, recent relevant legislation, and implications of all these factors for the children, families and staff involved.

Industrialization and schooling

Following the 1870 Education Act, elementary schools were provided for children, perhaps more as a result of anxieties over vandalism by poor and street children, whose parents worked long hours in the fast-growing areas of industrialization, and the need for a basically literate workforce, than out of any real concern for a truly educated populace. A few enlightened philanthropists, such as Robert Owen (1771–1858), had attempted to begin humane educational movements, because they believed in the civilizing power of appropriate teaching in a benevolent environment, and some of the German immigrants who came to work in managerial positions in the textile industries of the North brought with them the ideas of Froebel.

That statutory schooling should begin when a child was 5, while in most other European countries the ages of 6 or 7 had already been decided upon, is thought to have been the result of the influence on parliament of manufacturers, who thought that if children were to be schooled, and thus unavailable as cheap labour, then better to get the process over as quickly as possible. An earlier entry would mean an earlier exit.

By 1900, 43 per cent of the country's three-, four- and five-year-olds were attending the elementary schools. The conditions in which these children were being taught, grouped in huge numbers in inadequate buildings, is detailed in a report by women inspectors of the time, and in particular, Katherine Bathurst's (1905) sensitive testimony, and the oral accounts handed on to us by our grandparents, provide many insights into what must have been inhuman and inappropriate provision.

Nursery pioneers in the first half of the twentieth century

The women inspectors advised the government that children under 5 should be barred from attending the elementary schools; their intention is thought to have been that special nursery schools would be opened, but in spite of the pioneering work of Margaret and Rachel McMillan in the years leading up to the First World War, little was achieved. The 1918

Education Act allowed local authorities to set aside funds for nurseries, but by this time only 15.3 per cent of children under 5 were in 'maintained' schools (i.e. publicly funded schools). Thus one has the beginnings of a policy that the provision of nursery education should be subject to local, rather than central, government decision-making.

During the years leading up to the Second World War, there was a strong influence from the ideology of motherhood and the belief that the best place for a young child was at home, unless 'fecklessness' and 'unsuitability' of parents led to a decision that a child needed rescue in the form of attendance at a day nursery (seen as 'care', not 'education'). This message was enshrined in the Hadow Report (Consultative Committee 1933) on infant and nursery schools, in spite of Susan Isaacs, another great nursery education pioneer, being a member of the Committee.

Isaacs' research and writing (e.g. 1929) was highly influential with practitioners, and she set up the first Department of Child Development, at London University. However, her efforts, together with those of Margaret McMillan and the Nursery Schools Association begun in 1923, did not succeed in convincing policy-makers of the need for universal nursery education. During the Second World War there was some expansion (see Blackstone 1971; David 1990; Riley 1983 for fuller historical accounts), but this was cut back and hours of opening reduced in the years that followed, with Bowlby's theory of maternal deprivation (1953) influencing the way many young mothers felt about their role. But the war years had made some policy-makers aware of the importance of developing nursery schools and classes in the effort to provide equality of opportunity in the education of young children.

Accordingly, the 1943 White Paper from the Board of Education, preceding the 1944 Education Act, was the first official statement to give any recognition to the value of nursery education for all. The 1944 Act actually imposed 'an obligation' on local authorities to provide nursery education, but this duty was lost in the other reforms of that momentous Act relating to older children, and no local authority was ever brought to book over its failure to implement this 'obligation', and this was revoked and replaced by 'a power' (i.e. not a legal requirement, more a kind of permission) in a 1980 Education Act, although the Children Act 1989, as we shall see later, does impose slightly stronger demands upon local authorities.

Deprivation

Until the 1960s, there was little thought for expansion, because the post-war 'baby-boom' had caused a shortage of places and teaching staff in the primary and secondary phases of statutory schooling, and all finances

were focused on this, save for a few nursery classes in primary schools
aimed at encouraging women teachers to continue their careers during
this time of need.

It was not until the publication of the Plowden Report (CACE 1967),
which called for the inception of Educational Priority Areas in areas of
'deprivation', that nursery provision was once again recommended. One
can relate this to the compensatory movement in both the UK and the
USA. Both countries took up the theory that by compensating children
for their 'deprived' home background, with parents and a community
who supposedly saw schooling as alien and irrelevant, they would be
enabled to learn and achieve in primary school. Thus, following this
Report there was some expansion of nursery school and class provision
in certain areas, largely the inner cities.

When Margaret Thatcher was Secretary of State for Education in the
early 1970s, she presented a White Paper (DES 1972) 'A Framework for
Expansion', in which she proposed that by 1980 there would be nursery
school places for 50 per cent of three-year-olds and 90 per cent of four-
year-olds. A recession was already looming, and its arrival dashed any
further hopes of implementation. In the intervening years any expansion
which has occurred has been the result of benevolent local authorities,
not central government policy. One of the most recent references by a
government minister to Thatcher's 1972 proposals was that of Kenneth
Clarke (BBC TV 22 January 1991) during his period in office as Secretary
of State for Education, when, in a television interview, he declared that
'nursery education for all children is not a realistic prospect' and he
asserted that if a woman wanted to go to work it was her responsibility
to sort out her own arrangements for her children. (I will return to this
confused thinking later.)

The resultant effect, as Gillian Pugh states (1992), of the government's
expectation that parents and their employers, together with private sector nurseries, will sort out the provision of daycare is

> leading to a three-tier service: children of working parents in private
> sector provision; children in need in local authority nurseries; and
> children for whose parents part-time provision is convenient in nursery
> schools in some areas and in playgroups in others . . . access to educa-
> tion has already become unequal for young children by the time they
> reach statutory age for starting school.
>
> (Pugh 1992, p. 13)

Incidentally, employers have not, on the whole, taken up the government
challenge to become involved in childcare provision, which they see as
the responsibility of the government itself.

Patterns of provision of public, local authority nursery schools and classes (usually half-day only for an individual child, free of charge to parents, run by Local Education Authorities for children aged 3 and 4), and day nurseries (full-day care according to need, earnings-related charges to parents, run by Local Departments of Social Services, for children from under 1 year old to 4) have continued in much the same way to this day. They are found largely in inner city areas, usually where there is a Socialist majority in the local council. Similarly, the small number of Combined Nursery Centres provided jointly by Local Education Authorities and Social Service Departments, (see Ferri *et al.* 1981), intended to have both a 'care' and 'education' role in their communities, have been developed in areas of disadvantage.

The dearth of nursery provision in more affluent or rural areas caused parents, on the whole mothers not seeking employment while their children were young, to become involved in a voluntary capacity, so providing their children with group play experiences before school. A letter to the *Guardian* newspaper in 1961 by such a mother, Belle Tutaev, began what was to prove a powerful movement – the Preschool Playgroups Association (PPA). For the first ten years of its life this voluntary organization's aims were: to lobby for the expansion of public nursery schooling; and to provide stop-gap playgroups, either in someone's home, for a small group of children aged between 2½ and 4, or in any available premises which would be passed as adequate according to current Social Services regulations. These were often church halls or sports clubs, where precious and often sparse equipment, acquired through fund-raising efforts, would have to be locked away at the end of each session. However, when Thatcher's White Paper was made public in 1972, the members of the movement suddenly realized that, despite difficulties over resourcing, premises, and so on, what they had developed was not only powerful as an organization, it had exerted a powerful, transforming effect on the lives of many women, since parents were involved in running groups, committees, fund-raising, and proselytizing. It was a role those in the movement decided they would not surrender after all, and the expansion advocated in the White Paper began to be seen as a threat rather than as the fulfilment of their original aims. The two major forms of provision, public nursery schools and classes, and the playgroups, began to be set in opposition for twenty years. The question which needs to be asked, however, is – do playgroups actually provide the high quality experiences children need during the years before school, or are some children 'deprived' in comparison with peers who attend maintained nursery education? Certainly research by Jowett and Sylva (1986) has shown that children from nurseries staffed by teachers, and with appropriate premises and resourcing, were better able to cope with the demands of becoming a primary school pupil at the start of their reception class careers, than their playgroup counterparts. They persevered on learning-oriented tasks for longer, even when meeting difficulties; spent more time on 'academic' tasks; were more autonomous and motivated to learn. Further, recent studies (Knight 1992; Shorrocks 1992) have shown that children who attended maintained education authority nurseries performed better than non-nursery peers on a number of the National Curriculum assessments at age 7.

Current statistics

In analysing the current situation from the point of view of:

1. What is available?
2. Is it educational?
3. Do parents really have access to a range of services so that they may choose what is best for them, as the government insists?

we need to briefly explore some statistics and describe some types of provision so far not included in this discussion. Table 8, below, sets out some of the figures for the principal forms of early education and care.

Table 8 Under-fives in England: population and use of services 1975, 1985 and 1990 (from Pugh 1992)

	1975	1985	1990
Population 0–4	3,227,900	2,973,400	3,189,400
Places per 100 children 0–4:			
LA day nurseries	0.8	1.0	0.9
Private registered nurseries	0.8	0.8	1.8
Childminders	2.6	4.7	6.4
Places per 100 children 3–4:			
Playgroups	23.3	33.8	33.2
Pupils as a percentage of 3- and 4-year-olds:			
Nursery schools and classes	10.0	22.5	24.5
Under-fives in infant classes (of primary schools)	18.9	20.7	21.6
Independent (i.e. private) schools	2.1	2.5	3.2

Source: Early Childhood Unit Statistics 1991, compiled from government sources.

To give brief details of the above-mentioned forms of provision:

Local Authority nursery schools, and *classes in primary schools* are regarded as the nursery education sector in the UK. They are open during school hours, school termtime, but most offer children only sessional (i.e. morning or afternoon) places. They are open to children aged 3 and 4, and are generally staffed by qualified teachers and nursery nurses. Fees are not charged for this provision, funding comes from the local authority, through government education budgets, and the Local Education Authority is responsible for overall administration. However, recent legislation, both actual and proposed (e.g. Children Act 1989, Education Reform Act 1988, Education Bill 1992), together with cuts in funds to local authorities, could have far-reaching effects on this form of provision in the near future.

Local Authority day nurseries are administered by local Social Services Departments, for children under 5, and are open for the working day, most of the year. They are usually staffed by those with a nursing or nursery nursing qualification. Although local authorities provide the majority of the funding, parents are usually assessed to estimate whether or not they should be charged fees.

Combined nursery centres are a combination of the two forms described above.

Reception classes of primary schools – the first/youngest class of the 5–16 schooling system but currently many four-year-olds are admitted early, and many attend full-time (school day).

Playgroups usually provide for children aged 2½ to 4 years old. The majority are run by parents or community groups, often with an elected committee appointing staff, raising funds, etc. The Preschool Playgroups Association has fostered the development of courses ranging from short introductory sessions, to longer part-time supervisors' courses, and an advanced diploma, run in conjunction with local colleges of further or adult education. Most parents have to pay fees for a playgroup place, which is often for only two or three sessions a week. In recent years, some playgroups have developed 'extended hours' provision to cater for working parents. Playgroups often depend on unpaid help during sessions from parents, on a rota basis, in order to meet the requirements of the Children Act 1989 concerning ratios. For some groups this, together with the current financial situation for many families, has created considerable anxieties as to their future existence.

Private nurseries – similar hours, etc., to the local authority day nurseries, but parents pay fees unless their employers are willing to fund their children's places, since these are run as private businesses.

Childminders – look after babies and young children, and school-age children outside school hours, in their own (the minders') homes. Social Services Departments have the responsibility for registering and inspecting provision, which covers the working day, all year round. Parents pay fees, although, again, some employers, or some local authorities may sponsor a few places with childminders. Childminders, private providers, playgroup supervisors, etc, have not always undergone training in the past. With the Children Act 1989 and the advent of new, workplace-based qualifications – the NVQs (National Vocational Qualifications) – there is growing recognition that to be an educator of someone else's children entails the development of knowledge, skills, concepts and attitudes.

Other forms of provision – the above are the main (numerically) forms of provision, but many others exist, for example, nursery classes in independent (private, fee-paying) schools, playbuses (for remote locations or those lacking a potential facility), etc.

From the statistics above, we can see that less than half the three- and four-year-olds in the country (England only in this table) are in educational provision, and many of those in the infant sector are regarded as attending classes where the curriculum is inappropriate. What the table also displays is the present trend upward in the birth rate, which is expected to continue so that by the turn of the century there will be around 7 per cent more under-5s than is currently the case. Additionally, with more women being forced or wishing to continue in employment after the birth of their children, the need for a coherent, comprehensive service is vital, and it must be one in which early childhood education is embedded.

Much of what is written on the UK applies largely to England, or to England and Wales, and this tends to mask the situation in Scotland and Northern Ireland. Scotland has a strong, and possibly different (Hartley 1993), early years tradition. Its commitment can be seen in the pioneering work of Strathclyde authority in co-ordinating provision.

Despite the Rumbold Committee's (DES 1990) recognition that anyone who works with young children should be called an 'educator', very scant attention has been paid in the UK to educational experiences for children under 2, although this situation is being improved by the work of Rouse and Griffin (1992), Calder (1990), and Drummond, Rouse and Pugh (1992), and the NCMA (National Childminders' Association) for example.

For the purposes of this chapter, therefore, while acknowledging the contribution childminders make to the overall patchwork of provision, I will not discuss this service any further here. (See Ferri 1992 for more detailed information.) Nor will this chapter discuss the many 'home-based' educators, that is, people who look after babies and young children while their parents work, in the children's own homes, for example, those who do not normally need to be registered with Social Services such as relatives, au pairs, or nannies. Naturally, many of these home-based educators take their charges to some form of group provision, perhaps a Carer-and-Toddler Club before they are 3, a public or private nursery school or class, or a playgroup, after they are 3. Some childminders look after school-age children during the vacations and outside school hours.

Recent government reports and legislation

Following in the footsteps of the Plowden Report (CACE 1967) and the White Paper 'Framework for Expansion' (DES 1972), support for nursery education has been reiterated in various more recent government documents. In 1985, 'Better Schools' was presented to parliament by the Secretary of State for Education and Science and the Secretary of State for Wales. In it they argue

> Nearly all children stand to benefit from some attendance at school before reaching the compulsory age provided that what the school offers is appropriate to their age and stage of development . . . The education of young children is founded on play . . . The government has encouraged the education and social service departments of local authorities to develop co-ordination between the provision of education and care for under fives.
>
> (DES 1985, pp. 38–40)

Following this, in 1989, a House of Commons Select Committee of Members of Parliament from all the main parties, reported their findings (HoC 1988), after conducting their own enquiries into the education of children under 5. They concluded that there should be an expansion of public nursery education, and that good quality provision benefits all children, but especially those from economically or socially disadvantaged backgrounds. Their report also stressed the benefit to children whose home language is not English.

Although this report raised hopes that the call for more nursery schools and classes would be heeded, particularly since there is evidence that it is the very children most in need of such provision who are least likely to attend (see Clark 1988; David, 1990), the government responded by convening yet another committee to inquire into the 'quality of educational experience offered to three- and four-year-olds.' (DES 1990 Opening letter from Mrs Angela Rumbold to the then Secretary of State at the DES.) This time it was a committee of experts, who were required

> To consider the quality of the educational experience which should be offered to 3- and 4-year-olds, with particular reference to content, continuity and progression in learning, having regard to the requirements of the National Curriculum and taking account of the government's expenditure plans. To take into account in this consideration:
> i.   the diversity of needs and types of provision;
> ii. demographic and social factors;
> iii. the nature of training for teachers and other professional staff involved in the education of children under 5.
>
> (DES 1990. par.1)

The 'expenditure plans' referred to in the first paragraph of their brief meant that the Committee had little room for manoeuvre in the sense that they presumably could not simply reiterate the House of Commons Select Committee call for expansion of publicly funded nursery education facilities, and the presence on the Committee of a representative from the Preschool Playgroups Association was an endorsement of the government's view that playgroups were being seen as part of the early childhood education system of this country. Yet playgroups continue to be substantially underfunded and dependent on the goodwill of poorly paid and volunteer workers, and fees paid by parents.

In the Rumbold Report itself (DES 1990), there is comment to the effect that during the 1980s there had been some dramatic changes: first, educationally, with the implementation, for the first time in the UK, of a national curriculum in the 5–16 sectors of schooling; second, that many four-year-olds were now found in infant classes; third, that the Children Act 1989 required greater collaboration between social services and education departments of local authorities; and finally, to some extent as a result of demographic changes and maternal employment, that there had been a significant expansion of private nursery provision.

The Rumbold Committee repeated the co-ordination demand of the Children Act 1989, providing guidelines for policy-makers, local authorities, and practitioners to develop effective liaisons, to ensure quality control, to recognize the importance of the curriculum experienced by the children, the training, status, conditions of service and recruitment of suitable staff.

Although the 1988 Education Reform Act, and the National Curriculum Programmes of Study and the Assessments which were part of this legislation, was largely concerned with children aged 5 to 16, there was little doubt that it would have a 'top-down' effect on children under 5. Research by Sylva, Siraj-Blatchford and Johnson (1992) has already demonstrated that children attending public nursery schools and classes where there are qualified teachers are more likely to be experiencing a curriculum which is not only appropriate for their age and stage, but it is also more likely to be a preparation for their encounter with the National Curriculum in primary school reception classes (Year R), than that experienced by children attending other forms of provision.

One of the other main bones of contention is the fact that children aged 7 (in what is called Year 2 of primary school) are assessed not only through ongoing diagnostic teacher assessments, but through special Standard Assessment Tasks, known as SATs (DES 1988), often referred to as 'tests' and becoming increasingly of that nature. One of the purposes of these assessments is to monitor standards in schools, so headteachers are becoming increasingly sensitive to the fact that they want some idea of the 'raw material', that is, the standard reached by the children when they are admitted to the school. From this, they feel they can argue their case even if the results for their individual schools, at age 7, are comparatively low, as long as they are able to indicate that the school has a notable 'value added' score – the amount the children have progressed during their three years in the system, in Years R, 1 and 2.

Thus what is happening is that some schools and local authorities are testing or assessing children by a variety of means at age 4, with what have become known as Baseline Assessments. These assessments are often narrowly focused on the subjects of the core National Curriculum, the subjects of the SATs – maths, science and English.

Additionally, the publicity in the press following the reports of standards reached by children in the test runs of the SATs, together with the fact that they want their children to succeed in any assessments, so as not to be labelled a 'failure' at an early age, is causing parents to feel very pressurized, and in their turn to pressurize educators, because they feel there is a need for more formal work earlier in their children's lives – in the nursery (David 1992).

One of the main problems arising from recent legislation, and confirmed in the 1992 Education Bill, which, incidentally, is this government's seventeenth piece of education legislation, is that schools are being encouraged to become 'grant-maintained' and answerable to central government and a central Funding Council, rather than their local authorities. Competition for pupils, because of the espousal to the theory of market forces, is also endorsed, rather than co-operation. So, on the one hand there is the Children Act 1989, exhorting co-operation, sharing of training, skills, and expertise, between educators, and the 1988

Education Act and the 1992 Education Bill making such co-ordination and co-operation much more unlikely.

Theoretical underpinning

The major influences on the philosophy informing nursery education in the UK were Pestalozzi, Froebel, and Montessori. McMillan and Isaacs, through the publication of their ideas which were based on their own experiences in running nurseries, provided an impetus to the notion that young children needed early educational provision of a kind which would enable them to become autonomous thinkers, through meaningful activities seen by the children themselves as play (for a fuller discussion of theoretical influences see Bruce 1987).

The research interests and writings of Jean Piaget, who corresponded with Susan Isaacs, furthered the focus on a child-centred philosophy, because, according to his theory, children needed to be active learners at this stage. During the last twenty years his work has been refined by the Post-Piagetians, the work of Donaldson (1978) and others (e.g. Grieve and Hughes 1990) has encouraged greater recognition for the adult role in helping children disembed concepts which they have developed in, and attached to, a specific context. Vygotsky's (1978) ideas about the social nature of learning, the need for an adult, or a more advanced peer, to provide appropriate next steps in a learning sequence (in the 'zone of proximal development') have also become more widespread. This ties in with the important theories of Jerome Bruner (e.g. 1974, 1980, 1983, 1986) and Nelson (1986) suggesting that adults should 'scaffold' children's learning experiences.

This means that over this period nursery staff have become more aware of the ways in which they need to intervene in children's learning, rather than simply providing the premises and equipment, and waiting to be invited to engage with children – though there may be times when this is the positive decision made by an educator, and it was certainly never the intention of pioneers like Susan Isaacs that adults should remain aloof from children's learning experiences (Curtis 1986).

During the 1970s a great deal of early years research which was highly influential with practitioners was funded in the UK, for example, Tough's (1976) research on language development; Matthews' (1984) on mathematics; Tizard's (Tizard, Philps and Plewis 1976) on staff behaviours; the Oxford team, led by Bruner (1980) which included Sylva *et al's* (1980) analysis of challenge in activities and led her to theorize about the ways in which children's cognitive development was most likely to benefit from learning activities which were largely child-directed and conducted in pairs, rather than teacher-directed. Another strand of the Oxford team was that led by Wood (Wood, McMahon and Cranstoun 1980) and, again, this work has influenced ideas about the ways in which adults need to interact with children in nurseries to foster cognitive development.

For various reasons, some of that research was a long time coming into the public domain. For example, a project based on the research methods of human ethology, with evidence derived from observations of children in nursery schools, nursery classes, day nurseries and playgroups, by Hutt *et al* (1989) confirmed the ideas which Corinne Hutt had developed, based on Piaget's theories, that children at this stage engage in two stages of play, the first 'epistemic' stage is the one in which children explore a material, toy, or situation, the second, the 'ludic' and perhaps true play phase, is when they rehearse the learning gained in that first stage. Both phases are necessary, children moving in and out of the two as their own dictates demand.

A further project which is becoming more widely known is that reported by Chris Athey (1991). What is exciting about this research is the involvement of parents of disadvantaged children. The children were observed over a two-year period by staff and parents who kept records of these observations so that they could respond sensitively to the particular 'schema' a child was currently developing. For example, if a child seemed preoccupied by the notion of horizontal and vertical, far from the child's interest and actions being treated as bizarre, they were explored and fostered. The children from this experimental nursery made significant gains in their cognitive development, compared with a control group. For further discussion of much of the research carried out over this twenty-year period, see Margaret Clark's (1988) survey.

Perhaps the three major factors which stand out in relation to all this research evidence are: firstly, that young children came to be accepted as capable, independent beings who are actively struggling to *make sense* of the world around them; secondly, that partnership with parents, recognition for parents as the primary educators of their children, is a crucial factor in achieving success in early childhood education; and thirdly, in the same way as teachers from other sectors, early years teachers have become involved in practitioner-research, either through collaboration with researchers, or independently, as a result of their own search for meaning in the life of early years classrooms (see for example, ILEA 1986, in which teachers describe their own explorations of gender bias, etc.).

The curriculum and assessment

The Rumbold Report (DES 1990) suggests that the curriculum for children aged 3 and 4 should be based on areas of experience, as documented by Her Majesty's Inspectorate (DES 1985), and these are as follows:

aesthetic and creative; human and social; language and literacy; mathematics; physical; science; spiritual and moral; and technology. Within each of these areas, educators are urged to have regard for the development of children's knowledge, skills, concepts, and attitudes. The Rumbold Report (DES 1990) also draws attention to the fact that each institution should have a policy outlining 'aims and objectives with a clearly articulated philosophy shared by educators and parents' (par. 13.3); a policy on equal opportunities with respect to race, sex, class and disability; and, among others, policies on parental partnership, liaison with other institutions, quality control, and staff development.

Following these guidelines, organizations such as PPA have published their own documents to help educators who have not been trained as nursery teachers, for example, 'What children learn in playgroup' (PPA 1991) offers ideas about the ways in which activities experienced by children in playgroup accord with the seven areas of experience outlined above, and it goes so far as to add an eighth, emotional development. Nursery schools and classes have for some time been expected to ensure equality of opportunity, for example, with regard to the issue of race, by developing multicultural and anti-racist perspectives throughout the curriculum. Both PPA and NCMA have anti-racist policies which they expect grass-roots practitioners to enact. (A discussion of the issue of young children and racial discrimination in the UK can be found in Siraj-Blatchford 1992.) However, in spite of good intentions of this kind, research evidence shows that in all types of provision, whether maintained nursery school/class or playgroup, practice is not always in line with policy in matters of equality of opportunity (e.g. Burgess, Hughes and Moxon 1991; Brophy, Statham and Moss 1992). (For a fuller resumé of the evidence concerning the ways in which different groups of young children experience discrimination see David 1990.)

Prior to the report of the Rumbold Committee (DES 1990), two of the most influential recent publications offering information about the curriculum in the nursery were Curtis's (1986) 'A Curriculum for the Pre-school Child' and the Early Years Curriculum Group's (1989) 'Early Childhood Education: The Early Years Curriculum and the National Curriculum'. Together with Hurst's (1991) work, these reiterate the understandings early childhood practitioners have traditionally articulated about the nature of learning in young children, and the ways in which a holistic approach could be adopted yet offer continuity with the government's subject-based view of the new National Curriculum for 5–16-year-olds.

During the 1970s and 1980s, many nursery teachers had been developing their school documentation, in which they described the curriculum in terms of children's development – cognitive, social, emotional, physical, and sometimes aims, objectives and learning strategies for moral and aesthetic development would also be delineated. There was no requirement for nursery phase children to receive religious education or to attend religious assemblies, as in the primary and secondary sectors, although sometimes children attending nursery classes in primary schools would join older children's classes for the daily act of worship, at least on special occasions.

In addition to having school documents concerned with aims, objectives and methods, teachers in nursery schools and classes would keep records of the activities which had been offered, planning would often be worked out according to a thematic approach, which has been further developed and endorsed by research (Meadows and Cashdan 1988). In accordance with both the child-centred traditions of British nursery education, and with evidence about children's learning at this stage, there tends to be an 'invisible' structure (Hutt *et al* 1989) in nursery classes, that is, teachers and nursery nurses may hold a planned agenda according to which they will offer children choices, personalize learning, and observe and record children's progress, thus evaluating their own performances, but to the children the whole session will seem to have been one in which they have had fun and 'just played'.

While nursery teachers are sensitive to the idea of danger in 'labelling' a child at this early stage, diagnostic assessment has been legitimized in nurseries for a long time, most particularly through the use and adaptation of packs such as the 'Keele Preschool Assessment Guide' (Tyler 1979) and Bate *et al*'s (1978) 'Manual for Assessment in Nursery Education'. In fact, it has always seemed a great pity to me that nursery teachers were consulted very little over the recent implementation of the National Curriculum Assessments, since they had already learned a great deal about the complexities of this topic. More recent materials for practitioners wishing to explore the topic of assessment in the early years are the Warwick University Early Years Team's (1990) pack, which looks at aspects related to continuity and the effects of the National Curriculum in schools for children aged 3–8, and Drummond *et al*'s (1992) 'Making Assessment Work', which explores the values and principles involved in assessing children's learning for educators working with children from birth to eight.

Curriculum and assessment in other types of under-5s provision, where qualified teachers are not employed, has been more haphazard. This has been partly due to the focus of the group, for example, playgroups originally seeing themselves as more of a social institution, but as educational for parents, day nurseries seeking to ensure their charges' physical and emotional well-being – partly the result of issues such as staffing, ages of children cared for, frequency of sessions.

The impact of the Children Act 1989, implemented on 14 October 1991, and the publication of the Rumbold Report (DES 1990) has been significant during the first part of this decade. Many local authorities have begun to use the reviews of under-5s provision, required of them by the new law, to plan and co-ordinate services. Some, for example, Manchester, Leeds, Humberside and some of the London boroughs, have actually integrated their services within the remit of the Local Education Authority. Others, such as Merton and Solihull, have co-ordinated in-service training, so that 'education' staff learn about closer work supporting families from those educators working in social services daycare facilities and playgroups, and in their turn, daycare staff learn about the curriculum and providing appropriate, challenging learning activities from the teachers and nursery nurses of the nursery schools and classes. This is extremely important work, because we know that at present 'not all children have access to a high quality curriculum, and the most needy are often in the poorest provision' (Pugh 1992b p. 2), and the discrepancy in parental–educator understandings of learning and curriculum indicate the crucial nature of closer liaison. In the current multi-professional situation the Children Act 1989 calls for collaboration and for the efficient utilization of the differentiated expertise brought to the situation by the range of early childhood educators from different backgrounds. It has long been known, however, (Ward 1982) that those who have undergone teacher training courses have a deeper understanding of both children's learning and the elements of a subject-based curriculum, compared with educators from other services, who have not had the benefit of this type of education. If early childhood services are expected to be 'educational' in the cognitive sense, as well as in the socio-emotional sense, then the input of these professionals is vital – but so too is their willingness to adopt the strategies of the other sectors, by learning about positive involvement of parents and communities. Part of the problem may lie in the fact that certain types of knowledge pass unrecognized, and thus undervalued, in our society.

A session in an education/care setting in the UK
There is probably no such thing as a 'typical' session in an early childhood care and education setting in the UK. However, most forms of provision attempt to emulate the models provided by nursery schools and classes, although one must acknowledge the difficulties faced by playgroups operating in rented premises where they may not allow the children any 'messy' activities, and the long day, with mealtimes and quieter

periods, for children attending private and public daycare. The model adopted will usually include: spaces intended for messy play, for example with paint, water, clay, sand and so on; quiet areas, for example, a story corner with books, comfortable chairs; areas for large and small construction toys, blocks, etc; areas for fantasy play, perhaps a home corner set up as a house, or occasionally converted or added to with office, hairdressing, garage, or other experiential equipment, together with appropriate dressing-up clothes, and emergent literacy resources such as appointment cards, note-paper, etc., as props. Gross motor play will often be provided for outdoors, rather than inside, and many items of equipment such as climbing frames and rope ladders, trolleys, trikes, as well as smaller equipment such as balls and hoops, are available, weather permitting. Where possible, the outdoor play area will have both a hard and grassy section, a sandpit, small garden, and shrubs as exciting 'cover' for outdoor fantasy play.

The start of a session is usually a flexible, relaxed affair, and although the session will probably begin at nine, in the case of a morning session, children and their carers will usually arrive during the first half-hour period, carers often lingering to engage in talk with children or staff, to look at what is happening. Some parents/carers may stay for the whole session, either because their child is a new entrant and needs to settle, or because they are a parent-helper for that morning or afternoon, and have been delegated particular tasks, perhaps sitting at a construction table and encouraging conversation, or involving a small group of children in a cooking or baking activity, or sitting in the story corner and sharing books or other story resources, such as puppets.

While engaging with children in these different ways, nursery staff will also be storing information which they will discuss and enter in the children's records of assessment. In some schools, children themselves, and their parents, contribute to these folders (profiles of achievement), either by choosing certain items, a painting or some emergent writing perhaps, or by answering a user-friendly questionnaire with the teacher (Wolfendale 1987), to go into their file.

In many nurseries this first part of a session will be relatively free for children to choose which activities they wish to engage in, and with whom they wish to play. There may be a time at which a drink is available, mid-session, and if the weather is bad, outdoor play may be limited to a brief slot after this. In some nurseries an adult-directed group-time, during which children will be allocated to undertake a particular task with one of the staff, will take place. This might be something like preparing a fruit snack for the rest of the group, but the adult will have in mind clear objectives for the learning which can be derived from the activity, and will personalize it for each child in the group. On some days there may be a part of the session set aside for music and movement, or a PE-type activity, for the whole/majority of the class, especially when the weather has been too bad for any outdoor activity. Often the end of a session, after everyone has helped with tidying up, is marked by a story or singing activity, when most, if not all, of the class will come together in the story corner.

Some local authorities or individual nurseries have adopted a version of the High/Scope (1986) curriculum model and, as a result, the session begins with each child planning a chosen activity, carrying it out by collecting the necessary resources, negotiating with peers if it is a joint activity, then reporting back at the end of the session, often to the whole class. The cognitive demands of planning and negotiating, of recalling and sequencing one's activities, and the social and emotional demands of taking responsibility for one's own actions, contribute to making this style of working attractive. This type of 'plan, do, review' approach was often adopted informally by nursery practitioners before the more systematic programme was imported from the USA.

Educators in other forms of provision do their best to provide children with a commensurate curriculum to that in maintained nursery education, but it must be remembered that they do so without some of the benefits accorded Local Education Authority nursery schools and classes, for example, they may see the children far less frequently, have less space and equipment, less suitable premises and have little training (playgroups); or they may have other priorities, an over-representation of children from families experiencing severe difficulties, less favourable funding for equipment, less curriculum-focused training (day nurseries).

Children with special educational needs

One of the most thought-provoking statements to be reported by the Warnock Committee (DES 1978), set up to explore the education of 'handicapped children and young people', was the fact that at any one time 20 per cent of our children have special educational needs. This means that one child in five requires specialist help, which could be diagnosed in a nursery, and with support for parents, might obviate the need for much more costly intervention at a later stage. Among these children there will be some with severe learning difficulties, for example, children with cerebral palsy, or a hearing loss, or other condition. Following the Warnock Report, the 1981 Education Act was implemented to provide what was expected to be a better deal for all children with special needs, but especially for these children. Parents were to be able to call on local authority services when their child reached the age of 2 years, and there was the hope that extra funding would be provided to 'ordinary' schools, so that children with such difficulties would be accepted, with benefits for all accruing from this integration process. However, many parents and practitioners fear that in the current economic situation, and with the current pressure for schools to become grant-maintained, the rights of all children with special educational needs will be seriously restricted. At present many nurseries and playgroups operate a 'comprehensive' system – that is, children with special needs are integrated in their local provision. Sadly, some do not accompany their nursery peers on to their local primary school because of financial, staffing and other constraints. In some areas there are places in nursery classes of Special Schools, Opportunity Groups (playgroups for children with severe learning difficulties), and local hospitals usually run an assessment unit which children would attend for a short period of time.

The Children Act 1989 requires workers in all professional and voluntary agencies (e.g. medicine, law, social services, NSPCC, education, etc.) to work effectively together to support families, especially ensuring early educational provision for 'children in need'. While the definition of 'in need' was not intended to encompass only children with severe learning difficulties, it is feared that this narrowing of the criteria will result from current spending restrictions and shortages of nursery places.

Evaluation and monitoring
External monitoring and evaluation is carried out by different groups depending on the sector to which the type of provision belongs. For example, local education inspectors and Her Majesty's Inspectorate have traditionally undertaken this type of work in education settings, although the effects of recent changes by central government may mean that in future such inspections are carried out by people who may not have had experience in this particular sector. Inspections and reviews are required in other types of provision, relating to premises and staff training, etc., under the Children Act 1989. Nursery teachers also evaluate their own work, by reflecting on both the breadth, balance, differentiation and progression offered in the curriculum, and children's individual progress, through observation and continuous, diagnostic assessment of their play.

The role of parents

The part played by parents in early childhood provision varies among the different forms. In maintained nursery schools and classes parents will be represented on the school's governing body, the Parent-Teacher Association Committee, if there is one, and they may be involved in a variety of ways in the day-to-day running of the group. They will also help when children go out on visits or trips to places of interest.

In playgroups the parental role may be considerably more onerous, since the group may be actually run by a parents' committee which raises a large proportion of the group's funding. Parents may be obliged to take part regularly in a rota for helping in the sessions, to avert the need for more paid staff yet remain within the law regarding adult : child ratios. Some playgroups have found complying with the new ratios of the Children Act 1989 almost impossible, because they cannot afford extra paid staff, and parents in employment cannot afford the time to help.

Private nurseries and childminders are the least likely to involve parents, since these services are usually run as a business and provide facilities for working parents. Public day nurseries and combined centres often encourage parents to stay to their sessions, as part of their supportive work for and with families experiencing difficulties.

Current issues

In this final section some of the remaining issues concerned with early childhood care and education in the UK will be raised.

First, there are issues related to children from ethnic minority groups. Afro-Caribbean children are seen as disadvantaged and are over-represented in local authority day nurseries, where they are more likely than others to spend long hours because their parents are in low-paid jobs. Children from a linguistically different home background are not very likely to encounter educators who speak their language, yet early learning is more efficient in one's own language. Children from ethnic minorities may encounter institutional racism because, although policies exist, educators often lack the training needed to recognize and deal with unequal opportunities. However, the UK is the only European country with an anti-racist law, and this exerts a positive influence which is being developed through education and training.

Between 1980 and 1991 there was a 32 per cent increase in the number of places for children under statutory school age in the reception classes of primary schools, which is 'often inappropriate for this young age group, due to inadequate resources for staff and equipment' (Sylva and Moss 1992). Research, by Osborn and Milbank (1987) in the UK and abroad (Zigler 1987) has indicated the inadvisability of inappropriate, too-formal early schooling. Studies by Barrett (1986) and Cleave and Brown (1991) have demonstrated the crucial nature of the need for the school being prepared for the children, not the children for the school.

Although co-ordination has been called for, compartmentalization is compounded by differences in qualifications of educators involved in different services. Yet we have research evidence (Whitebrook, Howes and Phillips 1989) that the better educated the adult, the better educated the children. While recognizing the contributions made by non-teachers working in early childhood services, such research needs to be highlighted, especially at a time when central government is said to be considering proposals to allow those with no qualifications, or less academic, lower level qualifications, to take both nursery and infant classes (TES 1993). Although the argument in favour of a move away from degree-level qualifications for early years teachers is likely to hinge on the belief that they do not need academic expertise in a National Curriculum subject, cynics are likely to claim the exercise is for cost-cutting, or to ensure a biddable populace. Further, while the new NVQs are intended to remedy the situation to some extent, the possibility of educators proceeding up some kind of qualifications 'ladder' (or 'climbing frame'), and building on both qualifications already held and experience, remains a Sisyphean task.

The fact that there is no national policy for early childhood care and education in the UK compounds difficulties experienced by parents in trying to make sense of provision in their area. While the government stresses its belief in choice and the market, parents are finding there is, in reality, no choice (Pugh 1988; David 1992). Costings of a nationally organized system by Holtermann (1992) and by Cohen and Fraser (1991) have shown that financial investment by the government would bring dividends in taxation from the increased participation of women in the workforce. Further, the availability of free or inexpensive, high quality services would enable more single parents to work, those who are currently better off staying at home and living on benefits than finding work, because their earnings would be insufficient to cover edu-care charges.

So, instead of comprehensive, multi-functional, affordable provision, the UK muddles on, and instead of investing in its future citizens, helping them early in their lives to learn how to learn, and at the same time ensuring equality of opportunity for women, one is left with the questions 'How important are young children and their parents in this society, and does this government really want to improve educational standards?' Further, the continuing fragmentation of services, with different affiliations and philosophies may not be in the best interests of all children in the UK. While the playgroup movement claims to have substantial support from its parent advocates, and it must be acknowledged that it is a vibrant and important movement, early childhood educators must challenge its reasons for protecting its own existence – in the light of research evidence that the better educated the staff, the better educated the children. The view that playgroups involve parents in ways other forms of provision do not can be remedied and, in fact, only a small percentage of parents benefit to the degree claimed by the PPA (Ward 1982). Self-help in some circumstances may be highly laudable, but in the end one must ask the question, what is meant by self-help – can it be so 'self-focused' it denies help to others who are in greater need?

Early childhood educators in the UK must help central government clarify its thinking about early childhood services. High quality care facilities are definitely needed so that women are enabled to operate in the world of work on an equal footing with men. Many other changes in UK attitudes and legislature, for example relating to parental leave, are also needed if schemes like Opportunity 2000 are to work – for women, for men, and for the country. However, what happens to *children* during their sessions in early childhood services, whether their parents go out to work or not, is of supreme importance if we really care about educational standards, educational continuity, and the psychological well-being of new generations. Early childhood educators must come together to decide whether they are really working in the best interests of all our children, or simply carrying on squabbling over the crumbs thrown to divert them.

10

Overview: Issues and Implications

Tricia David

The importance of central government policies

In his discussion of some of the issues affecting early childhood services in the European Community, Peter Moss (1992) argues that one of the problems lies in the use of different terminology – 'daycare' 'childcare', 'preschool' and 'nursery education' – because these terms raise problems 'reflecting and encouraging a fragmented way of thinking about provision for young children and their carers' (Moss 1992, p. 30). Certainly what has happened as a result of separating out the 'care' and 'education' aspects of provision for young children is a lack of co-ordination, coherence and continuity for many children. Further, if the divisions and the way the services operate are fairly inflexible, some governments can use this as an opportunity to capitalize on the resulting divisions of interests, for example, setting parents who want or need to work against those who are able to afford to stay at home and look after their own young children, since their requirements will differ. While each may provide a high quality service as measured by specific criteria, any prioritization of government funding favour one type of provision over another creates feelings of frustration and injustice in the rest. Add to this the differences in training and status of educators in sectors divided as a result of labels, and the effects on children's differentiated experience, and one begins to ask exactly what that society believes about young children; their right, in a democracy, to an appropriate education; and whose responsibility it is to ensure the fulfilment of that right.

Central government policy can be seen to be crucial in terms of the resultant effects on the services to which children and their families ultimately have access. For example, in France and Belgium, although there is less certainty about babies and children under 2½, children over this age have, almost universally, the experience of a system seen as a voluntary precursor to obligatory primary school, and as such, part of the education system of the country. Teresa Odina, in the chapter on Spain, discusses the central government intention that all children aged from birth to 6 shall have educational experiences, and the ways which are being sought to provide this, even for the very youngest.

It is interesting to note that historically there have been examples of governments preventing the provision of early childhood education and care services, such as the 1851 ban on Froebel's development of the kindergarten and his training of young women to become educators, a ban imposed by the King of Prussia; in 1936 parts of Spain already possessed nursery schools, but these were closed by the Franco regime, which saw the role of women as home-making and mothering, and thus, the place of young children in that home too; and Hedi Colberg-Schrader and Pamela Oberhuemer, in their chapter on Germany, recount the fact that the Nazis halted the earlier developments of early childhood education and care, and the professionalization of educators. The implications to be drawn seem to be three-fold – firstly, that some regimes see the education of young children, encouraging them in learning how to learn, to be independent and autonomous, as unnecessary – or threatening; secondly, that educating educators to a high standard is unnecessary – or threatening; that providing women who are mothers with the means to be independent of husbands and/or the State is unnecessary – or threatening.

Delegation to local government

The ways in which central governments delegate responsibility for the provisions of services to local authorities, or to other bodies, is also a factor which results in variations and unfairness. For example, while children in Denmark have access to the most comprehensive system of childcare services in the EC, there are variations in the contributions parents pay to costs, as a result of this delegation. In the UK the implications of delegation have been much more marked. Some authorities have extensive, free, public nursery schools and classes, others, especially many of the rural counties, rely on the voluntary provision of the playgroup movement, which is largely for two or three sessions a week, and for which parents must pay fees. In neither case, apart from a few combined nursery centres and specially developed daycare playgroups, is this type of provision any help to a working parent, even if there are thought to be benefits for the children. In fact it is likely that the complications of combining employment and parenthood are increased, rather than being alleviated, by these forms of provision. While it may be argued that such variety assures choice, in reality most parents in the UK have little or no choice (Pugh 1988; David 1992). Even in Sweden there are variations in levels of provision in different local authorities as a result of differing political affiliations.

The question of whether or not provision for the youngest children should be free of charge, part of a country's education entitlement, or whether parents should pay fees highlights this divide in thinking about what exactly the services are for. In countries where specialized early childhood provision for the majority of the children, at least those over 3 years old, is indeed recognized as part of the national education system, in the same way as the primary phase (e.g. Belgium, France), no fees are charged in the public sector, apart from the costs of extra services, such as out-of-hours care before and after the school day.

Studies of costing by Cohen and Fraser (1991), Rudebeck (1989) and by Holtermann (1992) indicate that where a State provides funding for a service enabling more women to become employed there is a 'flow-back' of taxes, which, over a ten-year period, will ultimately more than repay the initial investment by the State. Further, in some countries those parents particularly hit by high-cost services, for example single parents for whom employment is out of the question because of fees for any early childhood services they may need, are thus given the opportunity to be independent of State benefits, with obvious financial advantages to the State, as well as advantages experienced by the family in terms of increased self-esteem, the development of support networks through the workplace, and so on.

Public and/or private provision

Although fees are charged in some countries for early childhood services within the public sector, especially where this is regarded primarily as 'care', rather than as part of the State education system, the existence of private provision naturally raises the issue of fees because in some cases the service will be a business as far as the provider is concerned. In Italy and Denmark, for example, there are government subsidies for private providers, in the UK some playgroups are eligible to apply for grants to help towards costs, although these are usually very small and in some local authorities no longer possible because of cut-backs in the current economic climate. In several countries one of the main types of private sector provider is religious groups, and this can be seen in one sense as philanthropic concern and positive community involvement, on the other, it may be viewed as a way of ensuring early affiliation to a particular denomination, although naturally this will depend on whether any pressure is exerted on the parents or children in this way.

In a somewhat disturbing study from the USA, Whitebrook *et al.*
(1990) demonstrated that private, profit-making services tended to have
less advantageous outcomes for children than those which are publicly-
funded or non-profit-making (for example church-based groups). The
difficulties arose principally because staff in the private provision tended
to be less well-educated (and therefore cheaper to employ), poorly paid,
and as a result to be less contented in their work and more likely to
change jobs frequently. Children not only had poorer levels of stimulation because staff did not have appropriate education and training, they
had few opportunities to build long-term, meaningful, high quality relationships with their educators.

In countries where governments feel unable to commit sufficient funds
to early childhood services so that all children are catered for entirely free
of charge, those which grant subsidies and encourage staff development
through financial or other support are more likely to be avoiding the
pitfalls of the system in the USA.

The aims of provision

The ways in which policy decisions are made will depend upon the
consensual view of early childhood and family roles held by the group in
power in that country. Where early childhood services are provided they
will also reflect these views, not simply in the existence of provision, but
also in the ways in which any policies are translated into practice through
the actual experiences offered the children.

In societies in which there is a belief in democracy and equality of
opportunity, and at the same time a belief that young children and early
learning are important, there will be a commitment to provision for those
children which will be intended to fulfil those beliefs. A survey of some of
the different political regimes in the world (UNESCO 1980) provides an
insight into the ways in which early childhood is seen as an important
phase of development, during which group provision outside the home
can have the effect of 'binding the children to the state ideology'
(Colberg-Schrader and Oberhuemer 1989, Chapter 5). However, it must
be recognized that not providing services can be a way of 'binding children to the state ideology' in a different way. In the UK and the USA
some theorists have argued that group provision (institutionalization)
may be harmful to children (see Mortimore and Mortimore 1985), and
despite calls to move the debate on to a new level (Moss 1990), there are
still those who suggest that the fact of group care, rather than its quality,
actually damages very young children (Belsky 1988).

The ways in which this 'harm' is defined varies, in some cases it is related to later achievement, and the more recent research indicating that this 'harm' does not occur if high quality provision is experienced during the early years (Hwang 1991, Whitebrook *et al.* 1990) provides evidence contradicting the view that all services other than home will be harmful.

A second notion is that early childhood provision will prevent children becoming autonomous individuals, if they are members of a group for such a high proportion of their day. Research carried out in the USA by Speekman-Klass (1986) and Lubeck (1985) demonstrates that it is the nature of the curriculum, its organization and processes more so than content, and role modelling by the adults concerned which determine the outcomes for the children, and that encouraging children to make choices, to direct their own learning with the support of parents and educators will foster autonomy and individualism, if that is what the society wants and needs of its children. Equally, children can learn to be co-operative, and to provide sympathy and support to others who need this, if the overt and the hidden aspects of the curriculum promote these characteristics.

In some cases early childhood provision is regarded as preparing the child for primary school, and is then often given the name preprimary, or preschool, provision to reinforce this view. What this may entail is a quite overt preparation of children for the primary school, with appropriate liaison between the sectors, and Madeleine Goutard points out that the French system has moved closer to this model in recent years. Karin Vilien's description of Denmark shows how her country has developed better links between the phases, but here one has the impression of the opposite model – the school prepared for the children. In the UK the fragmentation of services has meant that with the introduction of a National Curriculum in the post-5 sector, children attending certain kinds of early childhood provision are experiencing a foundation for this National Curriculum which is not only more appropriate to their current needs, but is also ensuring they are at an academic advantage compared with children coming from other types of under-5s settings (Sylva, Siraj-Blatchford and Johnson 1992; Shorrocks 1992; Knight 1992).

In some of the countries discussed here early childhood provision has been strongly influenced by empirically derived child development theories and evidence from research studies, particularly those concerned with cognitive development. In others, the pragmatically derived theories of early pioneers continue to influence practice. However, one needs to ask the question – is the research which influences policies and practices a) value-free, b) popular because it reinforces the current thinking and ideology of a particular group, or groups, in that society?

The type of early childhood education which has evolved in Western Europe, through the influence of pioneers and research on child development, is criticized for example by Walter Barker for the van Leer Foundation (Barker 1987). He argues that the philosophy and practices in the technically developed societies

> may be suited to the needs of the middle-class child, but fails to offer to the disadvantaged child the structured experiences which she or he may need in order to develop the skills, concepts and understanding that will fit the child for coping with school and wider community experiences . . . the adult caregivers do not spend sufficient time inter-acting with children individually . . . the quality of the educational experiences provided in preschool settings is primarily a function of the ethos and curriculum, the level of adult–child interaction, and the degree to which the setting is a skilful blend of both the indigenous culture and the wider mainstream or societal culture into which the child will be moving . . .
>
> (Barker, 1987)

Barker argues further that the level of academic qualifications of the caregivers is not a crucial factor in determining children's success as long as educators are committed to and aware of the purposes of the curriculum offered. In fact research (e.g. Tizard, Mortimore and Birchell 1981; Ward 1982; Whitebrook, Howes and Phillips 1989) has shown that better-educated staff are more able to understand the objectives of particular aspects of the curriculum, but unfortunately, as Barker himself points out, they often fail to communicate these understandings to parents, carers, or other educators who have not had opportunities for the same levels of curriculum and child development study.

Bronfenbrenner's (1979) ecological model of child development charges early childhood services with a responsibility to continue to place children and their optimal development at the centre of their concerns, but to be sensitive to all the interactions and conditions affecting children's lives. This means paying attention not only to the provision of appropriate, meaningful learning opportunities, but recognizing the context of dynamic, reciprocal relations between children, parents, educators, other services, community groups, employment and housing conditions, cultures and ideology, and so on. One area which has attempted to put this philosophy into practice is Strathclyde, in Scotland, where co-ordinated services of all kinds, and community-oriented early education have been planned for the 1990s (SRC 1985), as in Germany where a number of similar projects have been implemented.

While no-one is suggesting educators can actually be responsible for this development of co-ordination, their positive involvement, abandoning territorialism, is vital. In this respect, as Watt (1990) points out, the first step would be to accept that other forms of provision have qualities which may be lacked by their own service, we can all learn from each other. But in order to facilitate that learning and co-ordination, it may be necessary in those countries where this has not yet happened, for central governments to take a lead and place all services for young children under one government department or ministry (Pugh 1992a; Penn and Riley 1992). If this ministry were to be education, as in Spain, then a clear message about the aims of provision is part of the macro-level, the all-pervading ethos of that society (Bronfenbrenner 1979). Further, as Cochran's (1986) action research has shown, and Pugh (1992b) commented, community-based services which provide for all children, by being a combination of education and care facility, are more advantageous across the board, since their flexibility means they can cater for a range of needs, and certain children are not stigmatized by a start in life labelling them, or their families, as 'deficient' because they have some kind of special need, whether physical, cognitive, emotional or social.

Many European countries have recently passed laws concerning children's position in society (for example, Norway, Finland, Sweden, Ireland, UK) and in many cases this law has included requirements to address the educational needs of children in this earliest age group, and this adds further weight to the need for the co-ordination of services under one ministry.

The early childhood curriculum in practice

What we can see clearly in the various chapters of this book is the movement towards a delineation of an early years curriculum based on what we know about young children and their learning needs, from practical experience and from research.

On the whole, these curriculum guidelines are based on 'areas of experience', broadly defined to allow for interpretations which are appropriate to the groups' contexts and the personal needs of particular children. The interpretations are expected to epitomize educators' understandings of what is developmentally appropriate, while at the same time reflecting their awareness of what is to follow. In fact, what is to follow is potentially crucial to the actual curriculum experienced by children in this early phase. Compare, for example, the differences between the Danish and the British approaches. Not only is there a Gaderene rush to formalize, in the UK, with evidence that only 8 per cent of a four-year-old's day in the reception class of a primary school is spent on play (Bennett and Kell 1989) and parental belief that the sooner formal teaching of reading begins, the better (David 1992), there are often discontinuities in experience between the disparate under-5s settings, and between these and the reception class (Jowett and Sylva 1986; Sylva, Siraj-Blatchford and Johnson 1992). In Denmark, in contrast, there are co-ordinated approaches in both senses, aimed at enabling children to make sense of, and learn from, their experiences.

Some of the most acute failings in some of the countries' systems can be seen in their effects on children relating to discrimination in the areas of race, gender, class, special needs, linguistic and religious backgrounds, while in others, attention to these needs can provide models of successful integration of services. In addition, the ways in which all children are to be offered opportunities to learn and grow up together in a society which is free of stereotyping and bias can also be derived from official documents on the curriculum (e.g. DES 1990). As Moss (1992) states, 'Britain is unique in the relative prominence given to anti-racism as a basis for service development' (p. 41). The importance of putting these anti-discriminatory aims into practice (CRE 1991) cannot be underestimated in the current climate of increased racial harassment reported in several European countries.

Education and training of educators

At a policy meeting I attended fairly recently I was surprised and puzzled that planners thought they could take as their starting point for the provision of early childhood services the buildings and staffing requirements. Surely any service which purports to be appropriate for young children must start from their needs, and those of their families? Similarly, it can be argued that the educators need courses which will equip them to work with young children in ways which will best foster their development. This raises a host of issues related to the content of training, its length, the ultimate equivalent status, and so on – and we can see how this has differed from one country to another in the past. However, generally speaking, most European countries are moving towards better co-ordinated training, with the possibility of progression, and with equivalent status to teachers in other sectors of the education service of their country (Pascal, Bertram and Heaslip 1991). A society which argues that education and training for work with young children does not need to be at the same high level, nor involve equivalent academic rigour, to that of professional education for work with older pupils betrays the fact that it accords young children and their educators low status and low priority.

One of the aspects of work in early childhood settings which seems to have received little attention at initial training level is that relating to work with other adults. While the need to collaborate with parents in one way or another is seen as an essential part of the ongoing business of an early childhood educator, courses which engage with this requirement seem to be either embedded in other studies, or non-existent. In most of the countries discussed here educators tend to be recruited from the ranks of young women with either middle-class, or upper working-class backgrounds, and their own life experiences are likely to have been different from those of some of the parents and children they will be called on to support. Further, while students in all countries spend considerable proportions of their time during their course of study actually on placements in schools, daycare centres, children's hospitals, etc., there is often scant recognition in course content to the fact that they will work as a member of a team within their setting, and may have responsibilities of a multi-professional nature in various teams outside the setting – for example, in liaising with medical staff, educational psychologists and so on in work with children with disabilities, or in case conferences and meetings connected with child protection. The principal exceptions to this training neglect seem to be the Scandinavian countries (Hammershoj 1992), where the new 'pedagogue' training quite deliberately incorporates social work aspects, and theoretical and practical preparation to work with other adults.

Parents' wants and needs – access to low cost, educational provision

The EC Childcare Network is currently engaged in a survey of all the member countries, with respect to views of what constitutes 'quality' in early childhood services. The authors of their dissemination document – Irene Balageur, Juan Mestres and Helen Penn (1992) – have pointed out that the European Community is pluralist, so that the values of certain groups may be different from those of others. However, they hope to discover whether there are certain aspects, common threads, concerning which no government or agency should be prescriptive, but which do require attention in order that children receive the very highest quality experiences that can be provided. Their concerns then, range around aspects such as policies and their implementation, and as far as parents are concerned, aspects such as access, costs, flexibility with respect to hours to fit with employment requirements, power-sharing, accountability to and respect for the opinions of parents, and so on.

From the accounts in the chapters of this book one can see the ways in which some, if not all, of these issues have been addressed in the different countries concerned. Certainly for children aged 3 and over, access to publicly funded provision varies considerably, as Table 9, from Peter

Table 9 Places in publicly funded early childhood services as percentage of all children in the age group

	Date to which data refer	For children under 3	For children from 3 to compulsory school age	Age when compulsory schooling begins	Length of school day (including midday break)	Outside school hours care for primary school children
Germany	1987	3%	65–70%	6–7 years	4–5 hours (a)	4%
France	1988	20%	95%+	6 years	8 hours	?
Italy	1986	5%	85%+	6 years	4 hours	?
Netherlands	1989	2%	50–55%	5 years	6–7 hours	1%
Belgium	1988	20%	95%+	6 years	7 hours	?
Luxembourg	1989	2%	55–60%	5 years	4–8 hours (a)	1%
United Kingdom	1988	2%	35–40%	5 years	6½ hours	(–)
Ireland	1988	2%	55%	6 years	4½–6½ hours (b)	(–)
Denmark	1989	48%	85%	7 years	3–5½ hours (a,b)	29%
Greece	1988	4%	65–70%	5½ years	4–5 hours (b)	(–)
Portugal	1988	6%	35%	6 years	6½ hours	6%
Spain	1988	?	65–70%	6 years	8 hours	(–)

Key: ? = no information; (–) = less than 0.5%; (a) = school hours vary from day to day; (b) = school hours increase as children get older.

Notes: The table shows the number of *places* in *publicly funded* services as a percentage of the child population; the percentage of *children* attending may be higher because some places are used on a part-time basis. Provision at playgroups in the Netherlands has not been included, although 10 per cent of children under 3 and 25 per cent of children aged 3–4 attend and most playgroups receive public funds. Average hours of attendance – 5–6 hours per week – are so much shorter than for other services, that it would be difficult and potentially misleading to include them on the same basis as other services; however, playgroups should not be forgotten when considering publicly funded provision in the Netherlands.

Source: European Commission 1990.

Moss's work for the EC (European Commission 1990) shows. If access to publicly funded provision is limited, then it seems fair to conclude that parental choice is likely to be limited also – for all but the rich.

In many of the countries discussed here, we have evidence of both public and private sector provision but in certain countries there is little or no 'voluntary' provision. In France, for example, there are the *crèches parentales*, a fairly recent development, which boasted 30 parent-run nurseries in 1982 and 700 by 1991, many of these being found in rural areas and small towns (Moss 1992). Parents set up and run the service, usually for children under 3 years old, and including full-time care. As with most PPA groups in the UK, parents are expected to assist with the actual running of the group on a rota basis.

In Denmark, however, the concept of the British PPA, with its groups run by voluntary workers who are either paid nothing or very low wages, is incomprehensible. At the heart of this issue is a difference in interpretation and emphasis in values. In the UK voluntary work in a caring setting is seen as a vital part of a society which demonstrates its concern through acts of altruism, and a lack of expectation that one should be paid for every task one performs. In Denmark, on the other hand, the right of every family to what is conceived of as 'proper' provision is partly at the heart of their view, but so too is the feeling that it would be wrong for a society to exploit the goodwill of certain groups in that society.

While the playgroup movement has provided many women with experiences which have led them to gain further qualifications, and while its constant supply of 'new blood' from the waves of incoming parents has a dynamic effect which it seems difficult to replicate in the public sector where professionals can dampen parental ardour (Watt 1977), any system which achieves high quality in every respect, across the board, will by its very nature be expensive – in other words it is not acceptable to exploit playgroup supervisors, childminders, and nursery nurses, if one enacts laws requiring them to hold qualifications, etc., and to acquire ever higher levels in these. Similarly, in those countries where teacher education is undergoing review and upgrading, one needs to ask if governments will match their recognition of the need for highly educated adults to work with very young children with recognition that there will be implications for funding. Research evidence (e.g. Jowett and Sylva 1986; Whitebrook, Howes and Phillips 1989; Shorrocks 1992) points to the fact that the more one requires early childhood care and education services to have an impact on children's later educational achievements, the better educated the adults need to be.

There is some concern that current EC priorities, relating to childcare and parental employment rights and equality of opportunity, mean that the needs of children of unemployed parents are not taken into account. Shinman's (1981) study of children whose parents were in what would now be termed the 'underclass' were the least likely to attend some form of provision, yet were those in greatest need of early childhood education. As a result of the availability of provision in some of the countries of the EC, the needs of children from disadvantaged groups in society are more likely to be addressed than in those countries where public services are limited, and the implication, therefore, may be that it will be in those countries where early childhood education has not been properly addressed that effects compounding educational disadvantage over children's lifetimes will cause higher proportions of a European underclass to be located there.

The EC Network's task began as a women's rights issue, related to entitlement to childcare facilities as part of a policy enabling women to work outside the home. However, there is now recognition of the need to ensure that the children's needs and rights are also prioritized (see Sylva and Moss 1992). Unfortunately, earlier work often seemed to be setting one against the other, so opponents of women's equality of opportunity could argue that children were being neglected, that women, if they chose to become mothers, must make a sacrifice. Moss (1990) has long argued that provision for children is a societal and whole family issue – not the responsibility solely of women, and that in countries such as Sweden policies addressing parental, rather than maternal, needs and rights, and ways in which the whole society, including industry, must be geared to that ideology.

Karin Vilien, in her chapter on Denmark, has commented on concern expressed by researchers in Scandinavia about the dislocations experienced by children in today's society, where daycare and home appear to be two very separate worlds. However, we need to explore whether children themselves see their lives in this way, because children will attempt to make sense of their different environments and relationships. The lifestyles of this generation of children may be *different* from our own, but does this necessarily mean a less appropriate, or less fulfilling lifestyle?

Parental involvement in provision

Many of the systems of provision discussed here include parental involvement in management – for example, Italy and Denmark – but few engage parents in the day-to-day running of groups, working with the children, and this form of parental involvement, thought to benefit both children and families *and* staff whose links with home will be improved as a result, and this type of involvement is probably highest in the UK. Public provision in the UK has two causes to thank for this development, one is the Plowden Report (CACE 1967) for which background research was undertaken and this indicated the influential effect of parental engagement in children's education, the second is the preschool playgroup movement, which demonstrated parental eagerness to become involved at this grass-roots level. What is unfortunate is the fact that Lady Plowden's own espousal of the voluntary movement's aims, rather than suggesting that these be incorporated into public practice to a greater extent (Ward 1982) may have been a factor which contributed to the reluctance of central government to address the issue of improving access to publicly funded services.

Parental involvement as a way of educating parents is still seen as important in some developing countries (Fisher 1991), but although the compensatory movement made some impact in Western European countries during the 1960s and 1970s, the negative connotations of this approach are now generally avoided in EC countries and parents are recognized as bringing their own strengths to their children's learning. Services are expected to provide support and to work in partnership with parents. However, the need for educators to offer articulate accounts of the curriculum and play methods in early childhood settings as part of their accountability is still a central issue. Research in Belgium and the UK (David 1992) has shown that parents are affected by accounts in the media to the extent that they may begin to be dissatisfied with the services their children receive because they have not had opportunities to explore the aims underlying a curriculum based on play, nor to share in the observable, recorded outcomes as evidence of children's learning.

Curriculum, evaluation and monitoring of services

Most of the countries included in this study now have some sort of government document delineating the early years curriculum. In Italy, Spain, France, Belgium and the UK these are formulated in terms of areas of experience, rather than as subjects or disciplines, because it is considered to be important that young children learn through relevant and meaningful, real-life experiences. This is also the philosophy that characterizes the 'situation-oriented' approach in Germany. The challenge which may have to be faced by early childhood educators in the near future will be the demand to provide proof that this does in fact enable children later to access a more formally defined and 'delivered', subject-based curriculum, taught by professionals who are more likely to hold a degree in a subject such as mathematics, history, etc., than in child development. Countries where early childhood services are being, more and more, perceived as preprimary education and preparation of the child for the next phase, will be those where this debate could be most heated.

Monitoring and evaluation of services will, again, depend to a great extent on the basis on which the provision is made. If the service is seen as educational then there may well be inspections and monitoring by specialists in this field. However, the situation in several countries, e.g. Belgium and the UK, is in a state of flux as a result of changes in emphasis (see discussion about *maternelle*/preprimary above) or because recent legislation (such as the 1988 Education Reform Act, 1992 Education Bill and the Children Act 1989 in the UK) have altered the nature of those monitoring processes from inspection including an advisory role to one of inspection only.

The effectiveness of early childhood education

Provision for young children in some countries is made for social reasons, for parents to continue in employment, or to offer children opportunities which are rare nowadays in their everyday lives, of meeting with their peers and developing social and communication skills. However, if governments are encouraged to make an investment in high quality provision, in the current climate they are likely to expect some sort of return for that investment. Evidence concerning the long-term effects of early childhood education has been sought ever since the days of the compensatory movement, and some of the early research provided unfavourable results. However, in the USA researchers suggest that the wrong kinds of outcomes were being sought (Schweinhart, Weikart and Larner 1986) and that societies do stand to benefit substantially in financial terms, for the provision of educational programmes, but there is also evidence of positive long-term gains from some of the Western European countries too, for example, from Sweden (Hwang 1991), and from France (Jarousse, Mingot and Richard 1991).

Children's own influence on their lives

Both Bronfenbrenner's (1979) ecological model of child development and that of transactional theorists (e.g. Semeroff and Chandler 1975) put forward the view that child development is a dynamic process, with the children themselves portrayed as active participants in their own life processes. Children not only change as a result of their experiences and interactions, they cause change in those around them. However, young children attempt to make sense of their experiences in the context of what they already know. Attendance at some form of early childhood education and care facility may well be accepted as 'something we do' by children with no other experience. Children questioned in both Belgium and the UK (David 1992) did not, generally, have any other rationale for their attendance at nursery school, although one child who said he did not like attending concluded that his mother's employment was the element in his life forcing him (and, in his reasoning, his family) to accept this state of affairs.

No child in this study mentioned any facet of learning as a reason for engaging in the activities provided, in either country. While some may balk at the idea of discussing learning outcomes with young children, because they fear it may end up deadening the spirit of early years provision, encouraging children to engage in metacognition – recognizing not only what has been learned but the processes of that learning and their 'transferability' – might be ways in which early childhood educators can foster children's awareness and empowerment in their own learning, and at the same time provided them with the means of being advocates for a child-directed play curriculum.

Children in Finland (Huttunen 1992), asked about their memories of salient features of their earlier life in early childhood centres, provided overwhelming evidence that the quality of relationships is their central concern.

Finally, what is the future likely to hold for children and their early education and care facilities in Europe? Will all countries move towards a common age of primary school entry at 6? Will the signing of the Maastricht Treaty bring the different States' education services closer together, despite the fact that Denmark and the UK prefer the earlier Treaty of Rome 'hands off' policy with respect to education? There are those who believe that in any case, drawing education systems closer together will be a long, slow process because of their different and unique underlying philosophies, cultures and values (McLean 1991). For those of us in the field of early childhood provision, the question is – will our services be seen as part of the education system anyway?

If early childhood care and education is excluded from the education system, and is seen mainly as a social service, does the European Recommendation (that is, it is not a Directive) of 31 March 1992 (mainly focused on parental leave, the workplace, and gender relations) go far enough to ensure that those services, in caring for and about the children, in facilities offered to enable parents to work, provide them universally with the important early learning experiences which should be their right?

Sharing ideas and knowledge through increased involvement with representatives from other European countries should contribute to improvements in practice, better understandings about the ways in which services have developed and factors influencing decision-makers. Some early childhood educators from countries where provision has traditionally been of a high quality fear that 'Europeanization' could mean a fall in standards, because governments will use models from abroad which cost less if they can argue that this must be acceptable, since it is the norm in another Western European country (OMEP European Seminar 1992). We may in fact be humbled, and learn much to our advantage from closer links with countries of Eastern Europe, with their original tradition stretching back to Comenius, but that is another story. Children in Western Europe, despite the fact that an estimated 12 million of them in the EC countries are living in relative poverty (SCAFA 1992), are privileged in comparison with children in the developing countries. We need to offer them an education system which will prepare them to behave appropriately and justly when they grow up and are in positions of power relative to those from poorer nations.

In comparing the attention different countries pay to the needs of their youngest citizens we are left with many questions. The decisions made by governments need to be based not only on the evidence of research, the views of particular pressure groups, or those of experienced pragmatists in the field. They must also be based on arguments concerning the values espoused by a society which claims to care about its children and to require a highly educated workforce of the future. To fulfil questions about the implications of those values, policy-makers, parents and practitioners need opportunities to reflect on and discuss the place of the young child in European society, concepts of childhood, and the real worlds of childhood inhabited by all our children.

Bibliography

Achter Jugendbericht (1990) *Bericht über Bestrebungen und Leistungen der Jugendhilfe*, Bundestagsdrucksache 11/6576, Bonn.

Aguado, M.T. (1991) *Analisis evaluacion de programas al Plan Experimental para la Reforma de la Educacion Infatil*, Unpublished PhD Thesis, Universidad Nacional de Educacion a Distancia, Madrid.

AKN (1970) *Kvinnan i Sverige i statistisk belysning*, Stockholm, Arbetsmarknadens kvinnonämnd.

Arbeitsgemeinschaft für Jugendhilfe (1988) Fachberatung für Kindertageseinrichtungen – eine unverzichtbare Leistung für Erzieherinnen und Träger, in Arbeitsgemeinschaft für Jugendhilfe (Hrsg.) *Zur Situation gegenwirtiger Kindergartenerziehung*, AGJ, Bonn.

Arbetsmarknadsstyrelsen (1974) *Kvinnorna ach arbetsmarknaden*, Allmänna Förlaget, Stockholm.

Athey, C. (1991) *Extending Thought in Young Children*, Paul Chapman, London.

Ausubel, D.P. (1968) *Educational psychology: A cognitive view*, Holt, Rinehart and Winston, New York.

Ausubel, D.P., Novack, J. and Hanesian, H. (1989) *Psicologia cognitiva*, Trillas, Mexico.

Bagger, H. (1891) *Den Danske bornehave*, Roms Forlag.

Balageur, I., Mestres, J. and Penn, H. (1992) *Qualité des Services pour les Jeunes Enfants: Un Document de Reflexion*, Commission des CE, Bruxelles.

Balke, E. (1988) Svensk barnomsorg i internationellt perspektiv, in M. Chaib (ed) *Barnomsorg i utveckling*, Lund, Studentlitteratur.

Barker, W. (1987) *Early Childhood Care and Education: the Challenge*, Bernard Van Leer Foundation, The Hague.

Barrett, G. (1986) *Starting School: an evaluation of the experience*, AMMA, London.

Bate, M., Smith, M., Sumner, R. and Sexton, B. (1978) *Manual for Assessment in Nursery education*, NFER-Nelson, Windsor.

Bathurst, K. (1905) Report of the women inspectors on children under five years of age in elementary schools, in W. Van der Eyken (ed) *Education, the child and society: a documentary history, 1900–1973*, Penguin, Harmondsworth.

Beck-Gernsheim, E. (1987) Die Inszenierung der Kindheit, *Psychologie heute*, Vol. 14, No. 12, pp. 7–11.

Belsky, J. (1988) The 'effects' of infant daycare reconsidered, *Early Childhood Research Quarterly* 3, 235–272.

Bennett, N. and Kell, J. (1989) *A Good Start?* Blackwell, Oxford.

Bergman, M. (1991) Some aspects of the necessity for developing research in childcare and early childhood education. Paper presented at the 16th Annual Conference of ATEE, Amsterdam, September 1991.

Bergman, M. (1992a) Akademisering av lararutbildningen, in B. Södersten (ed) *Pendeln svänger – röster i högskoledebatten*, SNS Forlag, Stockholm.

Bergman, M. (1992b) The context of early childhood teacher education. Paper presented at the 17th Annual Conference of ATEE, Lahti, Finland, September 1992.

Bertolini, P. (1984) L'infanzia e la sua scuola, La Nuova Italia, Firenze.

Bertram, H. (Hrsg.) (1991) *Die Familie in Westdeutschalnd Stabilität und Wandel familiärer Lebensformen*, Leske und Budrich, Opladen.

Blackstone, T. (1971) *A Fair Start*, Allen Lane, London.

Boeckmann, B., Neumann, S. and Sebastia, U. (1991) Kindereinrichtungen – Erziehungstheorie und Erziehungspraxis im Wandel, in *Kinder und Jugendliche aus der DDR, Jugendhilfe in den neuen Bundesländern*, Berlin.

Bowlby, J. (1953) *Child Care and the Growth of Love*, Penguin, Harmondsworth.

Bronfenbrenner, U. (1979) *The ecology of human development: Experiments by natures and design*, Harvard University Press, Cambridge, Mass.

Brophy, J., Statham, J. and Moss, P. (1992) *Playgroups in Practice: self-help and public policy*, HMSO, London.

Browne, N. and France, P. (1988) *Hacia una educacion infantil no sexista*, Madrid.

Bruce, T. (1987) *Early Childhood Education*, Hodder and Stoughton, Sevenoaks.

Bruner, J.S. (1974) From communication to language, *Cognition* 3, p. 255–87.

Bruner, J.S. (1980) *Under Five in Britain*, Grant McIntyre, London.

Bruner, J.S. (1983) *Child's talk: learning to use language*, Norton, New York.

Bruner, J. (1984) *Accion, pensamiento y lenguaje*, Alianza, Madrid.

Bruner, J. (1986) *Actual Minds, Possible Worlds*, Harvard University Press, Harvard.

Burgess, R.G., Hughes, C. and Moxon, S. (1991) A curriculum for the under fives? Paper presented at CIDREE Conference, University of Leuven, Belgium, September 1991.

Busch, C., Dörfler, M. and Seehausen, H. (1991) *Frankfurter Studie zu Modellen betriebsnaher Kinderbetreuung*, Dietmar Klotz, Eschborn bei Frankfurt am Main.

CACE (1967) *Children and their Primary Schools* (Plowden Report) HMSO, London.

Calder, P. (1990) Educare can advantage under threes, in D. Rouse (ed) *Babies and Toddlers: Carers and Educators. Quality for Under Threes*, National Children's Bureau, London.

Carlsen, S. (1990) *Notat om behov og muligheder for offentlig bornespasning i Norden*, Ligesstillingsradets sekretariat, Copenhagen. (Danish Equal Opportunities Commission.)

Christensen, N. and Launer, J. (1989) *Über das Spiel der Vorschulkinder, Ein Beitrag zur Führung der Kinder im Spiel* (6. Auflage), Volk und Wissen, Berlin.

Christoffersen, M.N. (1987a) *Familien under forandringl en statistisk belysning af smaborn familie forhold 1974–1985*, Socialforskningsinstituttet, Copenhagen.

Christoffersen, M.N. (1987b) *Hvem passer vore smaborn. Dahpasning for 0–6 arige*, Socialforskningsinstituttet, Copenhagen.

Ciari, B. (1969) *Le nuove tecniche didattiche*, Editori Riuniti, Roma.

Ciari, B. (1972) *La grande disadattata*, Editori Riuniti, Roma.

Ciari, B. (1975) *I modi dell'insegnare*, Editori Riuniti, Roma.

Clark, M.M. (1988) *Children Under Five: Educational Research and Evidence*, Gordon and Breach, London.

Cleave, S. and Brown, S. (1991) *Early to School: four year olds in infant classes*, NFER–Nelson, Windsor.

CNREE/MEC (1992) Alumnos con necesidades educativas especiales y adaptaciones curriculares, Madrid.

Cochran, M. (1986) The parental empowerment process, building on family strengths, in J. Harris (ed) *Child Psychology in Action*, Croom Helm, London.

Cohen, B. (1990) *Caring for Children: the 1990 Report* (EC Report on the UK), Family Policy Studies Centre, London.

Cohen, B. and Fraser, N. (1991) *Childcare in a Modern Welfare System*, IPPR, London.

Cohen, B. (1993) A programme for Europe, *Child Education*, Vol. 70, no. 2, p. 11.

Colberg-Schrader, H. and Oberhuemer, P. (1989) Young children in a changing society. Child care and education in the Federal Republic of Germany, in *International Journal of Early Childhood*, Vol. 21, no. 2, pp. 45–48.

Colberg-Schrader, H. and von Derschau, D. (1991) Sozialisationsfeld Kindergarten, in K. Hurrelmann und D. Ulich (Hrsg.). *Neues Handbuch der Sozialisationsforschung* (4. völlig beu bearbeitete Auflage), Beltz, Weinheim und Basel.

Colberg-Schrader, H., Krug, M. and Pelzer, S. (1991) *Soziales Lernen im Kindergarten*. Ein Praxisbuch des Deutschen Jugendinstituts, Kösel, München.

Comité Francais de l'OMEP (1975) *Pauline Kergomard, un Cinquantenaire*, OMEP, Paris.

Consultative Committee (1933) *Report on infant and nursery schools* (Hadow Report), HMSO, London.

CRE (1991) *From Cradle to School: a practical guide to race equality and childcare*, (3rd edition) Commission for Racial Equality, London.

Curtis, A. (1986) *A Curriculum for the Preschool Child: learning to learn*, NFER-Nelson, Windsor.

Dahlberg, G. (1991) Empathy and social control. Paper presented at the ISSBD Conference, Minneapolis, USA.

Dahlberg, G. and Åsén, G. (1986). *Perspektiv på förskolan. Några utgångspunkter för en analys av den pedagogiska reformverksamheten i förskolan.* Rapport 2/1986. Institutionen för pedagogik, Högskolan för lärarutbildning i Stockholm.

Dahlberg, G. Lundgren, U.P. and Åsén, G. (1991) *Att utvärdera barnomsorg.* Stockholm: HLS Förlag/Socialdepartementet.

Danmarks Laererforening (1989) *Undersogelseom samordning af indskoling foretaget*, Denmark Teachers' Union, Copenhagen.

Das Bildungswesen der Deutschen Demokratischen Republik (1989) Akademie der Pädagogischen Wissenschaften (Hrsg.), (3. Auflage), Volk und Wissen, Berlin.

David, T. (1990) *Under Five – Under-educated?* Open University Press, Buckingham.

David, T. (1992) What do parents in Belgium and Britain want their children to learn in preschool? Paper presented at the OMEP XXth World Congress, North Arizona University, USA, August 1992.

De Bartolomeis, F. (1979) *il bambino dai tre ai sei anni e la nuova scuola infantile*, La Nuova Italia, Firenze.

Decat, M., Sant'Angelo, F. and Louveaux, H. (1989) *Droit des Jeunes Etrangers*, Service Droit des Jeunes, Bruxelles.

Delvaux-Furnière, A–M. and Malisoux-Gillet, M–J. (1985) *Special – Enseignement maternel: Enseignement Provincial Enseignement Communal*, No. 11. June 1985.

Demografiska rapporter (1992) *Fertility in a life-perspective*, Statistiska Centralbyrån, Stockholm.

Denmark (1990) *Cirkulaere om dagtilbud for born og unge efter bistandsloven. Nr. 203 26 oktober 1990*, Danish Government, Copenhagen.

Denmark (1991) *Lov om uddannelse af paedagoger*, Lov nr 370 af 6 juni 1991.

Denmark (1992) *Lov om aendring af lov om social bistand*, Lov nr. 350 14 mai 1992, Act nr. 350 14 mai 1992.

Derschau, D. von (1984) Die Ausbildung des pädagogischen Personals, in J. Zimmer (Hrsg.) *Erziehung in früher Kindheit, Enzyklopädie Erziehungwissenschaft*, Vol. 6, Klett-Cotta, Stuttgart.

DES (1972) *Education: a Framework for Expansion* (White paper: 5174), HMSO, London.

DES (1978) *Report of the Committee of Inquiry into the Education of Handicapped Children and Young People* (Warnock Report), HMSO, London.

DES (1985) *Better Schools*, HMSO, London.

DES (1985a) *Curriculum Matters 2: Curriculum 5–16*, HMSO, London.

DES (1988) *Report of the Task Group on Assessment and Testing* (TGAE Report) HMSO, London.

DES (1989) *The Education of Children Under Five*, HMSO, London.

DES (1990) *Starting with Quality* (Rumbold Report), HMSO, London.

Deutsches Jugendinstitut (1990) *Familiengründung im Wandel*. DJI-Bulletin, No. 16.

Deutsches Jugendinstitut (Hrsg.) (1990a) *Entwicklungsbedingungen und Perspektiven der Jugendhilfe in der früheren DDR nach Vereinigung der beiden deutschen Staaten*, Deutsches Jugendinstitut, München.

Deutsches Jugendinstitut (1991) *Projekt Orte für Kinder. Ansatze konzeptioneller Weiterentwicklungen von Einrichtungen fur Kinder und Familien*, Deutsches Jugendinstitut, München.

Deutsches Jugendinstitut (1992) *Tageseinrichtungen für Kinder, Zahlenspiegel*, erarbeitet von I. Berger, L. Miedaner, S. Pelzer and H. Permien, Deutsches Jugendinstitut, München.

De Vries, R. (1978) Early education and Piagetian theory, in *Knowledge and Development*, Vol. 2, pp. 75–92.

De Vries, R. and Kohlberg, L. (1987) *Programs of Early Education. The Constructivist View*, Longman, New York.

Donaldson, M. (1978). *Children's Minds*, Collins/Fontana, Glasgow.

Drummond, M.J., Rouse, D. and Pugh, G. (1992) *Making Assessment Work*, NCB/NES-Arnold Nottingham Group, London.

Ds U (1985) *Förskola och skola. En historisk återblick* (En rapport från Forskola-skola-kommittén), Socialdepartmentet, Stockholm.

Ds U (1992) *Alternativa verksamhetsformer inom vård och omsorg*, Rapport från en arbetsgrupp i Socialdepartementet/Statskontoret i Oktober 1992. Socialdepartementet, Stockholm.

Early Years Curriculum Group (1989) *Early Childhood Education: Early Years and the National Curriculum*, Trentham Books, Stoke-on-Trent.

Ebert, S. (1988) Erzieherausbildung als Persönlichkeitsbildung, *Sozialpädagogische Blätter*, Vol. 39, no. 5/6, pp. 153–161.

Erning, G., Neumann, K. and Reyer, J. (Hrsg.) (1987) *Geschitchte des Kindergartens*, Lambertus, Freiburg.

European Commission (1988) *Childcare and Equality of Opportunity*, European Commission, Brussels.

176   *Bibliography*

European Commission (1990) *Childcare in the European Communities, 1985–90*, European Commission, Brussels.

EURYDICE (1991) *Reform Educatif. Belgique: La Communautarisation de L'Enseignement* EURYDICE information, Bruxelles.

Evans, E.D. (1987) *Educacion infantil temprana. Tendencias actuales*, Trillas, Mexico.

Family Policy Studies Centre (1989) *Children Under Five* (Fact Sheet 7), FPSC, London.

Federal Law Gazette (1990) *Act for the Reform of the Law on Child and Youth Services (Child and Youth Services Act)*, 26 June 1990, Bonn.

Ferri, E. (1992) *What Makes Childminding Work?* NCB, London.

Ferri, E., Birchell, D., Gingell, V. and Gipps, C. (1981) *Combined Nursery Centres*, Macmillan, London.

Fisher, E.A. (1991) *Early Childhood Care and Education (ECCE): A World Survey*, UNESCO, Paris.

Fthenakis, W.E., Lehner, I.M. and Oberhuemer, P. (1990) Erzieher- Aus-, Fort- und Weiterbildung: zum gegenwärtigen Diskussionsstand, *KiTa aktuell*, Vol. 2, no. 12, pp. 175–179.

Grieve, R. and Hughes, M. (eds) (1990) *Understanding Children*, Blackwell, Oxford.

Hammershoj, H. (1992) Preschool teacher-paedagog training in Scandinavia, XXth World Congress of OMEP, North Arizona University, August 1992.

Hartley, D. (1993) *Understanding the nursery school*, Cassell, London.

Hatje, A.K. (1973) *Befolkningsfragan och valfarden*, Allmäna Förlaget, Stockholm.

Henckel, B. (1990) *Forskollarare i tanke och handling. En studie kring begreppen arbete, lek och inlarning*, (Akademisk avhandling Pedagogiska institutionen), Umeå Universitet, Umeå.

Hennessy, E. and Melhuish, E.C. (1991) Early day-care and the development of school-age children: a review, *Journal of Reproductive and Infant Psychology*, Vol. 9, pp. 117–136.

Herlth, A. and Schleimer, J. (1982) *Kinder im sozialen Umfeld*, Außerfamiliale Kontakte von Vorschulkindern, Campus, Frankfurt/New York.

High/Scope (1986) *Introduction to the High/Scope Preschool Curriculum*, High/Scope Educational Research Foundation, Ypsilanti, Michigan.

Holtermann, S. (1992) *Investing in Young Children*, National Children's Bureau, London.

Hopf, A. (1988) Eltern-Selbsthilfegruppen in der Früherziehung, *Zeitschrift für Pädagogik*, 23. Beiheft, Erziehung und Bildung als öffentliche Aufgabe, Beltz, Weinheim und Basel.

Hössl, Alfred (1988) Entwicklungen integrativer Erziehung im Elementarbereich, in H. Eberwein (Hrsg.) *Behinderte und Nichtbehinderte lerner gemeinsam. Handbuch der Integrationspädagogik*, Beltz Verlag, Weinheim und Basel.

House of Commons Select Committee Education Science and Arts (1988) *Educational Provision for the Under Fives*, HMSO, London.

Hultquist, K. (1990) *Forskolebarnet. En konstruktion for gemenskapen och den individuella frigorelsen*, Symposion, Stockholm.

Humblet, P.C. (1992) Communaute Française: le point de la situation, *Generation O.N.E.: L'Accueil de l'enfant en Europe* p. 32–33, Office de la Naissance et de l'Enfance Communaute Française de Belgique, Bruxelles.

Hurst, V. (1991) *Planning for Early Learning: Education in the First Five Years*, Paul Chapman, London.

Hutt, S.J., Tyler, S., Hutt, C. and Christopherson, H. (1989) *Play, Exploration and Learning*, Routledge, London.

Huttenen, E. (1992) Children's experiences in early childhood programmes, *International Journal of Early Childhood* 24, 2, p. 3–11.

Hwang, P. (1991) Day care in Sweden, in P. Moss and E. Melhuish, *Current Issues in Day Care for Young Children*, HMSO, London.

ILEA (1986) *Primary Matters*, London, ILEA.

Isaacs, S. (1929) *The Nursery Years*, Routledge and Kegan Paul, London.

Jarousse, J-P., Mingat, A. and Richard, M. (1991) *La scolarisation maternelle a deux ans: analyse des effets pedagogiques et sociaux*, Université de Bourgogne, Bourgogne, (Research report).

Johansson, J.E. (1983) *Svensk forskola – en tillbakablick* (Socialstyrelsen, kompletterande material till pedagogiskt program for forskolan), Liber, Stockholm.

Johansson, J.E. (1992) *Metodikamnet i förskollärarutbildningen. Bidrag till en traditionsbestamning* (Göteborg Studies in Educational Sciences 86), Acta Universatis Gothoburgensis, Göteborg.

Jowett, S. and Sylva, K. (1986) Does kind of preschool matter? *Educational Research*, 28, 1, p. 21–31.

Kamii, C. and De Vries, R. (1982) Piaget for early education, in M.C. Day and R.L. Parker (eds) *The Preschool in Action* (2nd Ed.), Allyn and Bacon, Boston.

Kamii, C. and De Vries, R. (1989) *El conocimiento fisico en la educacion preescholar. Implicaciones de la teoria de Piaget*, Siglo XXI ed., Madrid.

Kärrby, G. (1992) *Kvalitet i pedagogiskt arbete med barn*. Allmänna Förlaget, Stockholm.

Knight, C. (1992) Work in progress for M.Phil. University of Warwick, Coventry.

Krappmann, L. (1985) Das Erprobungsprogramm und seine Folgen, in J. Zimmer (Hrsg.) *Erziehung in früher Kindheit. Enzyklopädie Erziehungswissenschraft*, Vol. 6, Klett-Cotta, Stuttgart.

Langsted, O. and Sommer, D. (1988) *Borns opvaekstforhold i 80'erne*, Reitzels Forlag, Copenhagen.

Le Soir (1992) La 'meilleure école', un mythe: l'enseignement prescolaire. Epanouir et eduquer les petits des l'age de 2,5 ans, *Le Soir* 4.6.92 p. 8–9.

Lipski, Jens (1989) Integrative Erziehung im Elementarbereich in der Bundersrepublik Deutschland, in Technische Universität (Hrsg.) *Approaches Towards the Integration of Handicapped Children and Adolescents in the Countries of the European Community*, Universitätsbibliothek der Technischen Universität, Berlin 1990.

Lubeck, S. (1985) *Sandbox Society*, Falmer Press, London.

Lund, S. (1992) *Facts and Figures about Early Childhood and Youth Education in Denmark*, BUPL, Copenhagen.

Macbeth, A. (1984) *The child between*, Commission of the European Communities, Brussels.

McLean, M. (1990) *Britain and a Single Market Europe*, Bedford Way, London.

Matthews, G. (1984) Learning and teaching mathematical skills, in D. Fontana (ed) *The Education of the Young Child*, Blackwell, Oxford.

Meadows, S. and Cashdan, A. (1988) *Helping Children Learn: Contributions to a cognitive curriculum*, David Fulton, London.

Ministère de l'ERF (1985) *Programme des activities: Enseignement prescolaire de la Communaute Française*, Ministère de l'Education, de la Recherche et de la Formation, Bruxelles.

Ministerio de Educacion y Ciencia (MEC) (1969) *La educacion en España. Bases para una politica educativa*, Madrid.

Ministerio de Educacion y Ciencia (MEC) (1970) *Ley 14/70, General de Educacion y financiacion de la Reforma educativa*, Madrid.

Ministerio de Educacion y Ciencia (MEC) (1973) *Orientaciones Pedagogicas para Educacion Preescolar*, Madrid.

Ministerio de Educacion y Ciencia (MEC) (1981) *Programas renovados de Educacion Preescolar y Ciclo Inicial*, Ed. Escuela Espanola, Madrid.

Ministerio de Educacion y Ciencia (MEC) (1986) *Anteproyexto de Marco Curricular para la Educacion Infantil*, Madrid.

Ministerio de Educacion y Ciencia (MEC) (1987) *Ley Organica del Derecho a la Educacion y disposiciones reglamentarias*, Madrid.

Ministerio de Educacion y Ciencia (MEC) (1987a) *Proyecto para la Reforma de la Ensenaza*, Madrid.

Ministerio de Educacion y Ciencia (MEC) (1989) *Diseno Curricular Base, Educacion Infantil*, Madrid.

Ministerio de Educacion y Ciencia (MEC) (1990) *Ley de Ordenacion General del Sistema Educativo*, Madrid.

Ministerio de Educacion y Ciencia (MEC) (1992) *Informacion sobre la educacion no universitaria en Espana durante el curso 1991/92*, Madrid.

Ministero della Pubblica Instruzione (1991) Orientamenti dell'attività educativa nelle scuole materne statali, *Gazzetta Ufficiale* no. 139 – Serie generale, 15 June.

Moon, B. (1990) Patterns of control: school reform in Western Europe in B. Moon (ed) *New Curriculum – National Curriculum*, Hodder and Stoughton, Sevenoaks.

Mortimore, J. and Mortimore, P. (1985) Benign or malignant? The effects of Institutions, *Child care, health and development* 11, 267–80.

Moss, P. (1990) Work, family and the care of children: equality and responsibility, *Children and Society* 4.2, p. 145–166.

Moss, P. (1992) Perspectives from Europe, in G. Pugh (ed) *Contemporary Issues in the Early Years*, Paul Chapman, London.

National Institute for Research and Pedagogical Documentation (1972) *The Architecture of Nursery Schools*, Cahier de Documentation, Paris.

Nelson, K. (1986) *Event knowledge: structure and function in development*, Erlbaum, Hillsdale NJ.

Oberhuemer, P. (1989) Kindergarten im Wandel: Flexibilisierung mit und nicht gegen Erzieherinnen, in W.E. Fthenakis (Hrsg.) *Handbuch der Elementarerziehung*, Kallmeyer'sche, Seelze-Velber.

Oberhuemer, P. (1991) Praxisfeld und Professionalisierung, in *Familien von heute – Kindergärten von gestern?* Sonderheft der Zeitschrift Theorie und Praxis der Sozialpädagogik, Luther, Bielefeld.

Official Statistics Sweden (1989) *The labour market figures*, Statistics Sweden, Stockholm.

OMEP (1992) *OMEP European Seminar*, La Hulpe, Belgium, May 1992.

Osborn, A. and Milbank, J. (1987) *The Effects of Early Education*, Clarendon Press, Oxford.

Pascal, C., Bertram, T. and Heaslip, P. (1991) *ATEE Comparative Directory of Initial Training for Early Years Teachers*, Worcester College of HE, Worcester.

Peers, M. (1942) *Ovide Decroly*, Collection National Office de Publicite, Bruxelles.

Penn, H. and Riley, K.A. (1992) *Managing Services for the Under Fives*, Longman, Harlow.

Piaget, J. (1961) The genetic approach to the psychology of thought, in *Journal of Educational Psychology*, 52, pp. 275–281.

Pierre, R., Terrieux, J. and Babin, N. (1991) *Orientations, Projets, Activités pour l'école maternelle*, Hachette, Paris.

Pistillo, F. (1987) Educazione e custodia dell'infanzia in Italia, Profilo storico, *Ricerca Educativa*, Vol. 4, no. 2.

Pistillo, F. (1989) Preprimary education and care in Italy, in P. Olmsted and D. Weikart (eds.) *How Nations Serve Young Children*, High/Scope, Ypsilanti, USA.

Plaisance, E. (1977) *L'ecole maternelle aujourd'hui*, F. Nathan, Paris.

PPA (1991) *What Children Learn in Playgroup*, Preschool Playgroups Association, London.

Prop. (1975/76: 92) *Regeringens proposition om utbyggnad av barnomsorgen*, Swedish Government Papers, Stockholm.

Prop. (1981/82: 106) *Regeringens proposition om forskning*, Swedish Government Papers, Stockholm.

Prop. (1984/85: 209) *Regeringens proposition. Förskola för alla barn,* Swedish Government Papers, Stockholm.

Prop. (1989/90: 90) *Regeringens proposition om forskning,* Swedish Government Papers, Stockholm.

Prop. (1990/91: 115) *Regeringens proposition om flexibel skolstart,* Swedish Government Papers, Stockholm.

Prop. (1991/92: 65) *Regeringens proposition om valfrihet i barnomsorgen,* Swedish Government Papers, Stockholm.

Pugh, G. (1988) *Services for Under-fives: Developing a Co-ordinated Approach,* National Children's Bureau, London.

Pugh, G. (ed) (1992) *Contemporary Issues in the Early Years,* Paul Chapman, London.

Pugh, G. (1992a) 'A country that couldn't care less?' *Times Educational Supplement* 13.11.92, Section 2, p. 1–2.

Pusci, L. (1988) Training of pre-school teachers in Italy. Recent developments and perspectives, in M. Ojala (ed.) *The Social Role and Evolution of the Teaching Profession in Historical Context.* Vol. VI: The History of Preschool Teachers' Profession, University of Joensuu.

Pusci, L. (1990) La ricerca comparata trasnazionale sull'educazione dell'infanzio: problemi e prospettive *Scuola e Città,* Vol. 61, no. 12, pp. 513–520.

Reisby, K. (1991) Educational research in Denmark – status and perspectives, *Nordisk Pedagogik,* 1, 91.

Rouse, D. (ed) *Babies and Toddlers: Carers and Educators. Quality for Under Threes,* National Children's Bureau, London.

Rouse, D. and Griffin, S. (1992) Quality for the under threes, in G. Pugh (ed) *Contemporary Issues in the Early Years,* Paul Chapman, London.

Rudebeck, K. (1989) Barnomsorgsutbyggnad och arbetskraftsutbud. In *Barnomsorgen i ett samhallsekonomiskt perspektigv.* En seminarierapport. Stockholm: Delegationen for social forskning.

Saunders, R. and Bingham-Newman, A. (1987) *Proyecto 0–6 de Educacion Infantil. Informe Piagetiano,* MEC, Madrid.

SCAFA (1992) *Scottish Families Today,* SCAFA/HMSO, Edinburgh.

Schwarz, B. (1992) Barnomsorg och skola skadas, *Dagens Nyheter* 31.1.92.

Schweinhart, L., Weikart, D., and Larner, M. (1986) Consequences of three preschool curriculum models through age 15. *Early Education Research Quarterly,* p. 15–45.

Scuola materna in Italia (LA) (1982) *Studi e documenti degli Annali della Pubblica Istruzione,* no. 19, Le Monnier, Roma.

Semeroff, A.J. and Chandler, M.J. (1975) Reproductive risk and the continuum of caretaking casualty, in F.D. Horowitz, M. Hetherington, S. Scarr-Sala Patek and G. Siegel (eds), *Review of Child Development Research 4,* Chicago University Press, Chicago.

Shorrocks, D. (1992) Evaluating Key Stage 1 Assessments: the testing time of May, 1991, *Early Years* Vol. 13, No. 1, p. 16–20.

Shinman, S. (1991) A Chance for Every Child, Tavistock, London.

Simmons-Christenson, G. (1977) Förskolepedagogikens historia, Stockholm.

Singer, E. (1992) Child-care and the psychology of development, Routledge, London.

Siraj-Blatchford, I. (1992) Why understanding cultural differences is not enough, in G. Pugh (ed) Contemporary Issues in the Early Years, Paul Chapman, London.

SOU (1955: 29) Samhället och barnfamiljerna (Betankande av 1954 års familjeutredning), Socialdepartementet, Stockholm.

SOU (1967: 8) Barnstugor, barnarvårdsmannaskap, barnolyeksfall (Betänkande från 1962 års familjeberedning) Socialdepartementet, Stockholm.

SOU (1972: 26) Förskolan. Del 1 (Betänkande från 1968 års barnstugeutredning) Socialdepartementet, Stockholm.

SOU (1972: 27) Förskolan. Del 2 (Betänkande från 1968 års barnstugeutredning) Socialdepartementet, Stockholm.

SOU (1981: 25) Bra daghem för små barn (Betänkande från 1968 familjestödsutredningen) Socialdepartementet, Stockholm.

SOU (1985: 12) Skolbarnsomsorgen (Betänkande av fritidshemskommittén) Socialdepartementet, Stockholm.

SOU (1985: 22) Forskola-skola (Betänkande av förskola-skola-kommittén) Utbildningsdepartementet, Stockholm.

SOU (1990: 80) Förskola för alla barn 1991. Hur blir det? Socialdepartementet, Stockholm.

Socialstyrelsen (1982) Utvecklingsplan för barnomsorgen (Socialstyrelsens rapport till regeringen den 14 maj 1982) Socialstyrelsen, Stockholm.

Socialstyrelsen (1987) Pedagogiskt program for forskolan (Allmäna råd frän socialstyrelsen 1987: 3) Socialstyrelsen, Stockholm.

SoS (1991: 22) Flyktingbarn i Sverige Socialstyrelsen, Stockholm.

SoS (1991: 28) Barnomsorgen i siffror 1990 Socialstyrelsen, Stockholm.

Speekman-Klass, C. (1986) The autonomous child, Falmer Press, London.

Staatsinstitut für Frühpädagogik und Familienforschung (Hrsg.) (1991) Handbuch der integrativen Erziehung behinderter und nichtbehinderter Kinder, Ernst Reinhardt, München und Basel.

Statham, J., Lloyd, E. and Moss, P. (1989) Playgroups in Three Countries, Thomas Coram Research Unit, London.

Statham, J., Lloyd, E., Moss, P., Melhuish, E. and Owen, C. (1990) Playgroups in a Changing World, HMSO, London.

Statistics Sweden (1992a) About women and men in Sweden and the European Community (EC). Facts on Equal Opportunities 1992, SCB–Förlag, Stockholm.

Statistics Sweden (1992b) Fertility in a life-perspective, SCB–Förlag, Stockholm.

Statistisches Bundesamt (Hrsg.) (1990) Bevölkerung und Erwerbstätigkeit, Fachserie 1, Reihe 3: Haushalte und Familie 1989, Wiesbaden.

Statistisches Bundesamt (Hrsg.) (1990), *Statistisches Jahrbuch 1990*, Wiesbaden.

Statistiska meddelanden: Am SM 9212 (1992) *Labour Force Survey: November 1992*, SCB-Forlag, Stockholm.

Statistiska meddelanden: S10 SM 9201 (1992) *Preschools, after-school hour centres, daycare in private homes on December 31, 1991*, SCB-Forlag, Stockholm.

Statistiska meddelanden: S11 SM 9201 (1992) *Survey of childcare needs 1992. Among preschool children (3 months–6 years old)*, SCB-Forlag, Stockholm.

SRC (1985) *Under Fives*, Strathclyde Regional Council Report, Glasgow.

Stenhouse, L. (1981) *Research as a basis for teaching*, Heinemann Educational, London.

Svenska Kommunförbundet och Statistiska centralbyrån (1992a) *How much do local public services cost in Sweden? A comparison between 280 urban and rural districts in Sweden 1991*, Statistiska centralbyran och Svenska Kommunförbundet, Stockholm.

Svenska Kommunförbundet (1993a) *Kommunernas skatter och bidrag. Systemskiftet-93*, Svenska Kommunförbundet, Stockholm.

Svenska Kommunförbundet (1993b) *Kommunernas ekonomiska lage Aktuell prognos 1992–1994*, Svenska Kommunförbundet, Stockholm.

Sylva, K., Roy, C. and Painter, M. (1980) *Childwatching at Playgroup and Nursery School*, Grant McIntyre, London.

Sylva, K. and Moss, P. (1992) Learning before school, *NCE Briefing*, No. 8, p. 1–4.

Sylva, K., Siraj-Blatchford, I. and Johnson, S. (1992) The effects of the National Curriculum on the Preschool, *International Journal of Early Childhood*, 24, 1, p. 41–51.

TES (1993) Ministers seek non-graduate staff, *Times Educational Supplement*, 5.3.93.

Tietze, W. and Roßbach, H.G. (1991) Die Betreuung von Kindern im vorschulischen Alter, *Zeitschrift für Pädagogik*, Vol. 37, no. 4, pp. 555–577.

Tietze, W. and Uferman, K. (1989) An international perspective on schooling for 4-year-olds, *Theory and Practice*, Vol. XXVIII, no. 1, pp. 69–77.

Tizard, B., Philps, J. and Plewis, I. (1976) Staff behaviour in preschool centres, *Journal of Child Psychology and Psychiatry*, Vol. 17, pp. 21–33.

Tizard, B., Mortimore, J. and Birchell, B. (1981) *Involving Parents in Nursery and Infant Schools*, Grant McIntyre, London.

Tough, J. (1976) *Listening to Children Talking*, Ward Lock, London.

Tyler, S. (1979) *Keele Preschool Assessment Guide*, NFER, Windsor.

Ulich, M., Oberhuemer, P. and Reidelhuber, A. (1992) *Der Fuchs geht um ... auch anderswo. Ein multikulturelles Spiel- und Arbeitsbuch* (3. Auflage), Beltz, Weinheim und Basel.

UNESCO (1980) *International Yearbook of Education*, UNESCO, Geneva.

Vedel-Petersen, J. (1992) *Daycare Institutions for Children Under School Age in Denmark: structure, evaluation, and perspectives*, Social-forskningsinstituttet, Copenhagen.

Vigy, J.L. (1988) *Organizacion cooperativa de la clase. Talleres permanentes con niños de dos a siete anos*, Cincel, Madrid.

Vilien, K. (1990) Co-ordinated school start in Denmark, *OMEP Northern European Newsletter* (2), pp. 6–8.

Vygotsky, L. (1978) *Mind in Society*, Harvard University Press.

Walch, J. (1988) Svensk barnomsorgspolitik – en översikt, *Forskning om utbildning*, 1, 1988.

Ward, P. (1982) Parental involvement in preschool provision. Unpublished MA thesis, University of Keele, Dept. of Psychology.

Warwick University Early Years Team (1990) *Developing Your Whole School Approach to Assessment Policy*, NFER-Nelson, Windsor.

Watt, J. (1977) *Cooperation in Preschool Education*, SSRC, London.

Watt, J. (1990) *Early Education: the current Debate*, Scottish Academic Press, Edinburgh.

Weber, E. (1984) *Ideas influencing early childhood education*, Teachers College Press, Columbia University, New York.

Weil, M.S. and Murphy, J. (1982) Instruction processes, in H.E. Mitzel (ed.) *Encyclopedia of Educational Research*, Vol. 2 (5th ed.) New York.

Whitebrook, M., Howes, C. and Phillips, D. (1990) *Who cares? Child Care Teachers and the Quality of Care in America* (Report of the Childcare Staffing Study), Childcare Employee Project, Oakland.

Winkler, B. (Hrsg.) (1992) *Zukunftsangst Einwanderung*, Beck, München.

Wolfendale, S. (1987) The evaluation and revision of the ALL ABOUT ME preschool parent-completed scales, *Early Child Development and Care*, 29, p. 473–558.

Wood, D., McMahon, L. and Cranstoun, Y. (1980) *Working with Under Fives*, Grant-McIntyre, London.

Zeiher, H. (1983) Die vielen Räume der Kinder. Zum Wandle räumlicher Lebensbedingungen seit 1945, in U. Preuss-Lausitz (Hrsg.), *Kriegskinder, Konsumkinder, Krisenkinder. Zur Sozialisationsgeschichte seit dem Zweiten Weltkrieg*, Beltz, Weinheim und Basel.

Zigler, E. (1987) Formal schooling for four-year-olds? No, *American Psychologist*, Vol. 42, No. 3, pp. 254–60.

Zimmer, J. (1985) Der Situationsansatz als Bezugsrahmen der Kindergartenreform, in J. Zimmer (Hrsg.), *Erziehung in früher Kindheit, Enzyklopädie Erziehungswissenschaft*, Vol. 6, Klett-Cotta, Stuttgart.

Zimmer, J. (1991) Eine Politik für Kinder als reale Utopie: Auf der Suche nach einer humanen Gesellschaft, in S. Ebert (Hrsg.), *Zukunft für Kinder, Grundlagen einer übergreifenden Politik*, Profil, München.

Appendix

Useful contact organizations' addresses/information concerning early childhood education in the countries included in this text:

Belgium

OMEP Belgium
Av de Montalembert 27
1330 Rixensart, Belgium

Denmark

BUPL
Blegdamsvej 124
2100

LSF
Sankt Hans Torv 26
2200 Copenhagen N

Ministry of Social Affairs
Slotsholmgade 6
1216 Copenhagen K

France

CFEP
Comité Français pour l'Education Préscolaire (Comité national d l'Organisation Mondiale pour l'Education Préscolaire – OMEP –)
190 rue d'Alésia
75014 Paris

AGIEM
Association Générale des Instituteurs et Institutrices des Ecoles
Maternelles
9 rue Méchain
75676 Paris Cedex 14
(adresse de la Présidente: La Tillaie, La Héronnière, 62500 Clairmarais)

ANPDE
Association Nationale des Puéricultrices Diplômées d'Etat
132 avenue du Général Leclerc
75014 Paris

FNEJE
Fédération Nationale des Educateurs de Jeunes Enfants
60 rue François Peissel
69300 Caluire

Germany
Associations:

Arbeitsgemeinschaft fur Jugendhilfe (AGJ)
Fachausschuss Kindheit und Familie
Am Neutor 2
5300 Bonn 1

Arbeitsgemeinschaft fur Jugendhilfe
OMEP-German National Committee (DNK)
Am Neutor 2 5300 Bonn

Pestalozzi-Froebel-Verband, e.V.
Barbarossastr. 64
D – 1000 Berlin 30

Italy
Journals:

Bambini Via Pescara 32, 24100 Bergamo BG, Italy
Ricerca educativa CEDE, Villa Falconieri, 00044 Frascati, RM
Il Quadrante scolastico Via Degasperi 34/1, 38100 Trento TN
La vita scolastica Via Campo nell'Elba 27, 00138 Roma RM
Ricerche didattiche Via Crescenzio 25, 00193 Roma RM

Spain

Organizacion Mundial para la Educacion Preescolar (OMEP-Spain)
Federacion Espanola de Escuelas Infantiles (FEDEI) C/Espanoleto, 19.
28010 Madrid

Sweden

OMEP Sweden, Dept of Education and Educational Research
University of Gothenburg
Box 1010, Molndal, 43126, Sweden

UK
Organizations:

BAECE (British Association for Early Childhood Education)
111 City View House
463 Bethnal Green Road
London E2 9QY

National Children's Bureau Early Childhood Unit
8 Wakley Street
London EC1V 7QE

OMEP (UK)
c/o The Hon. Secretary
144 Eltham Road
London SE9 5LW

VOLCUF
(Voluntary Organisations Liaison Council for Under Fives)
77 Holloway Road
London N7 8JZ

Index

academic success 55
accueil 12, 41
Achter Jugendbericht 171
admissions 46, 99
Afro-Caribbean 152
Agazzi Carolina and Rosa 80, 82
Aguado, T. 93–111, 97, 156, 171
AKN 120, 121, 171
Andries, J. 7–17
apprentissages/cycles of learning 43,
    94, 95, 98–99, 100, 107, 109
Arabic 124
Arbeitsgemeinschaft für Jugendhilfe
    74, 171
Arbetsmarknadsstyrelsen 119, 171
architecture 48, 70
areas/fields of experience 11, 83, 89,
    104, 123, 145, 161, 167
Arhus 33
asili infantili 81
assessment 11, 51, 52, 67, 90, 98,
    106, 107, 138, 142, 143, 145,
    147, 151
assessment units 151
Association Generale des Institutrices
    des Ecoles Maternelles 39
Athey, C. 145, 171
Ausubel, D.P. et al. 96

Baccalaureat 54, 55
Bagger, H. 24, 171
Balageur, I. et al. 163, 171

Balke, E. 115, 171
Barker, W. 160, 171
Barrett, G. 152, 171
Bate, M. et al. 147, 171
Bathurst, K. 134, 172
Beck-Gernsheim, E. 59, 172
Belgium 2, 7–17, 155, 157, 164, 167,
    168, 169
Belsky, J. 158, 172
Bennett, N. and Kell, J. 161, 172
Bergman, Monica 4, 112–132, 113,
    125, 126, 127, 129, 172
Berlin 63, 74, 114
Bertolini, P. 172
Bertram, H. 58, 172
birth rate 19, 41, 61, 119, 120–121,
    140
Blackstone, T. 172
Boeckmann, B. et al. 58, 172
Bolzano 85
British 161
Bowlby, J. 172
Bronfenbrenner, U. 160, 161, 168,
    172
Brophy, J. et al. 146, 172
Browne, N. and France, P. 111, 172
Bruce, T. 144, 172
Bruges 8
Bruner, J. 105, 144, 172
Brussels 8, 16
Burgess, R.G. et al. 146, 172
Busch, C. et al. 77, 173

CACE (Plowden Report) 136, 167, 173
Calder, P. 140, 173
Carer-and-Toddler Clubs 141
Carlsen, S. 21, 173
Catholic 7, 17
Centro Europeo dell'Educazione 92
child abuse and neglect/protection 54, 163
child as being/project 6
childhood 19, 68, 170
children 'in need' 151
children's culture 61
children's lives 60
Christensen, N. and Launer, J. 68, 173
Christofferson, M.N. 19, 20, 23, 29, 173
church 25, 38, 62, 100, 114, 158
Ciari, B. 82, 173
Clark, M.M. 141, 145, 173
Clarke, Kenneth 136
Cleave, S. and Brown, S. 152, 173
CNREE/MEC 110, 173
co-ordinated school start 30–31
Cochran, M. 161, 173
COFACE 6
cognitive 10, 13, 24, 25, 65, 92, 97, 102, 104, 105, 108, 144, 147, 150, 159, 161
Cohen and Fraser 157
Cohen, B. 6, 173
Cohen, B. and Fraser, 153, 173
Colberg-Schrader, H. 56–77
Colberg-Schrader, H. and Oberhuemer, P. 76, 156, 158, 173
Colberg-Schrader, H. and von Derschau, D. 76, 173
Colberg-Schrader, H. et al. 66, 174
Colson, Caroline 8
Comenius 170
Comite Francais de l'OMEP French Committee of (OMEP) 39, 174
Commission de Renovation de l'Enseignement Fondamental (CREF) 12

Commission on Nursery Provision (Sweden) 117
communication skills 10, 89, 123
Community Education Development Centre 17
Compensatory Education Scheme (Spain) 110
competition 81, 83
continuity and transition 10, 12, 29, 43, 125, 154, 155
Copenhagen 28,33, 34
Council of Europe 6
Consultative Committee (Hadow Report) 174
CRE 162, 174
creche 68, 72, 114, 115, 165
cultural minorities 32, 68
cultural pluralism 69
curriculum 10, 25, 37, 47, 53, 54, 65, 66, 67, 83, 88–90, 91, 93, 94, 101–103, 110, 113, 118, 123, 131, 134, 138, 140, 142, 143, 145, 146, 147, 148, 150, 153, 159, 160, 161, 162, 167, 169
curriculum development 103–104
curriculum review 151
Curtis, A. 144, 146, 174

Dahlberg, G. 5, 174
Dahlberg, G. and Asen, G. 131, 174
Dahlberg, G. et al. 131, 174
Danish National Union of Preschool Teachers (BUPL) 19,20
Danish Research Council 33
Dansmarks Laerforening (Danish Teachers' Union) 31, 174
Das Bildungswesen der DDR 68, 174
David, T. 1–6, 7–17, 9, 133–154, 141, 143, 146, 153, 155–170, 157, 161, 167, 169, 174
daycare 1, 8, 18, 19, 23, 24, 25, 26, 27, 30, 50, 56, 58, 60, 61, 67, 83, 95, 112, 115, 122, 133–134, 139, 147, 148, 153, 155, 156, 161, 165, 169
De Bartolomeis, F. 174
Decat, M. et al. 15, 174
Decroly, Ovide 8, 14, 39

Delvaux-Furnière, A. and Malisoux-Gillet, M-J. 8, 9, 11, 13, 15, 17, 174
Demografiska rapporter 122, 174
Denmark 2, 18–34, 156, 157, 159, 162, 164, 165, 166, 169, 174
Department of Children's Affairs 27
Derschau, D. von 73, 175
DES 133, 136, 140, 141, 142, 143, 145, 146, 148, 150, 162, 175
Descoudres 39
Deutsches Jugendinstitut 58, 60, 64, 76, 175
De Vries, R. 107, 175
De Vries, R. and Kohlberg, L. 97, 102, 175
discrimination 88, 111, 162
Donaldson, M. 144, 175
Dottrens 39
drug problems 60
Drummond M.J. 147, 175
Drummond, M.J. et al. 140, 175
Ds 130, 175
Ds U 115, 175

Early Years Curriculum Group 146, 175
Eastern Europe 2, 170
Ebert, S. 73, 175
EC Childcare Network 34, 163, 166
EC/European Community 155, 156, 165, 166, 167
école a tricoter 35
école maternelle 7, 8, 35, 36, 37, 38, 39, 40, 41, 42, 43, 44, 45, 46, 48, 49
école normale 37
Edinburgh University 5
edu-care 153
educational priority areas 53, 136
EFTA 2,6
emergent literacy 1, 13, 53, 83, 89
England 35, 140
English language 141
equal opportunities 2, 22, 58, 59, 84, 95, 111, 119, 129, 132, 146, 153, 158, 165
equipment 48–49, 70, 81, 108, 144

Erikson, E. H. 117
Erning, G. et al. 57, 175
ethnic group 79
minorities 15, 124, 152
European Commission/EC 3, 6, 69, 127, 133, 164, 175
society 6, 170
Eurydice 7, 176
evaluation 11, 51, 67, 90, 97, 147, 151, 167, 168
Evans, E.D. 107, 176
ex-Soviet Union 69
ex-Yugoslavia 68, 124

Family Commission (Sweden) 116
family daycare/childminding 8, 26, 29, 58, 63, 112, 113, 121, 122, 124, 131, 138, 140, 152
family life 6, 58, 61, 76, 84
Family Policy Studies Centre 176
family structure 60, 80
Federal Law Gazette 62, 176
femme de service/auxiliary 39
Ferri, E. et al. 137, 141, 176
Finland 161, 169
Fisher, E.A. 167, 176
Flemish-speaking 7
France 2, 35–55, 155, 157, 164, 167
Franco regime 156
Frankfurt 74
French-speaking 7
Froebel, F. 8, 30, 57, 114, 115, 131, 134, 144
Fruizi-Venezia Giulia 85
Fthenakis, W.E. et al. 74, 176
funding 10, 63, 84–86, 99, 116, 121, 125, 130, 135, 150, 155

garderies 35
German-speaking (Belgians) 7
Germany 2, 38, 56–77, 156, 160, 164, 167
German Education Council 65
Ghent 16
Goteborg 124
Goutard, M. 35–55, 159
governing body 26
grandparents 63, 134

Index

Greece 2, 164
Grieve, R. and Hughes, M. 144, 176
group size 72, 100, 123

haltes-garderies 35
Hamburg 63
Hammershoj, H. 163, 176
Hartley, D. 140, 176
Hatje, A.K. 115, 176
Henckel, B. 118, 176
Herbinière-Lebert, S. 39
Hennessy, E. and Melhuish, E.C. 176
Herlth, A. and Schleimer, J. 59, 176
Hesse 63
High/Scope 150, 176
Holtermann S. 153, 157, 176
home-school links/relations 12, 14
Hopf, A. 76, 176
Hössl, A. 70, 176
House of Commons Select
    Committee/HoC 141, 177
Hultquist, K. 114, 115, 177
Humberside 148
Humblet, P.C. 8, 177
Hurst, V. 146, 177
Hutt Corinne 145
Hutt, S.J. et al. 145, 147, 177
Huttunen, E. 169, 177
Hwang, P. 159, 168, 177

ILEA 145, 177
immigrant children 119
inspection/inspectors/advisers 16, 38,
    51, 74, 111, 134, 145, 151, 167
integrated/combined nursery centres
    28, 30, 34, 44, 64, 137, 139, 152
integration (SEN) 70, 151
inter-agency work 54, 106
intercultural education 42
International Year of the Family 6
Ireland 2, 161, 164
Isaacs, Susan 135, 144, 177
Italy 2, 68, 78–92, 157, 164, 166, 167

jardin d'enfants 8, 35
Jarousse, J-P. et al. 17, 39, 168, 177
Jesuits 5
Johansson, J.E. 114, 115, 177

Jowett, S. and Sylva, K. 137, 162,
    165, 177

Kamii, C. and De Vries, R. 97, 102,
    177
Karrby, G. 126, 177
Kergomard, Pauline 37, 42
kindergarten 25, 28, 30, 32, 56, 57,
    60, 61, 62, 63, 64, 65, 66, 68,
    69, 70, 71, 72, 74, 75, 76, 94,
    99, 114, 115, 121
kinderkrippe 63, 64
Kinderläden 75
Knight, C. 138, 159, 177
Köhler 115
Krappmann, L. 67, 177

Lady Allen of Hurtwood 39
Laeken 8
Länder 62, 63, 64, 72, 75
Langsted, O. and Sommer, D. 21, 22,
    177
Le Soir 9, 177
Leeds 148
Legge Casati 79, 91
Liege 8, 14, 16
linguistic group 79
    minorities 15, 68, 124, 152, 162,
    167
Lipski, J. 70, 178
London 148
Louvain 16
Lower Saxony 63
Lubeck, S. 159, 178
Lund, S. 19, 28, 27, 178
Luxembourg 2, 164

Macbeth, A. 9, 178
Malmo 124
management 26, 79, 118
Manchester 148
maternal employment 8, 20, 22, 23,
    31, 58, 59, 60, 61, 63, 81, 84
maternity leave 21
Matthews, G. 144, 178
McLean, M. 169, 178
McMillan, Margaret 134, 135, 144
McMillan Rachel 134

Meadows, S. and Cashdan, A. 147, 178
MEC (Ministerio de Educacion y Ciencia) 94, 95, 96, 100, 101, 102, 103, 104, 105, 110, 111, 178
men in early childhood education 43, 126
Merton 148
metacognition 4, 169
migrant children 117
  families/workers 42, 54, 68
Ministère de l'ERF (Belgium) 11, 178
Ministero della Pubblica Instruzione (Italian Ministry of Education) 89, 178
Ministry of Labour 10
Moberg, Ellen and Maria 114
Montessori, Maria 8, 30, 38, 39, 80, 82, 115, 144
Moon, B. 2, 178
Mortimore, J. and Mortimore, P. 158, 179
Moss, P. 34, 155, 158, 162, 165, 166, 179
Munich 65
Myrdal, Alva 39, 115

National Board of Health and Welfare (Sweden) 117, 118, 127
National Childminders' Association (NCMA) 17, 140, 146
Nazi 57, 156
Nelson, K. 144, 179
Netherlands 2, 164
Norrkoping 114
North-Rhine Westphalia 63
Norway 5, 161
NSPCC (National Scoiety for the Prevention of Cruelty to Children) 151
Nursery Schools Association 135

Oberhuemer, P. 56–77, 74, 179
Oberlin J-F. 35, 36
OMEP 108, 170, 179
Osborn, A. and Milbank, J. 152, 179

out-of-hours care 10, 14, 26, 44, 46, 122–3
Owen, Robert 134

Pape Carpentier, M. 36
parents 3, 18, 19, 30, 45, 46, 50, 65, 69, 95, 105, 107, 138, 147, 150, 152, 153, 154, 155, 157, 159, 162, 165
  attitudes to school 97
  choice 165
  contributions/fees 29, 50, 63, 85, 130, 140, 152
  employment 6, 19, 109, 152, 156, 165; participation 9, 11, 16, 62, 75, 86–87, 105, 145, 149, 151, 166, 167; leave 6, 119, 120, 154, 169
Parent-Teacher Association 151
Paris 36
Pascal, C. *et al.* 162, 179
pedagogues 34, 38, 46, 53, 163
pedagogy 67, 68, 113, 116, 131
Peers, M. 8, 179
Penn, H. and Riley, K.A. 161, 179
Pestalozzi 114, 144
Pharsee 124
physiotherapists 31
Piaget, Jean 39, 97, 117, 144, 179
Pierre, J. *et al.* 179
Pieron 39
Pistillo, F. 179
Plaisance, E. 179
play 24, 39, 52, 57, 71, 89, 106, 109, 123, 145, 147, 149, 151, 167, 169
playgroups 61, 138, 139, 142, 147, 148, 151, 152, 153, 154, 157
Poland 69
Polish 124
Portugal 2, 164
Post-Piagetians 144
pouponnieres 35
PPA/Preschool Playgroups Association/playgroup movement 137, 146, 154, 156, 165, 179
Preschool Education Reform Project (Spain) 95

primary school admission 1, 4, 5, 31, 47, 65, 87, 113, 125–126, 133, 134, 169
private provision 7, 18, 25, 26, 29, 35, 44, 61, 78, 79, 80, 81, 85, 99, 121, 138, 139, 140, 149, 152, 157, 158, 165
profiles of achievement 149
Prop. (Swedish Government Papers) 118, 128, 129, 130, 179–180
provision on demand 132
Pugh, G. 133, 136, 138, 148, 153, 157, 161, 180
Pusci, L. 78–92, 180

racial harassment 162
racism 152
ratios (staff:child) 9, 29, 41, 50, 64, 88, 100, 101, 110, 126
reception class 139
refugees 124
Reggio Emilia 82
Reisby, K. 34, 180
religious communities and minorities 36, 157, 162
religious institutions 79, 80, 81, 85
research and development 16, 33, 64, 65, 66, 127–9
resources 5, 11, 41, 49, 70, 98, 102, 107, 138, 150
Romania 69
Rouse, D. and Griffin, S. 140, 180
Royal Danish School of Educational Studies 33
Rudebeck, K. 125, 180
Rumbold, Angela 142
  Committee 142
  Report 133, 140, 142, 145, 146, 148
rural areas/communities 40, 117, 123

salle d'asile 8, 36, 37
Sardinia 85
Saunders, R. and Bingham-Newman, A. 97, 102, 108, 180
SCAFA 170, 180
scaffolding learning 144
Scandinavia 4, 5, 23, 166

SCB (Statistiska meddelanden) 117, 182
schema 145
school doctor 51
Schrader-Breymann, Henriette 114
Schwarz, B. 130, 180
Schweinhart, L. *et al.* 168, 180
Scotland 140, 160
scuola materna statale 79, 81
scuole pratiche magistrali 92
Semeroff, A.J. and Chandler, M.J. 168, 180
Shinman, S. 166, 181
Shorrocks, D. 138, 159, 165, 180
Sicily 85
Simmons-Christenson, G. 116, 117, 181
Simon 39
Singer, E. 2, 181
Siraj-Blatchford, I. 146, 159, 181, 182
situation-oriented approach 65
Socialstyrelsen 118, 123, 128, 181
Solihull 148
SoS-rapport 120, 124, 181
SOU 116, 118, 119, 125, 128, 181
Spain 2, 3, 93–111, 156, 161, 164, 167
  Civil War 93
Spanish language 124
special educational needs 14–15, 31, 41, 50, 69–70, 88, 110, 150, 161
Speekman-Klass, C. 159, 181
SRC (Strathclyde Regional Council) 160, 181
Statham, J. *et al.* 181
Statistics Sweden 120, 181
Statistisches Bundesamt 59, 60, 69, 181
Statistiska medderlanden 120, 121, 122, 124, 182
Stenhouse, L. 98, 182
Stockholm 114, 124
Strathclyde 140, 160
Svenska Kommunforbundet 123, 125, 130, 182
Sweden 2, 5, 39, 112–132, 157, 161, 166
Swedish Froebel Foundation 114

Swedish Social Research Council 128
Sylva, K. *et al.* 143, 144, 159, 162, 182
Sylva, K. and Moss, P. 152, 166, 182

teacher/staff education and training/ qualifications 3, 6, 14, 15–16, 33, 37, 49, 72–74, 90, 97, 98, 99–100, 118, 126, 132, 140, 148, 150, 153, 155, 158, 162
TES 153, 182
Thatcher, Margaret 136, 137
Tietze, W. and Rosbach, H.G. 64, 182
Tietze, W. and Uferman, K. 64, 182
Tizard, B. *et al.* 144, 160, 182
Tough, J. 144, 182
Trento 85
Trevarthen, Professor C. 5
Turkey 68
Turkish community 16
    language 124
Tutaev, Belle 137
Tyler, S. 147, 182

UK 1, 2, 3, 39, 133–154, 156, 158, 157, 161, 164, 165, 167, 168, 169
Ulich, M. *et al.* 69, 182
Ulin, Carin 115
UN Convention on Children's Rights 3
UNESCO 158, 182
Unione Nazionale delle Educatrici dell'Infanzia 92

USA 136, 150, 158, 159, 168

Valle d'Aosta 85
Van Leer Foundation 16, 160
Vedel-Petersen, J. 32, 183
vertical grouping 12
Vigy, J.L. 108, 183
Vilien 166
Vilien, K. 18–34, 31, 159, 183
Vygotsky, L. 144, 183

Walch, J. 131, 183
Wales 140
Warburg, Anna 114
Ward, P. 148, 160, 167, 183
Warwick University Early Years Team 147, 183
Watt, J. 6, 160, 165, 183
Weil, M.S. and Murphy, J. 107, 183
Whitebrook, M. *et al.* 153, 158, 159, 160, 165, 183
Winkler, B. 69, 183
Wolfendale, S. 149, 183
women's employment 114, 115, 116, 119–120, 132, 140, 142, 154, 166
    position in the family 115
    role 56, 135
Wood, D. *et al.* 145, 183

Zeiher, H. 59, 183
Zigler, E. 152, 183
Zimmer, J. 64, 65, 183

Printed in the United Kingdom
by Lightning Source UK Ltd.
102086UKS00001B/157